AVCE
Information and Communication Technology
Units 4 - 6

R. P. Richards, B.Sc. (Hons), M.A.
&
P. M. Heathcote, B.Sc. (Hons), M.Sc.

Published by
Payne-Gallway Publishers Limited
26-28 Northgate Street
Ipswich IP1 3DB
Tel: 01473 251097   Fax: 01473 232758
E-mail: info@payne-gallway.co.uk
Web site: www.payne-gallway.co.uk

2001

Acknowledgements

We are grateful to Cygna and particularly Jeff Dummett for his help with photographs for Unit 4.

Cover picture © 'December' reproduced with the kind permission of James Judge
Cover photography © Mike Kwasniak, 160 Sidegate Lane, Ipswich
Cover design by Tony Burton

First edition 2001

10 9 8 7 6 5 4 3 2 1

A catalogue entry for this book is available from the British Library.

ISBN 1 903112 48 6
Copyright © R.P. Richards and P.M. Heathcote 2001

Printed in Great Britain by
W.M.Print, Walsall, West Midlands

Preface

Vocational A Level qualification

The AVCE (Advanced Vocational Certificate of Education) in Information and Communication Technology is one of several vocational A Level qualifications offered by the Examining Boards. The mandatory units and specification for each one is the same for all Boards but the assessment may be different for different Boards.

This book covers three of the mandatory units for the 12-unit award, which may also be chosen as optional units for the 6-unit award. All the theory given in the specifications is covered, as well as guidance for both internal and external assessments. Unit 4 is a very practical unit and students are shown how to perform all the tasks that they will need to describe or give evidence of in their portfolios. In Unit 5, practice is given in answering examination-style questions similar to those that are set by Edexcel. In Units 5 and 6, a sample systems specification and database project are given which will help students who are required (e.g. by AQA) to complete a practical project for their assessment.

How to use this book

The book is designed to be used in the classroom, and for practice and revision sessions. Suggestions for activities and discussions are found throughout, and questions and exercises to test students' understanding and recall can be used either as homework or as class work. In Unit 6, students can work through the sample application at their own pace, learning the capabilities of MS Access as they work through, so that they can then design and implement their own projects.

Extra resources

Extra resources for teachers can be found on our web site www.payne-gallway.co.uk.

Table of Contents

Unit 4

System Installation and Configuration

In this unit you will be taking the lid off a computer, taking it apart and then – more difficult – putting it back together again. You will also be learning how to install and customise software to make a computer function in just the way a user wants. There are a lot of technical terms to learn but you will pick these up as you go along, especially if you are doing a lot of practical work with hardware components. Learning how to work safely so that you do not damage either yourself or the computer is a very important part of this unit!

For the assessment you need to set up a working computer system to meet a given specification, modify existing hardware and software systems and keep comprehensive records to show what you have done. Check Appendix B for more detail about the assessment evidence you have to produce. Sample portfolio material can be downloaded from www.payne-gallway.co.uk/avce.

Chapter 1 – Introduction to Hardware

Objectives

- ✓ To learn about the basic structure of computer systems
- ✓ To identify the major hardware subsystems
- ✓ To learn how major subsystems are interconnected
- ✓ To investigate the hardware configuration of PCs

1.1.   Introduction

A computer system consists of *hardware* and *software*. Hardware is the physical machinery – the components that make up the computer. Software consists of the computer programs (sequences of instructions) that tell the computer what to do in response to a command or some event. In this chapter we'll take an introductory look at hardware.

1.2.   Major subsystems

Computer systems come in many different shapes and sizes, but they nearly all have the same overall basic structure and components. These components are often represented in a block diagram.

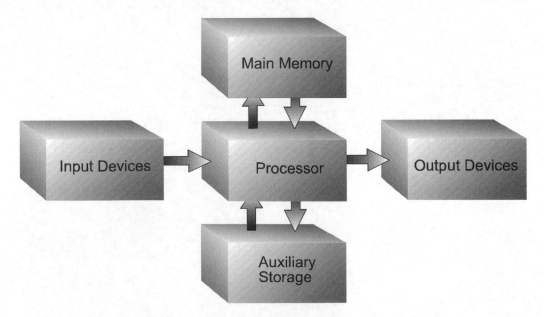

Figure 1.1: Block diagram of a computer system

This basic structure of a computer system consists of :

❑ a processor or Central Processing Unit (CPU) which is capable of obeying the instructions within the programs held in the memory system and thus processing the associated data.

❑ a storage system for storing information either on a temporary basis (main memory) or on a long-term basis (backing store).

❑ an input/output (I/O) system which provides the means of control to transfer information i.e. data and programs, both in and out of the system. The transfer takes place between the computer system's memory and a variety of different *peripheral devices* (meaning any input, output or storage device attached to the computer such as a screen, printer, scanner or disk drive).

In order to function correctly and perform useful work or tasks, these hardware subsystems need to be:

❑ controlled and driven correctly. This is achieved by means of software called *operating systems* and *drivers*.

❑ interconnected so that they can communicate with each other effectively. This is achieved through the internal *bus* structure of the computer and defined *external interfaces*.

> **Note:** The name *bus* originates from the analogy of carrying many people at once around town in a double-decker, but in this case it is simply a set of wires connecting components which provide a high-speed system for transporting data to and from different parts of a computer.

The characteristics of devices connected to the computer system can vary enormously and so cannot be connected directly to the processor by a simple bus. Instead, each device is connected via an *interface* which in turn is connected to the bus (these are discussed in more detail later).

The bus structure is shown in very simplified form in Figure 1.2. Data is transferred across a *data bus* between the processor and locations defined by the *address bus* in the main memory. A *control bus* synchronises the data flow to and from devices.

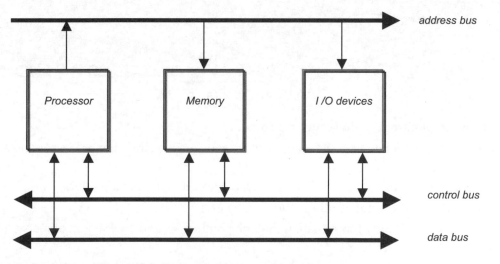

Figure 1.2: Basic interconnection of subsystems

1.3. Types of computer

The best-known form of computer system is the *desktop personal computer*.

Figure 1.3: A Desktop PC

This, in its basic form shown above, consists of:

- ❑ a *system unit* which houses the main memory and backing store, the processor and the I/O subsystem;
- ❑ a *monitor* or *screen* to provide human-readable text and graphical output;
- ❑ a *keyboard* for the input of information by the user;
- ❑ a *mouse* for the input of information through pointing to, and clicking on objects on the monitor screen.

The PC shown above has a *tower unit*, which is so called because it stands upright, usually on the floor or in a frame under the desk. A *desk unit* is usually smaller and sits on the desk under the monitor. The amount of space taken up on the floor or the desk is sometimes referred to as the computer's *footprint*, so a computer with a small footprint is simply one which takes up less space on the floor or desk.

A *laptop* computer has exactly the same structure as the desktop model but is packaged differently. It is designed to be easy to carry and to function for prolonged periods without mains electricity, using only a battery contained within the unit.

Figure 1.4: A Laptop computer

Network servers are system units capable of running a network of PCs and holding data and programs used by every user on the network. They are usually much more powerful devices than an average PC, often containing:

- large amounts of main memory;
- large hard disk systems;
- multiple processors;
- data backup devices.

Figure 1.5: A typical server

There are many other forms of computer systems, such as large supercomputers used to solve complex problems found, for example, in weather forecasting, to so-called embedded systems used to control video recorders and microwave ovens. However these are very specialised systems and will not be investigated further here.

1.4. Managing hardware in Windows

In this unit we will be discussing the management of hardware in Windows-based systems. As you work through the chapters, you need to have access to a PC so that you can try out the different facilities being discussed. It's time to log on to your PC and experiment.

Windows **Control Panel** provides facilities for finding and adjusting hardware settings and adding and removing peripherals. Within Control Panel, **Device Manager** keeps track of resource settings and installed devices.

To access Device Manager do the following:

- Select **Start**, **Settings**, **Control Panel** and double-click the **System** icon.
- Click on the **Hardware** tab and then **Device Manager**.

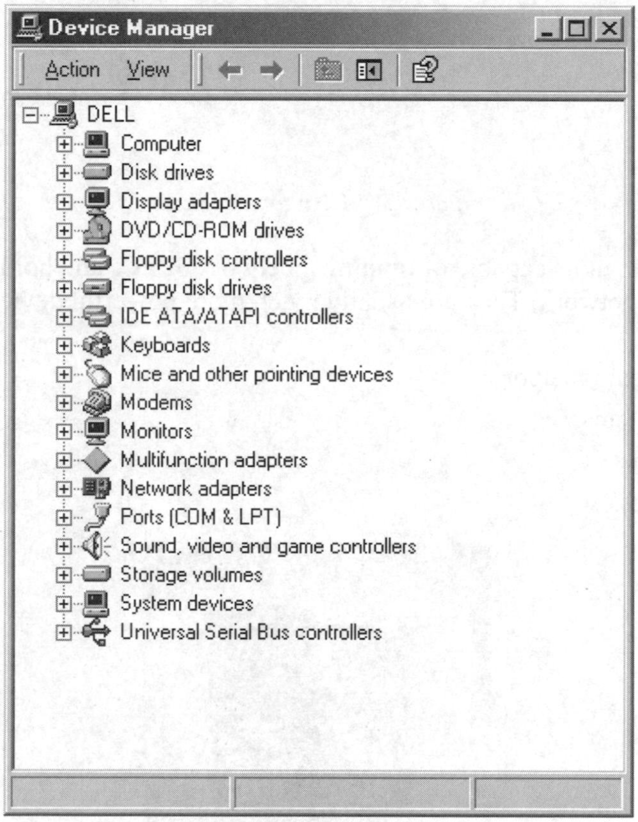

Figure 1.6: Device Manager

Device Manager lists all of the various hardware devices associated with your PC. By clicking on the + symbol next to the desired device type, you can see what hardware is installed on your system in the selected device category. Double-click the revealed devices and you will get a configuration sheet that includes information for that device.

You can also print out your current system configuration from Device Manager.

- Access **Device Manager** as described above and browse through the information about your computer.
- With the settings shown in Figure 1.6 click on **Print** from the **View** menu, check that the **System Summary** option is selected and click **OK**.

You will get several pages of information about your system, most of which may not be very meaningful. Hopefully you will be able to make more sense of it by the end of this unit.

Plug and Play (or **PnP**) was developed by Microsoft, Intel, Compaq and others to provide automated recognition and configuration of hardware in PCs – in other words, to make it simpler to install devices such as a new printer. There are three components:

❑ The hardware – circuit boards and devices that are to be connected to the PC must be PnP compatible. They include some memory that stores unique identifiers providing the operating system with key information.

❑ BIOS (Basic Input/Output System) – this is the lowest level of software running on the PC (discussed in more detail in Chapter 3) which must be set up to handle PnP hardware.

❑ Operating system – e.g. Windows 95 or 98 which interacts with the BIOS to ensure devices are properly configured and which can automatically detect new PnP devices.

1.5. Electrical Safety

You should read the Appendix **Standard Ways of Working** which discusses safety issues in detail. For this unit in particular you must be able to work safely and take precautions not to damage yourself, others or the equipment you are working on.

Whenever anyone is carrying out work on electrical equipment there is some risk involved. However, assuming you have powered it off first, the PC system unit is relatively safe to work on. The greatest danger comes from large charges of electrical energy that are retained in power supply components. You should never remove the outer casing of a power supply because of this risk of electrical shock – it should only be replaced as a complete unit. The same applies to PC monitors – the casings should never be removed unless you are specifically trained to do so.

Static electricity stored in the human body can pose a serious threat to your PC components. It is possible to damage these devices simply by touching them. To combat this you should always wear an anti-static wrist strap before commencing work inside a PC case. In addition, anti-static mats which you place under the item you are working on are also recommended.

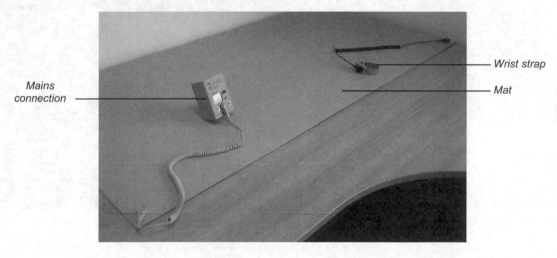

Figure 1.7: An anti-static kit.

Discussion: What details can you determine about the specification of the hardware you are using?

Chapter 2 – The System Unit

Objectives

- ✓ To learn what makes up a motherboard
- ✓ To be able to select and install a motherboard
- ✓ To understand the function of the processor
- ✓ To appreciate the different types of processor
- ✓ To learn about the bus architecture

2.1. The System Unit

The PC case holds all the vital electronics components as well as providing a housing for CD-ROM and floppy drives on the front, and various ports and fans along the back. The case also acts as an electromagnetic radiation shield and allows for channelled airflow to prevent the unit from overheating.

Small form factor   Traditional desktop design   Mini-tower

Figure 2.1 Different PC case designs

The PC case can be either the traditional desktop design (also available in SFF profile – Small Form Factor) or now often a mini-tower which provides easy access to the internal components while minimising the size of the footprint (this does not apply to laptop computers where the screen is integral with the case).

2.2. Motherboards

Inside the PC case almost everything is mounted on a single large circuit board called the motherboard (sometimes referred to as the system board). All components communicate with each other via this board and it determines how quickly and efficiently the PC will work. Other circuit boards, such as video, network or sound cards slot into the motherboard. It also contains the processor, memory, disk drive interfaces and the controllers that control the peripheral devices.

The components of a motherboard are discussed in more detail later in this unit. They are easy to identify and are shown in Figure 2.2:

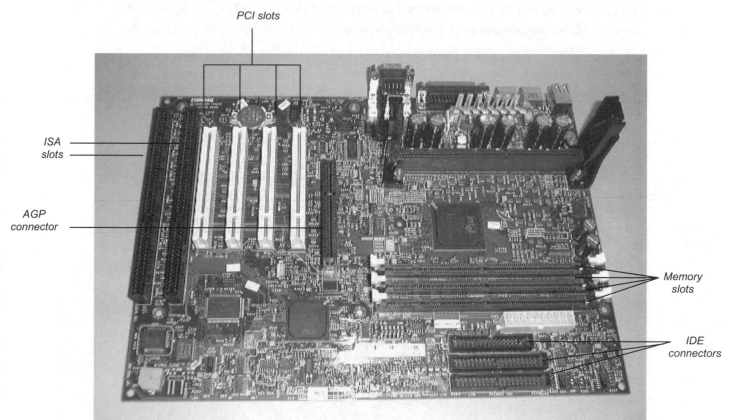

Figure 2.2: A typical motherboard

Selecting a new motherboard

The motherboard in a PC can often be replaced with a faster, more recent model, but before buying a new board it is best to check with the supplier that it will be compatible with the rest of your system. Some points to consider include:

- ❑ What size (or *form*) of motherboard does your PC use? (for example, an ATX motherboard requires an ATX-compatible case)
- ❑ Can your existing processor be used in the new motherboard?
- ❑ Will the memory on your current motherboard be compatible with the new one? (See chapter 3.)
- ❑ What features in the BIOS does the new motherboard include? (The BIOS is the Setup program stored in special integrated circuits on the motherboard which controls communication between your PC and its peripherals – see Chapter 3.) Examples include power management (allowing key components to power down after a set period of inactivity) and passwords.
- ❑ Can you use your existing expansion cards in the new motherboard? (See section 2.4 below.)

❑ Does the new motherboard have the same type of power connectors?

❑ Does it have the fastest and most up-to-date chipset you can afford? Sometimes referred to as the 'glue logic' these integrated circuits control the flow of data between the key parts of your motherboard.

❑ If your current motherboard has integrated I/O and video functions, you may still need to purchase these separately.

Removing the old motherboard

- **Always protect yourself by removing mains plugs from the unit and protect the components from electrostatic discharge by grounding yourself with a wrist strap or equivalent.**

- Note the position of all connectors and plug-in boards – make written notes if necessary.

- Carefully remove all plug-in expansion/adaptor cards and unplug all connectors.

- Unscrew and remove any screws holding the motherboard, noting which holes are used.

- Slide out the motherboard with the plastic standoffs still attached and place the motherboard on a table away from your work area.

Figure 2.3: Removing a motherboard

Setting up the new motherboard

Latest motherboards normally configure themselves automatically, but you should check the user guide supplied with the new motherboard to see if you are required to make any settings. This is usually done by re-siting small links called *jumpers*. For example you may have to set processor type, expansion bus speed, etc. You may also need to update information in your PC's setup BIOS program – this is discussed further in Chapter 3 but, again, you should consult the user guide supplied.

Installing the new motherboard

- Check all jumpers or switches are correct.

- Install any memory modules (see Chapter 3).

- Reinsert the motherboard ensuring plastic standoffs are sited correctly.

- Secure the screws holding the motherboard.

- Carefully reinstall all essential connectors and expansion cards such as the video card and serial I/O card. Take care not to apply too much pressure and bend the motherboard Check that the orientation of the board is correct (most connectors are *keyed* i.e. they will only fit one way). Make sure nothing is obstructing the card such as loose screws.
- Check over your work.
- Switch on the PC and test to ensure that the PC starts up correctly and can read from the hard drive.
- Switch off and refit your other non-essential cards.

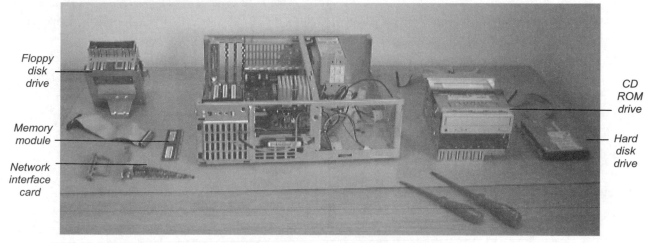

Figure 2.4 Breaking down a PC

2.3. Processors

The processor (or CPU) is the most important part of the PC, performing all the number-crunching and essential data processing. It is so important to the performance and pricing of a PC that computer manufacturers often market their products by the processor's type and speed.

The CPU keeps the processing of data in step using a very fast clock. Early CPUs worked in the kilohertz (i.e. thousands of hertz) range (KHz) but current Pentium IIIs clock data at 800 megahertz (MHz) – that means 800 million times/second or more: Pentium 4s now run at 1 gigahertz (GHz) – 1000 million times/second and more.

Companies that produce CPUs include AMD, Cyrix and IBM but the most popular types are the Intel Pentium II/III and their derivatives.

Figure 2.5: An Intel PIII processor in situ

Selecting a new processor

There are some important things to consider before buying a processor. Most importantly check with the supplier that it will be compatible with your existing system; you will have to tell them the type of motherboard fitted and whether it has a processor upgrade socket. Other elements of the system such as the memory may limit the true potential of a more powerful processor.

Types of CPU

Older types of CPU include:

- 486-type CPUs
  Before the Pentium processor arrived the Intel 80386 and 80486 were the most popular. However these processors would not now be capable of running today's software.

- 1st and 2nd generation Pentium CPUs
  The first Pentiums came in a variety of types and speeds. They used the Intel Zero Insertion Force (ZIF) socket 7 which can also accept most equivalent Cyrix and AMD CPUs.

- The Pentium Pro CPU
  This was designed for applications such as graphics and multimedia.

- Pentium MMX CPU
  This was essentially a supercharged Pentium 'tuned' for multimedia applications.

The current generation of CPUs include the following:

- Super-fast Pentium II/III and 4s
  A variety of speeds are now available up to an amazing 1GHZ + at time of writing.

- Celeron
  This is Intel's cheaper alternative to the Pentium.

- AMD
  These competitors to the Intel processors also range in speeds up to 1GHZ +. Various models include AMD K6, AMD Athlon and AMD Duron ranges.

Figure 2.6: Typical PC advertisements

2.4. Interface/bus architecture

As discussed in Chapter 1 buses are sets of interconnecting links which move information between different components. A bus is a set of typically 8, 16 or 32 parallel wires along which data and memory addresses are transmitted.

Several buses are used in PCs including:

- **Data bus**

  The data bus transfers data to and from memory locations. The size of the data bus determines how much data is transferred into or out of the CPU at any time, and has a significant impact on the computer's speed.

- **Address bus**

  These are the electrical connections that enable the CPU to send address information to the system. The size of the address bus determines the maximum size of the computer's memory. A 16-bit bus can transmit an address up to 2^{16}-1, or 65535. A 32-bit address bus can transmit an address up to 2^{32}-1 – a very large number! Don't worry if you are confused by bits and bytes – they are explained in the next chapter.

- **Control bus**

  Because data and address buses are shared by all of the system components, their actions need to be synchronised. The control bus carries the signals that tell devices when they can use the bus and controls the data flow.

- **Expansion bus**

  The expansion bus (sometimes referred to as the Input/Output bus) links the processor to those parts of the PC that are not on the motherboard. Expansion cards like sound cards and network cards fit into expansion slots which are directly connected to this bus. Figure 2.2 shows expansion slots which come in several types, the most common now being:

    PCI (Peripheral Component Interconnect) – A newer fast bus (generally running at 33MHz or 100 MHz) found on Pentium-class PCs. It is sometimes referred to as a local bus as it is connected near to the CPU.

    ISA (Industry Standard Architecture) – A common low-speed bus that was included on virtually all PCs in the past.

    AGP (Accelerated Graphics Port)– A new graphics-only connection running at two or four times the speed of PCI. It speeds up graphics performance and is particularly effective for 3D and video.

- **Universal Serial Bus (USB)**

  For use with Pentium MMX or faster systems running Windows 98 or higher, this is an external Plug and Play bus which replaces serial and parallel ports. This is discussed in more detail in Chapter 5, paragraph 5.5.

Discussion: Look through some computer magazines and identify the most 'powerful' PCs that are advertised.

Chapter 3 – Main Memory

Objectives

✓ To learn about system memory

✓ To learn how to upgrade system memory

✓ To learn about the system ROM BIOS

✓ To understand cache memory

3.1. Bits and bytes

Digital computers use the **binary** system for representing data of all types – numbers, characters, sound, pictures and so on. A binary system uses just 2 symbols to represent all information. The symbols could be anything like + and -, or 0 and 1. The great advantage of the binary system is that the digits 1 and 0 can be represented by electrical circuits that can exist in one of two states – current is either flowing or not flowing, and a circuit is either closed or open, on or off.

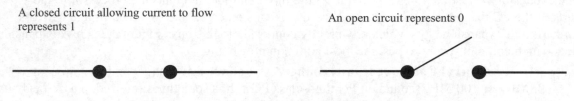

A closed circuit allowing current to flow represents 1

An open circuit represents 0

Figure 3.1: Electrical circuits can represent 1 or 0

A binary digit (1 or 0) is known as a '**bit**', short for **BI**nary digi**T**. In most computers today, bits are grouped together in 8-bit **bytes**. A byte can hold 2^8 different combinations of 0s and 1s, which means that, for example, 256 different characters can be represented.

One byte holds one character.

3.2. Computer memory

The memory of a computer can be thought of as a series of boxes, each containing 8 bits (1 byte), and each with its own unique address, counting from zero upwards. The memory capacity of a computer is measured in thousand-byte units called kilobytes, megabytes or gigabytes.

These measures can be abbreviated to Kb, Mb and Gb. These are all powers of 2; thus although 1Kb is often thought of as being 1,000 bytes, it is actually 1024 bytes.

Thus:

2^{10} bytes = 1024 = 1Kb   (1 kilobyte is about 1,000 bytes)

2^{20} bytes = 1024 x 1024 = 1Mb   (1 megabyte is about 1 million bytes)

2^{30} bytes = 1024 x 1024 x 1024 = 1Gb   (1 gigabyte is about 1000 million bytes)

2^{40} bytes = 1024 x 1024 x 1024 x 1024 = 1Tb   (1 terabyte is about 1,000,000 million bytes)

3.3. RAM

Random Access Memory or RAM is used as a temporary storage area for data during normal processing. The PC uses RAM in a similar way to how you use a desk. Things that are being worked on are placed in RAM where the processor can reach them quickly. The system assigns addresses to data specifying exactly where in the RAM the specific data can be found. Data that isn't being worked on is sent back to the hard disk (like a filing cabinet) or deleted. RAM therefore plays an essential part in a PC and nothing would work without it. Without enough memory, a PC can spend too much time reading data from the hard disk and starving the CPU in the process. Adding RAM to an older PC can give it a new lease of life and arguably increase the performance of the PC more than any other upgrade.

Windows requires at least 32Mb of RAM and preferably 64Mb which is the minimum that most new PCs are supplied with.

System memory is easy to identify – it is in the form of one or more low thin cards sitting in rows on the motherboard. These cards measure roughly 10cm long by 2cm high and include a number of small black chips mounted on them. Inside these black chips are many, many tiny transistors which the PC uses to store information in the form of 0s and 1s.

RAM is *volatile* – that is, the contents are lost when the system powers down. It is often referred to as dynamic RAM (**DRAM**) as it needs to constantly receive electrical signals to keep data present. Even a brief disruption in power forces the system to reboot. This is because the memory space is emptied and the PC forgets everything it knew and assumes that it has just been turned on.

RAM usually comes in standard formats, enabling you to plug new memory into the sockets on the motherboard.

Types of RAM

This is currently available in two forms: **SIMM** (Single Inline Memory Module) and **DIMM** (Dual Inline Memory Module) shown in Figure 3.2. All of these cards have connector pins on their lower edge. The fewer pins on the card, the fewer bits the system can move in and out of RAM at any one time, thereby affecting the performance of the PC.

SIMMs can have 30 or 72 pins although most manufacturers now use 72-pin SIMMs (referred to as **EDO** or Extended Data Out RAM). These offer capacities of up to 128Mb per module. When you purchase 30-pin SIMMs you generally need to do so in pairs, as for example a pair of 32-bit SIMMs are used to yield 64-bit access.

The current generation DIMMS are much faster and are currently available with 168 pins. These are available with capacities of up to 256Mb on a single card. Three types of DIMM are generally available: 66MHz EDO, 66MHz SDRAM or the new fast 100MHz SDRAM which is becoming the most popular. **SDRAM** or Synchronous Dynamic Random Access Memory is one of the fastest memory designs available and is particularly suited for multimedia tasks.

Figure 3.2: Example of a DIMM card

SIMMs and DIMMs and their respective motherboard sockets are made using two main technologies: gold-plate and tin-plate. The main difference is cost, with tin-plated connectors being much cheaper. For upgrades it is advisable not to mix the metals as this can cause problems. Fit only tin-plated SIMMs/DIMMs to tin-plated sockets and gold-plated SIMMs/DIMMs to gold-plated sockets.

Memory Banks

When fitting these memory modules in a motherboard, it is important to know the bank layout. Memory must be fitted in banks starting with bank 0, then bank 1, bank 2 and so on. Each bank must be full before the PC can use the bank.

3.4. Adding and removing RAM

Upgrading system memory

There are two common ways of increasing the amount of memory in a PC:

- ❑ add more memory to any vacant memory slots on the motherboard;
- ❑ replace existing memory with larger capacity memory modules.

Installing a SIMM/DIMM

You will need to practise installing memory modules. These instructions are for guidance only; you should follow the exact instructions supplied with the memory modules.

- **Ensure that the power is off and you have connected your anti-static wrist strap.**
- Make sure the SIMM/DIMM is facing the correct way before inserting. The module will fit in easily only one way, so do not force it.
- Pull open the plastic anchors at each side of the socket.
- Gently insert the card into its socket. For a SIMM you may need to insert at an angle of about 45 degrees to the vertical. A DIMM usually inserts vertically.
- Push the tabs at each side of the socket outwards, while pushing the card into position vertically until the tabs at each end of the socket lock the card in place. When you insert a DIMM it usually pulls the two anchors on each end of the DIMM back into place automatically.

Removing a SIMM/DIMM

- **Ensure that the power is off and you have connected your anti-static wrist strap.**
- Carefully push or pull the tabs on each side of the SIMM/DIMM socket outwards.
- Pull the SIMM/DIMM up carefully and remove from the socket. You may need to gently rock the SIMM/DIMM at an angle to remove it easily.

Figure 3.3: Installing a memory module

3.5. Cache memory

Today's processors often run too fast for even the fastest system RAM. Processors can run two to five times faster than the motherboard. To help the rest of the system catch up, motherboard makers began by putting a small store of very fast memory between the processor and RAM called secondary cache (or L2 cache). This L2 cache in Pentium and faster systems is made up of extremely fast silicon memory called Static RAM or SRAM which is about six to eight times faster than main system memory. Unlike system memory SRAM requires no refresh electrical signal from the system which cuts down access times and results in much faster performance. This cache memory is about ten times more expensive than system RAM which is one reason that caches tend to be small. Some Pentium processors have L2 cache built into the processor package which makes cache upgrades impossible unless the processor is replaced.

3.6. ROM

Motherboards contain a special set of memory chips quite separate from the main memory made up of SIMMs and DIMMs which are used for loading and running applications. This extra memory is the BIOS (Basic Input Output System). BIOS information may be stored partly in ROM and partly in CMOS (Complementary Metal Oxide Semiconductor) RAM.

ROM (Read-Only Memory) is non-volatile memory in that it keeps information intact even when the power is turned off, whereas CMOS RAM is maintained by a backup battery when the PC is turned off.

The BIOS is very important – without it nothing in the PC would work. It stores information about things like your hard drive, floppy drives, the amount and type of memory etc. When the PC is first switched on the BIOS is activated, checking the memory and performing other system checks (the Power On Self Test which is discussed further in Chapter 10). If the BIOS checks are successful, the operating system then loads.

There are two types of BIOS: *flash* and *nonflash*. Most recent systems use a flash BIOS which can easily be updated using software on a floppy disk, as opposed to nonflash BIOS which can only be upgraded by physically replacing the BIOS chip.

When a PC first boots up the BIOS information is briefly displayed. Hitting the **Pause** key gives the user time to read the information. Most systems also have a BIOS utility that can be accessed during the initial boot by pressing a particular key sequence that is specified in the system documentation. It is a text-based utility that provides choices for managing settings and capabilities. This is discussed in more detail in Chapter 10.

Chapter 4 – Backing Store

Objectives

✓ To understand the basic operation of a floppy disk drive and how to replace one
✓ To understand the basic operation of a hard disk drive and how to replace one
✓ To learn about options for optical drives
✓ To consider suitable media for a backup strategy
✓ To compare different types of removable storage media

4.1. Floppy Disk Drives

The floppy disk drive was the first removable storage device for the PC. It is still an important part of the standard PC as it allows you to remove relatively small amounts of data or programs between compatible computers. The term floppy came from the 5¼ inch disks which were actually flexible. The 3½ inch disks that are currently used are covered in a hard plastic case and hold up to 1.44Mb of data. They spin at a constant speed of 300rpm and there are 135 concentric tracks per inch on each disk.

A floppy disk drive contains the following components:

❑ **Magnetic read/write heads** read and write the data to and from the disk surface.

❑ A **head actuator** moves the heads in and out across the disk to position them over a specific track.

❑ A **spindle motor** spins the disk about its axis so that the track/sector data passes beneath the heads.

The two read/write heads are spring-loaded and actually grip the disk surface on both sides. The direct connection between the heads and the disk surface causes wear over time, which is why it is a good idea to replace disks frequently.

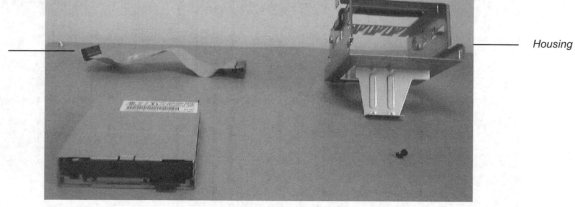

Cable ———————   ——— Housing

Figure 4.1: A floppy disk drive unit

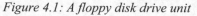

Discussion: What safeguards should be taken in the care of floppy disks?

4.2. Installing a floppy disk drive

Floppy disk replacements are not normally carried out to upgrade to a better version but just to replace a faulty unit.

A standard 1.44 Mb floppy disk has two main connection points to the motherboard or floppy disk controller. A 34-pin floppy disk cable is normally used to connect a floppy drive to the motherboard or drive controller card, for data flow. For power, a standard 4-pin keyed connector is used. Floppy drives have four main settings which you may need to be aware of when installing a drive. These are:

❑ Media sensor

❑ Drive Select (DS) sensor

❑ Drive Terminator

❑ Drive Ready sensor

Because floppy drives reside alone on their own controller ports these jumper settings should not need to be altered.

Refer to the user instructions which accompany the new floppy disk drive. Some general guidance is given below.

- **Ensure that the power is off and you have connected your anti-static wrist strap.**
- Before removing the existing drive, carefully note the alignment of the connectors, making notes if necessary.
- Carefully unplug the 4-pin power cable followed by the 34-pin data cable.
- Remove the drive mounting screws and the old drive.
- Attach the data and power cables to the back of the new floppy drive unit before inserting it into the drive bay – it might be difficult to access the ports after the drive is installed.

Figure 4.2: Installing a floppy disk drive

- Slide the floppy drive into the drive bay. Make sure the front of the drive is flush with the front of the PC unit. Make sure there are no gaps between the edges of the drive and the metal frame that surrounds it.

- Attach the screws that secure the drive in place making sure not to over-tighten them.

- Close the PC case and secure the case screws.

- Reinsert the power cable.

- If you have replaced the floppy drive with a similar unit, no BIOS adjustments should be necessary.

4.3. Hard disk drives

The hard drive on a PC is the central mass storage element of a PC system that holds all of your files and programs. Using a magnetic-based recording format, the disk retains the information even if the power supply is switched off.

When the operating system or any application is launched, its data is read from hard disk storage and loaded into RAM for processing by the CPU. For example if you choose to start Microsoft Word, the program is read from the hard disk and stored in RAM. If you then open a saved document, it too will be read from the hard drive and loaded into RAM. If you edit the document, the changes will be written back to the hard drive when you save the document. Operating systems also use the hard disk as an overflow for system RAM. When too many applications are loaded, those least recently used are stored back on the hard disk. Programs are tricked into thinking that these applications are still in RAM, but when the application is called up, the operating system goes to retrieve the information from the hard disk. This extension of the RAM, called Virtual Memory, can increase the functionality of the PC but it does reduce its performance, since hard disks are around 100 times slower than system RAM.

Hard drives are sealed units usually containing several circular platters which spin on a spindle at speeds ranging from 5,400 to 10,000 revolutions per minute. Moveable recording heads float above each platter, reading and writing data. Data is stored on both sides of each platter in concentric circles known as tracks which are then divided into sectors. The tracks that line up with each other on the various platters are collectively known as a cylinder.

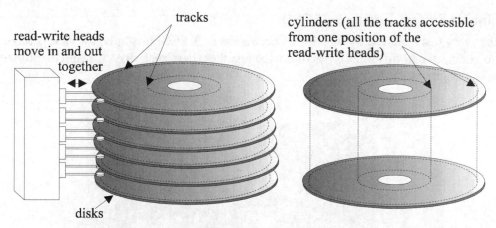

Figure 4.3: How data is stored on a hard drive

Hard disk drives are connected to the PC system via a disk controller which handles the transfer of the request to the drive and the passing back of the retrieved information over the PC's bus. These days the controllers are integrated directly into the motherboard and the two main controller types for PCs are called IDE and SCSI which are used to connect both internal and external devices.

Integrated Drive Electronics (IDE)

This type of hard drive has the electronic control circuitry built into the drive assembly and no additional board is necessary. Enhanced IDE (EIDE) drives have now replaced IDE drives which were limited in capacity. These use a fast system of data access called Logic Block Addressing (LBA). Several speeds or modes are possible providing up to 16.6Mbps (megabits per second) of data throughput. With EIDE two hard-drive channels are normally available allowing up to four devices to be connected to the motherboard. These need not only be hard drives but also CD-ROM/DVD-ROM drives and tape drives. One device on each channel is designated as the master and the other as the slave, and jumper settings may have to be configured to indicate this.

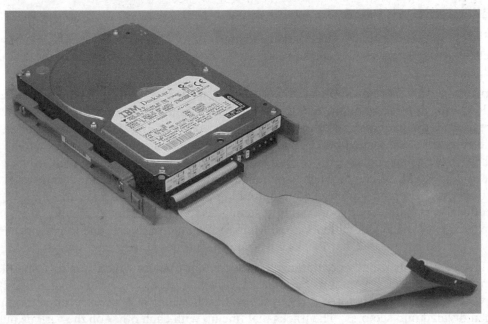

Figure 4.4: An EIDE hard disk drive and cable

Small Computer System Interface (SCSI)

This is another very fast standard by which PCs access data. A SCSI host adaptor card is required which allows you to chain several different types of device together (hard disk drives, printers, plotters, CD-ROM drives and scanners).

Figure 4.5: A SCSI host adaptor card

4.4. Upgrading a hard disk

The main reasons for upgrading a hard drive include the following:

- ❏ more room is needed for applications and/or data.
- ❏ the disk has crashed and needs replacing.
- ❏ a faster and more responsive drive is required.

The capacity of hard disk drives increases all the time and prices continue to go down, so this can often be an effective upgrade.

Hard disk upgrade kits are available which include all the necessary cables, brackets and screws and will probably include installation instructions. The steps below give a guide to installing a new internal hard disk.

Before you start:

- Backup your data, preferably onto tape, CD-Recordable, Zip or Jaz drives. The operating system, applications and all data will have to be copied onto the new drive after installation.

- If you are adding a second drive, open the PC case and check for available drive bays (your system documentation might help here). It is best to use a bay close to the other drive(s) to be within reach of the IDE cable.

- If you are replacing a drive without changing to a new controller you can use the old power supply connection and controller connection for the new drive. If you are adding a drive, check for free power supply (four wide-pin sockets) and controller connections.

- If you are installing an IDE device, set the jumpers on the disk to indicate if it is a master or slave drive.

- For a SCSI drive the jumpers must be set to a unique SCSI ID. The termination jumpers must also be set if the drive is at the end of a SCSI chain of devices.

Replacing the hard drive

- **Ensure that the power is off and you have connected your anti-static wrist strap.** Disconnect the power cable and open the case.

- Remove the data cable and the power cable from the old drive.

- Unscrew the mounting screws holding the old drive in place.

- Slide out the old drive and insert the new drive.

- Screw in the mounting screws for the new drive being careful not to over tighten them.

- Reattach power and data cables – both of these attach correctly in only one way. The ribbon data cable normally has a red line running along the edge corresponding to pin 1 of the connector. The hard drive should have a small 1 marking pin 1 on the data cable connector at the back of the drive. The power cable should have a rounded edge on the top two corners of the connector as does the top edge of the power supply port.

- Close the PC cover and connect the power cable.

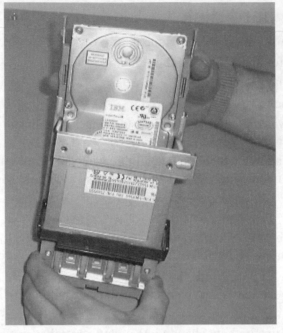

Figure 4.6: Removing a hard disk from its housing

Adding a second drive

- **Ensure that the power is off and you have connected your anti-static wrist strap**, disconnect the power cable and open the PC case.
- Mount your new drive in a free bay. Slide in the new drive so that its back end ports are closest to the data and power supply cable connections.
- Screw in the mounting screws, taking care not to over-tighten them.
- Connect the data and power supply cables. Internal cables have several connectors running along the length of one cable. Use one of the open connectors for both the data cable (coming from the controller) and the power supply cable (coming from the power supply).
- Close the PC case and reconnect the power cable.

Once the drive is physically installed you need to check that the BIOS updates to identify the new drive when you power the PC up again.

Partitioning, reformatting and installing files

Before using a new hard drive it must be prepared. Preparation includes:

- ❏ **Low-level formatting** (normally already completed by the manufacturer)
- ❏ **Partitioning**
  The new physical drive can be partitioned (or divided) into several *logical drives* (one hard disk can be divided into several logical drives which can be formatted and assigned a drive letter). Newer versions of Windows use a file system called FAT32 which does this very effectively. The disk can be partitioned using proprietary software supplied with the hard disk or the MSDOS **FDISK** command.
- ❏ **High-level formatting**
  The hard disk partitions now need to be formatted as you would a floppy disk (using **My Computer** in Windows). If it is your boot drive then the system files must be installed on it. Finally, copy the applications and data from the backup medium to the newly installed drive.

4.5. CD-ROM drives

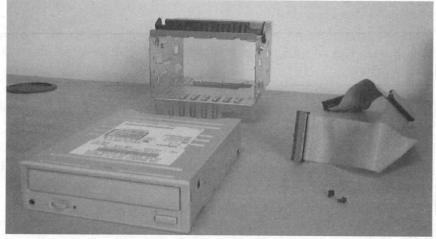

Figure 4.7: A CD-ROM drive

Compact disk read-only memory (CD-ROM) drives are now supplied with most PC systems. The CD-ROM is the preferred delivery medium of most software manufacturers: it provides a way in which large amounts of data can be stored for later retrieval and it has allowed software developers to include large sound and video data files in their applications and games. Up to 650Mb of data can be stored on the 4.72 inch disks.

Unlike magnetic-based recording formats such as floppy disks or hard disks, CD-ROMs use a laser light method for reading (and writing in the case of CD-Recordable drives) digital data from their discs. A laser scans the rotating disk surface and the light reflected back is interpreted as bit data.

The biggest change in CD-ROM drive technology relates to speed. Early drives had transfer rates of 150Kbps, called 1X speed. As manufacturers improved the drive mechanics and therefore the speed it became standard to refer to drive speed in multiples of this original transfer rate. Current CD-ROM drives are now mostly 12X to 40X speed – or even faster.

Like hard disks, CD-ROM drives come in both SCSI and IDE controller types and, as the transfer rates are slower than with hard disks, both types offer similar performance. Again IDE CD-ROMs will be internal so it is important to check that you have an available drive bay accessible via a removable space holder through the front of the machine. If you already have a SCSI controller or all the IDE controllers are full, you can consider either an internal or external SCSI CD-ROM.

4.6. Upgrading a CD-ROM drive

The main reasons for upgrading your current drive might include the following:

❑ It is slow (e.g. 1X or 2X).

❑ It has difficulty reading CD-Recordable discs.

❑ It is faulty, generating constant read errors.

❑ It is noisy.

❑ It is incompatible with popular CD-ROM formats such as Photo CD, Video CD etc.

Before you start:

• Consider purchasing a CD-ROM upgrade kit that will include all the necessary cabling, screws, rails (for sliding the drive into) etc.

- If the PC does not already have a sound card and speakers consider purchasing a full multimedia upgrade kit that will include everything.
- Choose a drive bay as discussed above.
- Check the cabling, making sure you have the necessary power cable (usually a white plastic moulding with four large pin openings) and controller cable (IDE or SCSI) and make sure they both reach the drive bay.
- Set up the drive. Remember that as for hard drives, an IDE device can be either a master or a slave and the jumpers on the device must be set accordingly (CD-ROM drives are normally already set as the master drive by default).

Installing a CD-ROM drive

- **Ensure that the power is off and that you have connected your anti-static wrist strap, then disconnect the power cable.**
- Open the PC case and remove the front placeholder panel.
- If the drive bay requires slide rails, attach them.
- Attach the controller cable and the power cable (they both only attach correctly in one position).
- Attach the audio cable from the CD-ROM drive to your sound card (or connector on the motherboard if there is no sound card). The audio port of the CD-ROM drive is normally adjacent to the power cable port. Read the maufacturer's documentation to find where the connector goes on the sound card. Slide the CD-ROM drive into the drive bay ensuring that the front edge fits flush with the front of the PC case.
- Close the PC case and reattach the power cable.

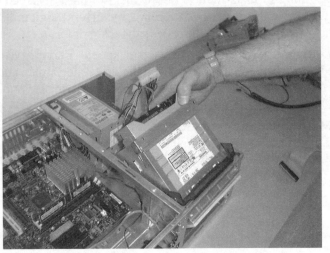

Figure 4.8: Installing a CD-ROM drive

- After physically installing the CD-ROM drive, power up the PC and Windows will automatically check for any hardware changes.
- When Windows detects the new CD-ROM drive, it will automatically install the appropriate driver. The Add New Hardware wizard may be displayed, in which case follow the on-screen instructions.
- When the system is rebooted, Windows should identify the new CD-ROM drive.

Figure 4.9: Automatically installing a new hardware device

CD-RW

Recently CD-R (CD-Recordable) and CD-RW (CD-Rewritable) drives have become available. These are optical recorders that provide a cheap and fast mass-storage option that can then be transferred to another compatible machine.

CD-R technology means that the disk can be recorded to only once. Although the data can be read back from the disk as long as the disk remains intact, you can never record over a track after it has been 'burned' by a CD-R drive (this is often referred to as **WORM** – Write Once, Read Many). A great advantage of CD-R discs is that they can be read by most other CD-ROM drives and so are useful for exchanging files and backup files.

CD-RW drives allow writing and rewriting on CD-RW discs. They can also write to CD-R discs which tend to be much cheaper. Unfortunately CD-RW discs cannot be read by older CD-ROM and CD-R drives: a drive conforming to the Multi-Read specification is needed to read them. CD-RW drives are also more expensive with relatively slow recording and playback speeds compared to CD-R drives. In addition CD-RW discs, although more expensive, only hold 650Mb of data compared to 700Mb on a CD-R disk.

Figure 4.10: A CD-RW drive

DVD-ROM

The DVD-ROM is now used in many homes as a replacement for video tapes and is becoming more widely considered as a medium for connection to PC systems. DVD-ROM drives are read-only and it is not possible to write or erase current content and re-record with new content. The drives use standard PC interface connectors – either IDE or SCSI. The discs are available in single or double-sided versions and each side can have a single or double layer. They offer a number of advantages over CD-ROMs:

❑ Higher capacity – a single-sided, single-layer DVD-ROM can hold up to 4.7Gb of information.

❑ A single-sided dual layer disk can hold up to 8.5 GB, with a double-sided single-layer disk can hold up to 9.4Gb. Double-sided, double-layered discs can hold an amazing 17Gb of information.

❑ Much greater speeds, giving faster response times. A DVD-ROM disk spins at about 3 times the speed of a single speed CD-ROM. The 2X-speed and 5X-speed drives are now well established and 10X-speed DVD-ROM drives are now available.

❑ DVD-ROM drives can also play standard CD-ROMs and audio CDs.

❑ Each DVD-ROM can hold up to 135 minutes of high quality video and CD-quality sound. Many films are now being released on DVD-ROM.

Figure 4.11: A DVD-ROM drive

4.7. Other backup media

In the commercial world today the information stored on computer systems is often more valuable than the equipment itself. It is therefore crucial for organisations to establish a backup strategy to protect data.

Data stored on a PC can be damaged in many different ways:

❑ Spikes in mains electricity can cause data errors.

❑ Lightning strikes can destroy a hard drive.

❑ RAM ICs can be stolen.

❑ Hard drives can simply wear out or crash.

❑ Computer viruses can damage programs or files.

❑ The entire PC could be stolen.

❑ Sabotage by unauthorised users.

The backup system should be specifically tailored to the particular organisation. However, more than one copy of each data backup should be kept in a different location (in case of fire or floods). It is also a good idea to keep a written log of what has been backed up, when and by whom.

If small amounts of data need to be backed up, floppy disks may be an appropriate medium. However, beyond this there are several other choices available which can be categorised into either tape- or disk-based backup systems.

Tape backup

A low cost option is tape backup which is used extensively particularly if time is not a major consideration (for example if you can back up overnight). Tape uses a sequential method of backup, so that Block A must be backed up before Block B and so on. Disk backup is random and so multiple blocks of data can be backed up apparently simultaneously. This is therefore a much quicker, but more expensive method.

Internal tape drives are normally the least expensive, but if you have no spare drive bays in your PC then an external device may be a solution.

There are several types of tape format – Sony's DAT (Digital Audio Tape) is one of the most popular and comes in two main formats, Digital Data Storage (DDS) and DataDAT.

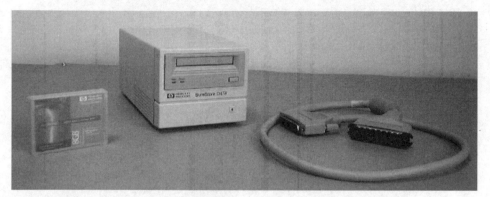

Figure 4.12: An 8Gb DAT external backup tape drive

Zip drives

Another option for removable storage is the Iomega Zip drive. These use 3.5 inch disks that are twice as thick as standard floppy disks and can store about 100Mb of data as standard, but recently a 250Mb version has been released and their capacity is bound to increase in the future. Zip drives have different interface options:

- ❑ SCSI internal
- ❑ SCSI external
- ❑ Parallel port external
- ❑ EIDE internal
- ❑ USB external

SCSI and IDE connections offer quite fast performance, but the parallel port option is quite flexible as it allows you to quickly connect up to different computers. The newer USB version is even faster and easier to install.

Figure 4.13: A Zip drive and Zip disks

Jaz drives

These are essentially the big brother of the Zip drive and are ideal if you want to back up your PC quickly and you are not too worried about the cost. The Jaz drive is basically a hard disk drive housing into which you can insert a 1GB or 2GB removable hard disk to back up your data. When a disk is full you can simply insert another disk when prompted.

The Jaz drive requires a SCSI controller interface card and is supplied as either an external unit or an internal unit which will fit into a floppy drive bay. A Jaz drive can back up 1Gb of data in about 6 minutes. The actual disks are relatively expensive.

Figure 4.14: A Jaz drive and Jaz disk

Removable Disk Storage Comparison

Device	Capacity (Mb)	Approx Price of Drive	Approx Price of Media
Floppy Disk	1.44	£20	£0.30
CD	650	£50	£0.99
Jaz	2000	£250	£60.00
Zip	250	£100	£15.00
DVD	5200	£200	£25.00

Online storage

Online storage is a relatively new concept. It can be thought of as a hard disk located on another computer that is accessed over the Internet. Providing you are online you can do all the things with a file stored on this virtual hard disk that you could do if it was stored on the disk inside your PC.

Online storage companies allocate 'blocks' of space to each user to store their files. The cost is set by the company itself but it is generally free, so long as you don't mind advertisements appearing while you work.

The advantages of this type of storage is that it cannot suffer the physical damage that a Zip or Jaz disk can. The data can also be accessed from anywhere in the world, without transporting removable disks or your complete PC with you.

> **Discussion: What do you think are the disadvantages of this type of storage?**

Chapter 5 – I/O Subsystems

Objectives

- ✓ To understand the different PC interfaces
- ✓ To learn how to upgrade a video card
- ✓ To learn how to install a sound card
- ✓ To understand the basic types of network and to install a network card

5.1. Interfaces

On the back of the system chassis there is a series of connectors (see Figure 5.1). There are serial and parallel ports as well as connectors for keyboards and mice. More recent Pentium systems will normally also include a pair of USB (Universal Serial Bus) ports. All of these connectors run directly from the motherboard and out of the back.

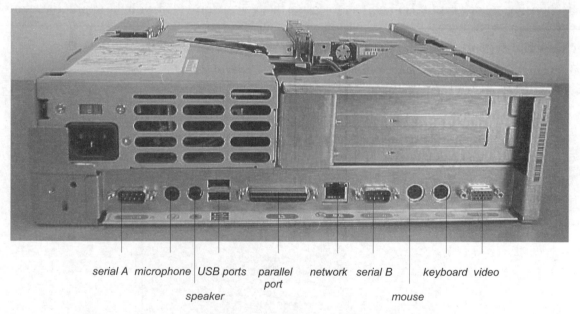

serial A microphone | USB ports parallel network serial B keyboard video
port

speaker   mouse

Figure 5.1: I/O connectors

5.2. Graphical interface

A video card (sometimes called a graphics card, display adaptor or graphics adaptor) generates the electrical signals which produce a picture on your PC screen. Upgrading a video card can speed up your graphics display and provide a wider range of display modes. The speed and range of resolutions of the video card are determined by the chipset and amount of memory on the card. However, adding more memory will not increase the speed but may provide more colours and better resolutions. The refresh rate of the card is important as this determines how steady an image appears on the screen. This is measured in hertz (Hz) and should be at least 72Hz at the resolution you are viewing.

Figure 5.2: A graphics card

2Mb of video memory is now an accepted minimum standard in order to provide 1600 x 1200 resolution in 256 colours. However for serious graphics or DTP work a minimum of 4Mb is recommended. Some high-performance cards are available with 16Mb memory providing millions of colours and very high resolutions.

When choosing a video card it is important to ensure that you are provided with the appropriate software drivers and the means to switch between different resolutions.

To check the type of video card in your PC

- From the **Start** menu, select **Settings** and click on **Control Panel**.
- Double-click on the **Display** icon.
- Select the **Settings** tab.

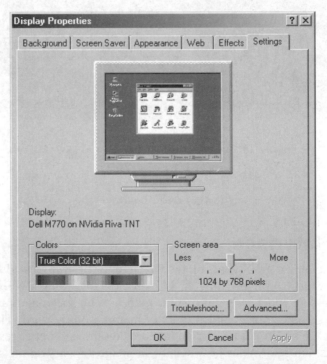

Figure 5.3: Investigating the properties of your display

The Display Properties box tells you the type of display you are using, the number of colours available and the screen resolution (1024 x 768 in this case). You can adjust these settings using this dialogue box.

- Click on the **Advanced** button.
- Select the **Adaptor** tab.

Information about your video card is displayed as shown below. In this example the video card has 16Mb memory.

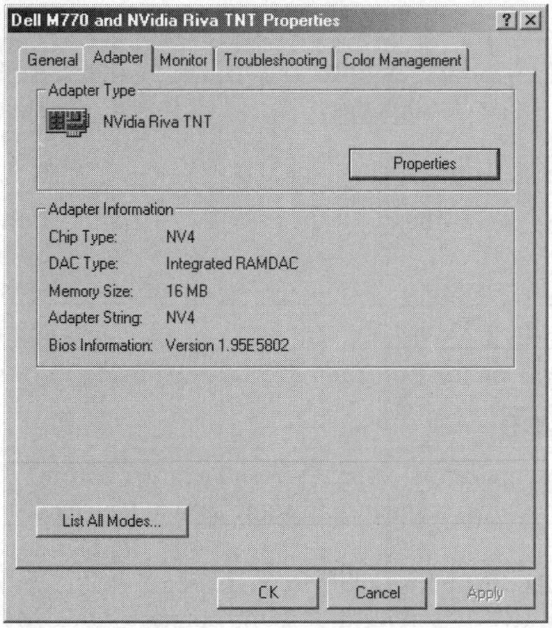

Figure 5.4: Video card settings

To install a new graphics card

Most new graphics cards are Plug and Play compatible so the job of installing one is made quite simple. However, these instructions are intended to be a guide only – you should also refer to the manufacturer's instructions.

- **Ensure that the power is off and that you have connected your anti-static wrist strap.**
- Unscrew any retaining screws and carefully unplug any leads connected to the old card (make a note of the connections if necessary) and remove it from its slot.
- Install the new card in the appropriate slot. If you are installing a VGA/ISA card use an ISA slot, or a PCI slot for a PCI card, or the AGP connector for an AGP card. Hold both ends of the card and if necessary carefully rock the card from end to end to push it fully home in the slot.
- Refit the securing screw into the metal mounting plate of the card.
- Reconnect the video card leads as before.
- Replace the PC case and switch on the PC.
- You may be prompted to insert the disk containing the software driver (this should be supplied with the card). However some later releases of Windows may automatically have it installed.

5.3. Parallel interface

On most desktop PCs the parallel port is used to connect printers. The parallel port is generally fast enough for data transfers such as printing jobs. Scanners, tape backup, external CD-ROM drives, Jaz and

Zip drives are also designed to be able to use the parallel port. Not all parallel ports are the same – the standard issue on earlier PCs was the centronics port, but newer systems feature an enhanced parallel port (EPP) or an enhanced capabilities port (ECP) which are able to provide duplex operation and higher data rates. EPP and ECP ports can cut down on print times but only if the printer can recognise the different signals.

The different types of parallel port are compared in the table below (bps stands for bits per second, the data transfer rate).

Parallel port type	Throughput	Description
Centronics	40-300Kbps	Standard issue on earlier PCs. Highest level of compatibility with all devices.
Enhanced Parallel Port (EPP)	2Mbps	Better performance and allows bi-directional communication but not supported by all printers.
Enhanced Capability Port (ECP)	2Mbps	Improved version of the EPP.

5.4. Serial interface

Most PCs have two serial port connectors – one 9-pin and a larger 25-pin. These ports are used by external peripherals such as modems, scanners and some slower tape back-up systems. Serial ports can transfer 1.5Kbps of data.

The serial ports use the logical COM ports to talk to the system. COM1 and COM3 service one serial port connector and COM2 and COM4 service the second connector. COM1 and COM2 are the best ports to use as the higher COM port addresses can change: this effectively limits the number of permanent serial-based peripherals to two.

5.5. Universal Serial Bus (USB)

USB ports have solved a real problem with many PC systems – a lack of serial and parallel ports to support all the peripherals now available for connection to the PC. Most desktop PCs include two USB connectors placed at the level of the motherboard. The peripherals themselves must be USB compliant but many are now supported as plug and play devices including mice, keyboards, scanners, printers, modems, joysticks, digital cameras and audio speakers. The advantages of USB connections include:

- The compact snap-in connectors will support up to 127 linked peripherals (daisy-chained).
- 12Mbps data transfer rate (considerably faster than most parallel ports).
- Allows hot-swapping of devices (i.e. swapping devices without restarting the PC).
- Allows low-power devices such as modems and scanners to run without their own external power supply.

5.6. Sound

A sound card can provide a PC with high quality audio functions and is a vital component in any multimedia system.

Sound cards handle several types of sound. They can handle wave audio, i.e. sounds that have been recorded outside the PC, generally called .WAV files. They can also support the Musical Instrument Digital Interface (MIDI) standard that allows musical instruments and the PC to share data. MIDI files

(.MID) are digital and contain codes that tell the PC system how to produce the required sound. Professional musicians use MIDI to compose electronic music.

Figure 5.5: An ESS 1868 sound card

For many years the Creative Labs Sound Blaster card has been the standard sound card installed in PC systems. Therefore before planning to upgrade a sound card it is advisable to check that the new card is Sound Blaster compatible to ensure maximum compatibility with most PCs. The older Sound Blaster cards ran on the ISA bus but newer sound cards run on the PCI bus and are plug and play compatible. Sound cards provide line-in and microphone inputs for recording analogue sound to digital files. Speaker and line-out ports send analogue sound to speakers or external recording devices. Many boards also include a MIDI port for controlling MIDI devices such as musical keyboards.

5.7. Installing a sound card

These instructions are provided as a guide only: you should refer to the instructions supplied with the sound card.

- **Ensure that the power is off and that you have connected your anti-static wrist strap.**
- Identify the slot into which you will install the sound card.
- Remove the screw holding the metal blanking plate next to the slot you are using.
- Hold the sound card by the metal mounting bracket and opposite card edge without touching any of the components or the edge connectors.
- Set any configurable jumpers to the correct positions by referring to the documentation provided.
- If the CD-ROM drive has a 4-pin audio cable, connect one end of this to the sound card and the other to the internal CD-ROM drive.
- Some CD-ROM drives allow for the main data connector to plug directly into a sound card rather than the IDE connector. Depending on your particular configuration, connect the sound card ribbon data connector to the correct place. Insert any other connectors.
- Holding the card by its edges, carefully push the card into the expansion slot and replace the mounting screw.
- Plug in your speakers to the appropriate jack socket on the sound card.
- Most sound cards are now Plug and Play compatible so when you switch on the PC and start Windows, a message should be displayed informing you that it has detected new hardware and is installing it.
- You may be prompted to install the driver disk supplied with the card. If so, follow the instructions.

5.8. Network interface

A computer network is a collection of interconnected computers and peripherals that enable users to share information and resources easily.

There are two main network models:

❑ Local Area Network (LAN) where all the network components are physically in the same location. In practice this usually means within say 100m of a central point.

❑ Wide Area Network (WAN) where various LANs or standalone devices at different locations anywhere in the country or world are connected together by means of telecommunications facilities.

There are two types of local area network: **peer-to-peer** and **server**.

A peer-to-peer network is generally a small network in which the individual PCs share their resources e.g. documents and printer(s).

A server network is used for larger systems and has one or more computers (servers) dedicated to the network that do nothing but service workstation requests. They also provide a central point for logging on to the network and controlling access.

The most widely used networking system is Ethernet which can run on a network using either twisted pair cabling or coaxial cabling. Most modern networks use Ethernet on UTP which is unshielded twisted pair cabling. It can achieve fast data speeds (100Mbps) and supports many different types of equipment. The network is usually configured in a star topology where each PC and the server is connected to a central hub. One of the advantages of this kind of configuration is that any cabling fault merely affects the single device using it (unlike a 'Bus' network where PCs are simply daisy-chained one to the next). The hub helps route data to the correct PC.

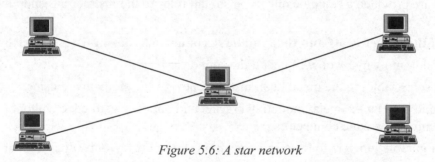

Figure 5.6: A star network

The alternative to Ethernet is a Token-Ring-based network which is more suited to larger organisations. In this type of network each PC is connected to the next PC in order to form a complete ring. Token-Ring networks can move data at a rate of 4-16 Mbps.

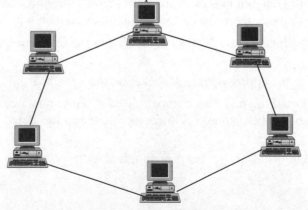

Figure 5.7: A ring network

Ethernet cards use:

RJ connectors (RJ45 for 10BaseT cables – 10 megabits per second)

DB connectors (DB15 D-shaped 15-pin used for ThickNet coaxial cable –rarely used now)

BNC connectors (for ThinNet coaxial cable)

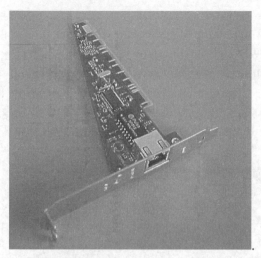

Figure 5.8: An Ethernet network card

Each networked PC needs a network interface card (NIC) installed on or connected to its motherboard. The network cable then plugs into the appropriate socket on the NIC. This network card translates information moving on to the network into standard-sized packets of data. These packets are translated into electrical signals which are passed onto the cable. The NIC in the receiving PC receives the electrical signal, then decodes the packet and delivers it to the computer.

When choosing a network interface card you must ensure that it is compatible with your type of network – most cards are designed for use on either Ethernet or Token Ring networks.

Ideally you would select the fastest possible network cards to help transfer information as fast as possible around the network. If you are installing an Ethernet network card in a Pentium PC, a PCI-type will be faster than ISA, providing you have a spare slot available. Most current network interface cards are available in 2 speeds: 10Mbps (also referred to as 10BaseT) or 100Mbps (also referred to as 100BaseT). Provided that all the cards are Ethernet compatible it is normally acceptable to mix different brands of network cards.

> **Discussion: What advantages are there to a user working on a networked system over a standalone PC?**

5.9. Installing a network interface card

Most network cards are Plug and Play compatible and one of the most popular configurations is the hub-based, star configuration. These instructions are intended to be a guide only, and you should refer to the manufacturers instructions.

- **Ensure that the power is off and that you have connected your anti-static wrist strap.**
- Find an empty expansion slot of the correct type for the card (ISA or PCI), in each PC.
- Insert the card into the first slot. Repeat in the other PCs.
- With one end of the network lead plugged into the card, plug the other end into the appropriate socket on the hub. Repeat with the leads from the other network cards.

- Plug in the power supply to the hub and switch on both the hub and the PCs.
- You may be prompted to insert the disk containing the software drivers (this should be supplied with the cards). However some later releases of Windows may automatically have them installed.
- Reboot each PC.

Setting up network interface cards

After installing a network card Windows 2000 detects it when you start your computer and then starts the local area connection automatically. To see the installed components:

- Double-click the **My Computer** icon and select **Control Panel** and then click on **Network and Dial-up Connections**.
- Double-click the **Local Area Connection** and then in the next dialogue box click on **Properties**. A number of components will have automatically been installed. You can install and enable additional components from this dialogue box.

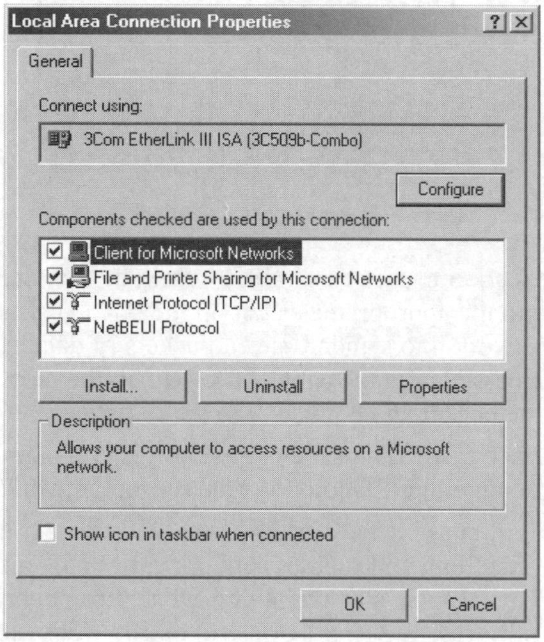

Figure 5.9: Configuring a network card

All computers in a Windows 2000 (or NT) network belong to either a domain or a workgroup. A domain is a group of computers that share a common security database and that can be administered as a group. If you are working on a smaller network you will probably not participate in a domain, but you will belong to a workgroup which is a named set of computers.

- To join a workgroup open the **Advanced** menu in the **Network and Dial-up Connections** folder.
- Click **Network Identification**.
- The **Network Identification** tab of the **System Properties** dialogue box shows your computer's current name and workgroup. Click the **Properties** button to make any changes.

Note: In Windows 2000, file and printer sharing is enabled by default. In Windows 98 and 95 it must be set from the **File and Printer Sharing** button on the window similar to Figure 5.9, accessed from **Start**, **Settings**, **Control Panel**, **Network**.

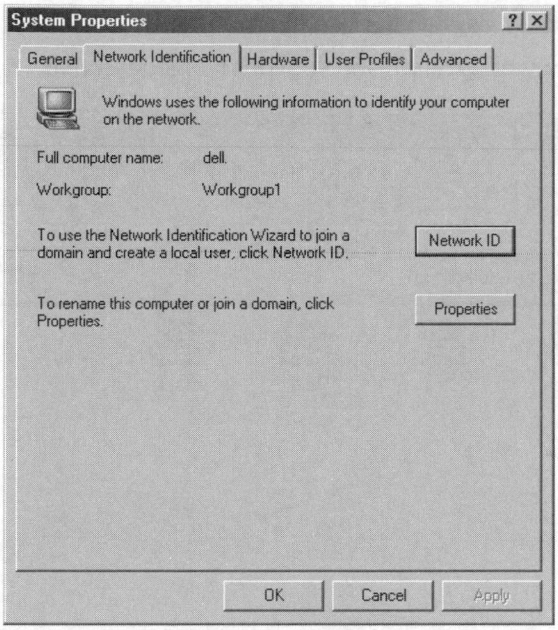

Figure 5.10: Identifying a computer on a network

- Restart the computer to ensure that Windows records the new settings.

- Repeat the above steps for each PC on the network.

- To test the local area network, reboot all of the PCs.

- On each PC double-click the **Network Neighbourhood** icon. You should be able to see all of the PCs on the LAN. You can double-click on each of them to view the files and folders on each networked PC.

- To allow sharing of a particular drive or folder right-click on a folder in Windows Explorer and select **Sharing**. Set the options on the **Sharing** tab in the dialogue box.

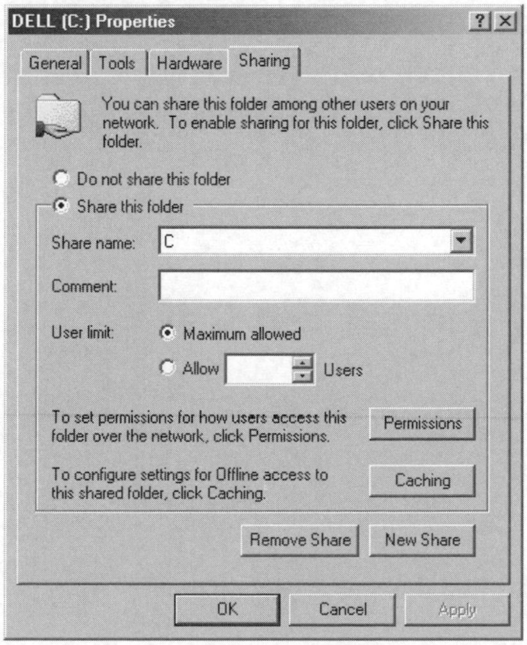

Figure 5.11: Sharing folders

The shared drive or folder then appears with a hand beneath it.

- View the computers in a workgroup from Network Neighbourhood.

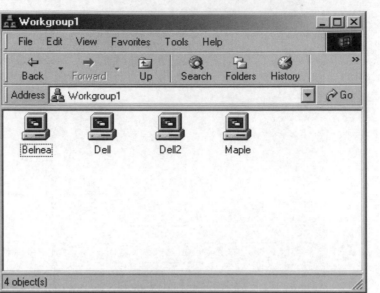

Figure 5.12: Viewing the PCs connected to the network

Chapter 6 – Peripheral Devices

Objectives

✓ To learn about different input devices
✓ To learn about different output devices
✓ To install a range of devices

6.1. Monitors

Computer monitors are similar to television sets in that both are cathode ray tubes (CRTs). Both displays are composed of individual dots on the screen called *pixels*. An electron beam constantly scans over the pixels which are coated with a phosphoric substance and are illuminated by the beam. However they do not hold this illumination for long so the beam constantly has to refresh them. The number of times per second is called the *refresh rate* and is measured in hertz (Hz). Originally the beam scanned the rows of pixels in order from top to bottom, but this could cause annoying screen flicker since by the time the electron beam reached the pixels at the bottom of the screen, the ones at the top had started to lose their illumination. Manufacturers found that they could reduce screen flicker by *interlacing*, that is, scanning the odd numbered rows and then the even numbered rows so that every part of the screen was scanned twice as often. Most monitors now run at refresh rates of at least 72Hz. At this rate, interlacing is not necessary as the beam hits the pixels often enough to prevent flicker.

Figure 6.1: An IBM 15 inch monitor

A monitor's **resolution** measures how many pixels make up the screen. All PCs also need a video card (see Chapter 5) which together with the monitor determines resolution. The size of the screen is also an important factor. Screen size is measured diagonally from the top left corner of the screen to the bottom right, but remember that this is not the viewing area because the case and fascia cover up part of the screen.

Generally monitor sizes match up with standard resolutions used by Windows. This is a guide to the best size for the different resolutions:

15-inch monitor	800 x 600
17-inch monitor	1024 x 768
19 or 21-inch monitor	1280 x 1024

Another factor that affects the clarity of the image is the **dot pitch** of the monitor. It is usually expressed as a decimal number, the smaller the better but preferably 0.28mm or less for a sharp image.

Other considerations include power consumption – choose one that conforms to the latest energy-saving criteria. The US Energy Star standard ensures that a monitor will power down to 30 watts or less in "sleep" mode. All monitors also emit some radiation and obviously the less the better. Many manufacturers meet the Swedish MPRII guidelines or the stricter TCO-92 standard. Most monitors also feature controls for straightening and resizing the screen image as well as the swivel and tilt features of an ergonomic design. Some monitors are also being produced with integral speakers which can help decrease the clutter on the desk. However these can reduce the display quality and this type of speaker often produces poor sound quality.

Although there are great advantages in having a large monitor, particularly for certain applications, there is a major drawback – they are huge, taking up lots of desk space and they also consume large amounts of power. The manufacturers' response to this has been the introduction of flat-screen displays like the one shown in Figure 6.2 below. These are LCD (Liquid Crystal Display) screens similar to those provided on laptop computers and although considerably more expensive, do have a number of advantages. As well as taking up less space on the desk, they consume a fraction of the power and emit much less heat and no electromagnetic radiation. Above all though is the display quality that is superior to virtually all CRT monitors. Unlike CRTs which refresh the image 70 or 80 times each second, pixels on an LCD screen remain constantly lit. They therefore offer greater clarity and sharpness and reduce the health risks of prolonged periods staring at the screen.

Figure 6.2: A flat screen display

6.2. Printers

A good printer can help you produce professional-looking output from your PC system. There are three main categories of printer and it is important to select the correct printer for the job.

Dot Matrix printers

A dot matrix printer is an **impact printer**, producing its image by striking the paper through a ribbon. Its print head consists of a number of small pins, varying between 9 and 24 depending on the manufacturer. A 24-pin print head will produce a better quality of print than a 9-pin print head because the dots are closer together.

As the print head moves across the page, one or more pins strike the ribbon and make a dot on the paper. The figure below shows how the letter F is produced.

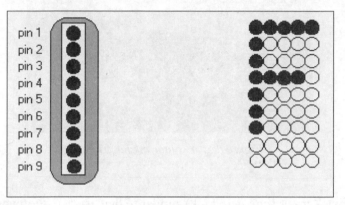

Figure 6.3: Dot matrix print head

In order to produce 'near letter quality' (**NLQ**) print, a line is printed twice, with the print head being shifted along very slightly in the second printing so that the spaces between the dots are filled in. The disadvantage of this technique is that the document then takes approximately twice as long to print. Many dot matrix printers are 'bidirectional', meaning that they can print in either direction, thus eliminating the need to start printing each line from the left hand side of the page.

Dot matrix printers are relatively cheap but have largely been replaced by newer technology, as the print quality does not compare with, say, laser-printed output. Also, they are noisy and are sometimes supplied with acoustic covers. They are useful for jobs (e.g. invoices) that require multi-part stationery which has holes down each side and is loaded onto sprockets on the printer. This is the cheapest method of printing multiple copies. Wide-carriage models are also available for printing on large custom stationery.

Figure 6.4: An Epson FX-1170 dot matrix printer

Ink Jet printers

These have become the most popular option for home printing as they are relatively cheap but provide reasonable quality text and graphics including colour printing. Ink jets work by forcing small dots of ink through tiny holes to form the text or graphics on the page. The ink is stored in replaceable cartridges, normally separate for colour and black ink. Most low-end ink jets do not have their own memory to store the page to be printed: instead they have a small buffer (from 128 to 512Kb) to hold incoming data which is printed on the page as soon as it arrives. This type of printer is capable of printing envelopes, labels, acetates and other specialist paper.

Figure 6.5: A colour ink jet printer

Laser Printers

Laser printers use fine black *toner* (powdered ink) similar to that used in photocopiers to produce high quality text and graphics.

A laser heats up a cylindrical drum and creates electrical charges on its surface which represent an image of the page to be printed. The toner sticks to the electrically-charged areas creating a 'negative image'. Paper is then rolled around the drum and the toner sticks to it creating a 'positive image'. The paper becomes heated which fuses the toner onto it.

The replaceable toner cartridges are expensive (typically £50 - £70), but can be refilled and recycled. Most laser printers have their own memory to store pages being processed which can make them quite expensive to purchase. However they are ideal for volume printing as they can print up to twelve pages per minute, with the larger network models like the one shown in Figure 6.9 able to print 30 to 40 pages per minute or more.

Figure 6.6: An HP laserjet 2100 laser printer

6.3. Installing a new printer

- Place the printer on a flat stable surface.

- Connect the 25-pin parallel port cable to the printer and the parallel port on the PC.

- Plug in the printer's power cable.

- Ensure that an ink or toner cartridge is installed in the printer.

- Power up the printer and do a test print (usually from a test button found on the outside of the printer).

If the printer you install conforms to the Plug and Play standard Windows should recognise it. If you connect a Plug and Play printer while Windows isn't running, at the beginning of your next Windows session Plug and Play detects the device and installs the requisite driver. Depending on the device the Add Printer Wizard may appear and ask you a few questions.

If the printer is not a Plug and Play device you should use the Add Printer Wizard to install it. This can be accessed from **Start**, **Printers**. **Add Printer**.

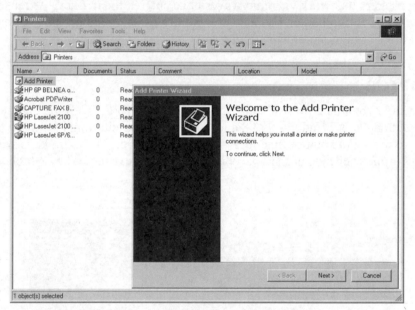

Figure 6.7: Installing a new printer

6.4. Speakers

Buying a good sound card will be a waste of money if you have poor quality speakers. Some of the important things to consider in their specification are as follows:

- ❏ Power output per channel in watts RMS – usually in the range of 10-30 watts per channel.

- ❏ Frequency response – a high-quality card will reproduce the low-frequency sounds at 20Hz through to the high-frequency sounds at 20,000 Hz.

- ❏ Distortion, measured in percent. The lower the figure the better.

When the volume of a sound is lower our ears can become less sensitive to extreme low and high notes. A switch on some speakers allows you to enhance the bass and treble sound quality to compensate for this.

Powered speakers are also available which have audio amplifiers built into the speaker boxes. These can give a greater level of sound with more control than is provided by the sound card.

Figure 6.8: Powered speakers

Recently, cordless speakers that work via radio waves have entered the market. A transmitter is plugged into the speaker socket on the computer's sound card and the speakers (containing batteries) are placed wherever you want them but not more than 100m away.

6.5. Keyboards

There are a number of keyboards now available mostly using the QWERTY-type layout with 101 keys, or 104 keys for new commands in Windows 95/98 and NT. The three additional keys are not essential but allow touch typists to use all the mouse functions from the keyboard. The extra keys are the two **Windows logo** keys – one each side of the Spacebar and the **Context menu** key which is situated to the right of the Spacebar.

Figure 6.9: A range of keyboards

Several ergonomic designs have been introduced that change the shape of the keyboard and provide wrist rests. Some have a 'soft' key action while others have a crisp mechanical action. Figure 6.10 also shows a trackball keyboard which saves space by providing a ball that performs the functions of a mouse and can minimise the amount of hand movement required.

6.6. Mouse

Together with the keyboard most PCs also have a mouse as an input device. They have a rubber-coated ball inside, which rolls against the surface of your desk or mouse pad as you move the mouse. As the ball rotates it drives two rollers, one for left-right movement and one for up-down movement. A motion digitiser reads the turning of these two bars, interpreting them as increments of travel (measured in hundredths of an inch). A message is then sent to the PC to tell it that the mouse has been pushed forward half an inch or right a quarter of an inch. Most mice have two or three buttons on the top which also have sensors that send a signal to the PC each time a button is pressed or released. A small software program called a mouse driver is required for the mouse to work, but this is included in Windows.

Mice generally operate over a dedicated PS/2 mouse port or the serial port (usually a 9-pin connector).

Figure 6.12 shows some variations on the standard mouse. They are available with a tracker ball or a scrolling wheel (found on the IntelliMouse) between the two buttons. In Windows applications the left button is usually configured for most actions with the right button reserved for special actions or short cuts. However reconfiguring the software will often allow you to reverse these actions. Some operating systems require a mouse with three buttons.

6.7. Installing a new mouse

- Plug in the new mouse
- Select **Start**, **Settings**, **Control Panel** and double-click the **Add New Hardware** icon.
- Follow the **Add Hardware** Wizard instructions.

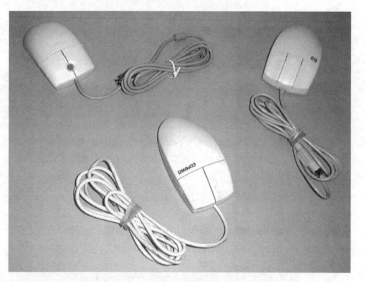

Figure 6.10: Two or three buttons?

To reconfigure your mouse for left-handed operation:

- From the **Start** menu select **Settings**, **Control Panel** and then click on the **Mouse** icon.
- In the **Mouse Properties** dialogue box click on the **Buttons** tab (Figure 6.11).
- Select **Left-handed**.

You can also drag the **Double-click** speed adjustment to make it faster or slower. If you click on the **Pointers** tab you can change the appearance of the pointer on the screen and adjust the motion of the pointer by clicking the **Motion** tab.

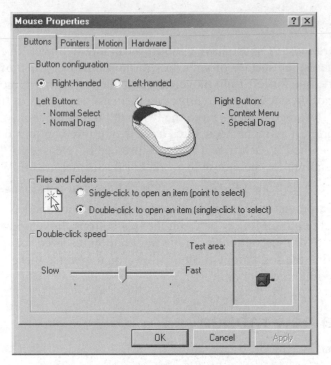

Figure 6.11: Changing the mouse properties

6.8. Scanners

A scanner is used to scan an original image or document and then to convert the information it picks up into a digital representation on the PC. Handheld models have now generally been overtaken by flatbed models. These record reflected light as the scanning apparatus glides beneath the glass window or 'bed'. When buying a scanner, look for ones labelled optical or true resolution. As a scanner sweeps a page the optics see it as a series of thin strips – the thinner the strips the higher the resolution. 600 strips per inch or an optical resolution of 600dpi is preferable and more expensive models can do much better – even 2400 dpi. Colour depth is also an important part of the specification: most scanners have 24-bit capability but some offer 42-bit colour depth for a similar price. '24-bit capability' means that 2^{24} (over 16 million) different colours can be recorded.

In the past scanners were connected to the PC via the parallel port or over a SCSI connection. However, recently more USB-based scanners have become available. Budget models tend to connect over slower parallel or USB ports as no extra card is required and most parallel-interface scanners feature a pass-through port, meaning that a printer and scanner can share the PC's single parallel connector.

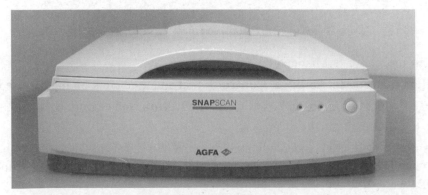

Figure 6.12: A flatbed scanner

6.9. Microphone

With the increasing use of Internet chat and cheap long-distance telephone charges, it is possible to talk to someone on the other side of the world using your PC with a sound card, microphone and speakers or a combined headset, the appropriate software and an Internet connection.

A microphone must be compatible with the sound card in the PC. The sound card documentation should specify the impedance required. The impedance of a common PC microphone is 600 ohms. Remember that they usually record in mono not stereo so the sound quality will not be great.

Usually a microphone attaches to a sound card via a small round jack socket labelled 'Mic in' (see Figure 5.4).

Figure 6.13: A microphone and headset combined

Once you have connected your microphone you can record sound/voice files in .wav format within Windows using software such as **Sound Recorder**.

- From the **Start** menu select **Programs**, **Accessories**, **Entertainment**, **Sound Recorder**.
- On the **File** menu, click **New**.
- To begin recording, click the **Record** button.
- To stop recording, click the **Stop** button.
- On the **File** menu, click **Save As** and save the sound file.

You can play your recording in **Sound Recorder** or in **Media Player**.

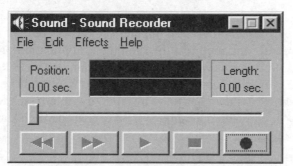

Figure 6.14: Recording a sound file

Discussion: Produce two lists of input and output devices.

49

Chapter 7 – Introduction to Software

Objectives

- ✓ To look at different categories of software
- ✓ To consider the organisation of files and folders
- ✓ To configure the ROM BIOS
- ✓ To modify operating system files

7.1. Types of software

Software is the general term used to describe all of the programs which run on a computer. There are three general categories of software:

- ❑ Systems software
- ❑ Special purpose applications software
- ❑ General purpose applications software

7.2. Systems software

This category itself covers several types of software:

Operating systems

An operating system must be installed on every computer. It allows the user to communicate with the computer hardware and it controls and monitors the running of application programs. The operating system consists of a number of programs which are typically 'bundled' with the hardware; in other words, when you buy a new PC, for example, you will also be supplied with a CD containing the latest version of the Windows operating system. This then has to be installed by running a special installation program supplied on the CD, which will copy the operating system to your hard disk and customise it to your particular hardware configuration.

All operating systems perform certain basic functions, including:

Memory Management – most computers nowadays are capable of holding several programs in memory simultaneously, so that a user can switch from one application to another (multi-tasking). The operating system has to allocate memory to each application as well as itself.

Resource allocation and scheduling – in larger computer systems capable of running several programs at once (multiprogramming), the OS is responsible for allocating processing time, memory and input-output resources to each one.

Backing store management – the OS controls the transfer of data from secondary storage (e.g. hard disk) to memory and back again. It also has to maintain a directory of the disk so that files and free space can be quickly located.

Interrupt handling – the OS detects many different kinds of interrupt such as, for example, a user pressing the **Enter** key on the keyboard, a printer sending a message that it is ready for the next block of data to be sent, the real-time clock interrupting to indicate that the processor should be allocated to the next user in a multi-user system, a hardware or software malfunction.

User interface – the user gives instructions to the computer to start a program, copy a file, send a message to another user and so on by typing in commands recognised by the operating system or, more usually nowadays, by using a mouse to point and click in a Graphical User Interface (GUI) such as Windows 95, 98, 2000 or Me.

7.3. Examples of operating systems

MS-DOS (Microsoft Disk Operating System)

This is a simple operating system that is only capable of executing a single program at any one time. When a program is run, it runs until it completes; only then can another program be run. It is a single-user operating system and offers little security.

It is essentially a command-driven interface, meaning that the user has to type in commands in exactly the correct syntax to perform any operation. These commands can be quite complex and while experienced users may be able to perform operations with some speed, the average user can find it a difficult interface to work with.

Windows 95, 98 or 2000

Some years ago Microsoft produced the Windows operating system which, although based upon pioneering work done by Apple in this field for their Mac range of machines, is by far the most widely used family of operating systems in the world today.

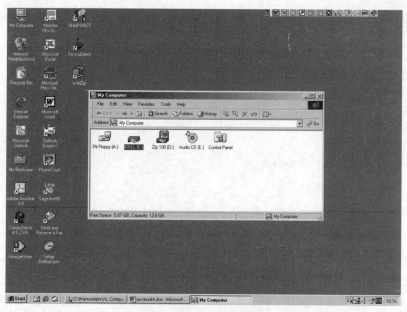

Figure 7.1: Windows 2000 GUI interface

Windows 95, unlike previous versions of Windows, was in itself a full operating system offering true multi-tasking (i.e. allowing the user to have more than one application running simultaneously and to switch between them) and taking full advantage of the 32-bit architecture of newer PCs (allowing applications to run faster). Other improvements include a completely redesigned GUI (Graphical User Interface) and the ability to use file names of up to 255 characters.

Windows 95 and subsequent versions also provide 'Plug and Play' support designed to make it easier to install peripherals such as a new printer. This has been discussed in the chapters dealing with hardware, earlier in this unit.

UNIX

This is a general-purpose, multi-user, multi-tasking operating system written in C which has been around since the early 1970s. It is generally used on mainframe computers and, unlike other operating systems, it can be used on different types of hardware produced by many different manufacturers (referred to as different **platforms**).

LINUX

This operating system was created by Linus Torvalds, a Finnish programmer. It is available entirely free and can be downloaded from the Internet. There are not currently many applications that will run under Linux; Microsoft have had a virtual monopoly with the Office suite of programs but rivals Corel and Borland are beginning to offer Linux versions of their software.

Networked operating systems

These are operating systems designed to control networked computer systems such as Windows NT and Novell Netware. This type of operating system controls users' access to shared resources on the network such as programs and data, and also physical devices such as printers and backing store. It uses login procedures to identify a user and request a password. The users are allocated network rights which are controlled by the operating system and which limit their access to the network.

7.4. Utility programs

Numerous utility programs are available to users such as:

Virus checkers – these check the disks and memory for viruses and clean them if detected (e.g. McAfee and Norton Utilities).

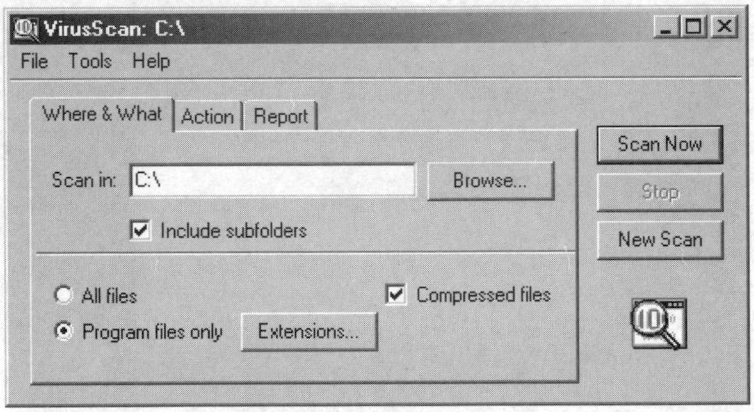

Figure 7.2: A virus checker

Security and accounting – this type of software is normally installed on a network to check user IDs and passwords, to count and report the number of attempts to log on under each user ID, the amount of processor time used at each session and so on.

File management utilities – these attempt to detect and repair corrupted files (e.g. ScanDisk), reorganise files on disk so that the space is defragmented and so improve performance (e.g. Defrag), 'Zip' (compress) files so that they occupy less space (e.g. WinZip).

7.5. Programming languages

Low-level programming languages such as machine code or assembly language are machine-oriented, designed to be close to languages that the hardware of the machines can understand. Because these are difficult for humans, high-level languages have been developed which are designed to be closer to English. General purpose programming languages include Pascal, Visual Basic, C and C++ amongst others.

Programming language **compilers** and **interpreters** are the programs used to translate the statements in a programming language such as Visual Basic, Pascal or C into a form that the computer can understand.

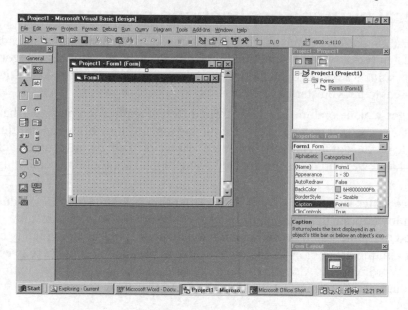

Figure 7.3: Visual Basic programming environment

7.6. Diagnostic software

This type of software is used to monitor, analyse and report on the performance of a computer and its components. It can provide information such as the overall utilisation of the processor and number of disk accesses over a given period of time. Some basic diagnostics are provided by Windows System Tools (e.g. ScanDisk and System Information). Some hardware manufacturers also supply additional diagnostic software (e.g. Compaq diagnostics). It is also possible to download free diagnostics software from the Internet (e.g. AMIDiag) or purchase alternative diagnostics packages (e.g. Checkit-Pro and Norton Utility Diagnostics). Diagnostic and trouble-shooting software is discussed further in Chapter 10.

7.7. Drivers

Drivers are pieces of software which undertake a most important task, providing the interface between hardware devices and subsystems and the operating system. Manufacturers of hardware all strive to make their devices the best in terms of value for money, functionality, flexibility and versatility. In order to do this, the various designs will often be quite different and will require to be driven in a particular way to get the best out of them. It would not be feasible for an operating system to be able to cater for all these variations. Thus manufacturers of printers, monitors and graphics cards etc. all supply a driver with their hardware which will interface correctly to the given operating system.

7.8. Special purpose applications software

This type of software is written to perform specific tasks such as order entry, payroll, stock control or hospital appointments. The software may be designed specifically for one particular company ('bespoke' software) and written for them using a programming language or software such as a database management system. Alternatively the software can be purchased 'off the shelf', for example Sage for accounting and Pegasus OPERA, an integrated package for accounting, stock control, sales and order processing.

7.9. General purpose applications software

All common application packages such as word processing, desktop publishing, spreadsheet, database, computer-aided design (CAD) and presentation graphics packages fall into this category. Most general purpose software is sold as a package, including a CD containing the software and either manuals or an on-screen help system to get you started.

Integrated packages which combined features from different application packages have been very popular in the past and can still be a good buy for the beginner as they offer capabilities from different packages in a single product at a relatively low price. However a single integrated package (e.g. Microsoft Works) has fewer and less sophisticated features than are found in separately-purchased packages.

Complete **Software suites** such as Microsoft Office offer four or more software products packaged together at a much lower price than buying the packages separately. A software suite such as MS Office can also be referred to as integrated in that the individual applications are completely compatible, so that there is no problem in importing or exporting data from one package to another (e.g. copying an Excel spreadsheet into a Word report). Also the packages have the same look and feel, with the same shortcut keys used for various operations (e.g. **Ctrl–S** for **Save**) and this makes learning new software an easier task.

PC vendors often offer one of these software suites as **bundled** software that is 'thrown in' with the price of the PC. These deals often seem very tempting but it is important to consider what is essential and what you can really do without.

Figure 7.4: Integrated packages and software suites

7.10. Application Service Providers

In the future more software companies may consider offering consumers the chance to subscribe for access to certain software applications instead of buying them outright. Application Service Providers (ASPs) already provide this service and Microsoft has recently announced that it will offer annual subscription fees for its Office software.

Discussion: What are the advantages and disadvantages of this type of service?

7.11. Generic software

This is a general term used to describe application packages that are used to perform operations that are an integral part of day-to-day business operations. The most common ones are word processors, spreadsheets, database management, graphics and electronic mail. Versions of these applications are available from many different software manufacturers, but they all have many features in common – these are summarised in the following paragraphs.

7.12. Word Processing

A word processing package is a program that is used to enter, edit, format, store and print documents. A document may be anything from a simple memo to a complete book. In addition to data entry and editing facilities, word processors have several important features:

Spelling and grammar checker – this allows all words in a document to be checked against the package's dictionary.

WYSIWYG capability – this acronym stands for 'What You See Is What You Get' and refers to the ability to display on screen exactly what you will get when the text is printed.

Creation of standard templates – these provide preset styles, margins, formatting, letterheads etc. to speed up the word processing task.

Import files – pictures, graphics, video and sound files can be imported from other sources and inserted into a document.

Mail merge – a document and a list of names and addresses can be merged to produce personalised letters.

Automatic creation of index and table of contents – in a long document any word can be marked for inclusion in an index. Headings and subheadings in a given style can be included automatically in a table of contents.

Examples of Word Processing packages include:

    Microsoft Word

    Corel WordPerfect

    Lotus SmartSuite

Figure 7.5: Word processing packages

Discussion: What word processing features would someone writing a technical manual need, that a secretary writing letters would not?

7.13. Spreadsheets

Spreadsheet packages allow the user to create worksheets representing data in column and row form. Spreadsheets are used for any application that uses numerical data, such as budgets, cash flow forecasts, profit and loss statements, student marks or results of experiments. Spreadsheets generally offer the following facilities:

Formatting – it is possible to format cells, rows and columns and to copy/cut and paste data. Rows and columns can be inserted, moved and deleted.

Formulae – use of the basic arithmetic operators allows calculations to be performed within and between cells.

What-if calculations – the effect of several hypothetical changes of data can be determined.

Functions – these can be used within formulae (e.g. SUM, AVERAGE, MIN, MAX etc.).

Templates – spreadsheets can be stored and retrieved that have formats and formulae already entered, into which new figures may be inserted.

Queries – a simple data base can be created and then certain records extracted in a report depending on certain criteria.

Macros – to automate common procedures.

3-D worksheets – one spreadsheet can consist of several worksheets and data can be copied between them.

Charting – many different types of chart and graph can be produced (e.g. pie charts, bar charts, histograms, line graphs).

Examples of spreadsheet packages include:

> Microsoft Excel
>
> Lotus 1-2-3

Figure 7.6: Spreadsheet packages

7.14. Database Management Systems

Database packages store a collection of data and enable the rapid retrieval and analysis of information. The main features of a database system include:

Editing of data – data can easily be edited to correct errors, add new records or delete old records.

Data validation – as data is entered into the database it can be validated to help ensure accuracy.

Sorting of records – records can be sorted alphabetically and numerically in a matter of seconds.

Queries – certain records can be extracted from the database depending on specified criteria.

Forms – these can easily be created to make data entry easier for the user.

Reports – different types of report analysing data can be produced from the system.

Macros – these can be developed to automate common procedures.

Examples of databases include:

MS Access

Filemaker Pro

Borland Visual dBase

MS Visual FoxPro

7.15. Bitmap graphics

Painting packages can be used to produce and edit pictures called bitmap graphics. When a picture or photograph is scanned using scanning software, the colour of each pixel is saved to produce a bitmapped image. This can be edited in great detail – down to pixel level. However the files created are large and sizing a bitmap can cause some distortion.

Examples of painting packages include:

Microsoft Paint

Corel Photo-Paint

Adobe Photoshop

Jasc Paint Shop Pro

7.16. Vector graphics

Drawing packages produce geometric objects called vector graphics (e.g. the drawing tools in MS Word, Corel Draw and CAD packages).

Vector graphics deal with *objects* which can be sized easily without distortion and are used in technical drawings or CAD applications that require great precision. The drawings are saved in a different way: instead of saving the colour of each pixel, information about each object is saved – for example the start and end points and thickness of a line, or the centre and radius of a circle.

Packages such as AutoCAD are used by architects and engineers to produce technical drawings. Objects can be scaled and rotated, shaded and shown in three dimensions, and have calculations performed on them to find, for example, volume or centre of gravity.

Examples of graphics packages include:

Drawing tools in MS Word

Corel Draw

AutoCAD

Figure 7.7: Corel Draw, a vector graphics package

7.17. E-mail

E-mail systems allow you to send memos, letters and files containing data of all types from your computer to any other computer with an e-mail address and a modem, simply by typing in the recipient's name and pressing the 'Send' button. Some of the standard facilities on offer include:

Address book – a list of contacts can be stored so that you do not have to remember e-mail addresses.

In and Out boxes – copies of all incoming and outgoing messages can be stored until deleted.

Reply feature – it is easy to send a reply to an e-mail as soon as it is received by using a 'Reply' button.

Attachment feature – data in files of many types can be attached to the e-mail message and transmitted electronically to the destination.

Send to lists of people – the same message can be sent simultaneously to a group of people.

Examples of e-mail packages include:

> Microsoft Outlook
>
> Microsoft Outlook Express
>
> Lotus Notes

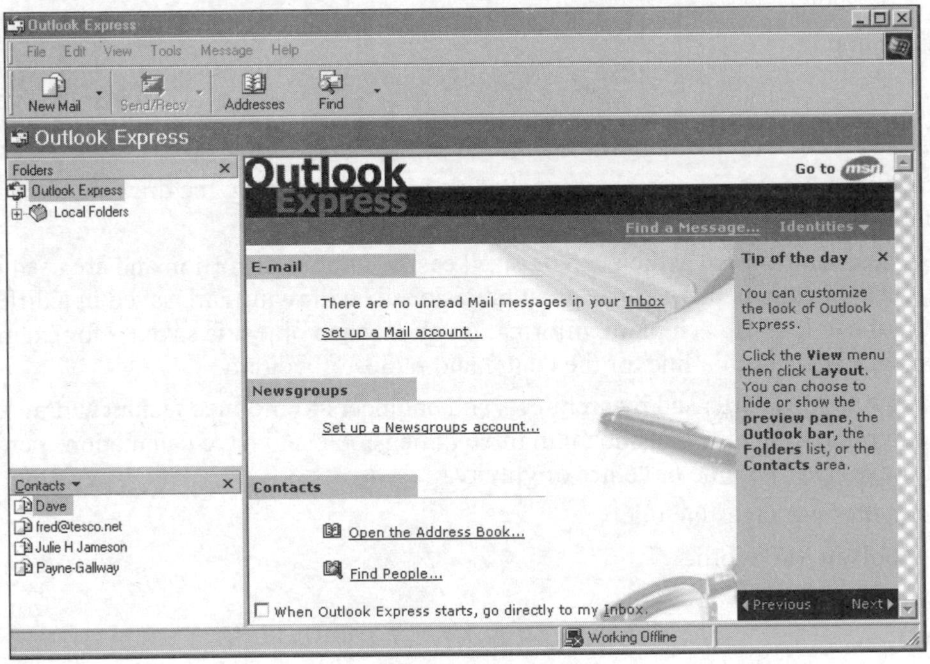

Figure 7.8: Microsoft Outlook

Discussion: What are the advantages of e-mail over "snail-mail"?

7.18. Organising files and folders

It does not take long before a PC has hundreds, probably even thousands, of files stored on the hard drive. It is therefore extremely important to keep your work organised so that you can easily find a particular file. Windows Explorer (don't confuse this with Internet Explorer) allows you to create folders and subfolders in which to store your files. To access Windows Explorer either click on it in the **Programs** list from the **Start** menu *or* right-click the **Start** button and click **Explore** *or* it may be displayed as an icon in your Office toolbar**.**

When Windows is first loaded onto your computer it names each of the drives – the floppy drive is usually A:, the hard drive C:, the Zip drive if you have one is probably D:, the CD drive E: and so on. The hard drive may also be partitioned into several 'logical drives' in addition to C: designated D:, E:, and so on (this process is usually done when formatting the disk). In this case the CD drive might end up as F: or G: Additionally on a network you can assign a drive letter to a shared drive or folder on another PC so that it appears as drive K: or Q:, for example. This, among other advantages, allows you to find it faster in a file dialogue.

On the C: drive Windows sets up a number of folders and every time you load on new software such as Word, Excel or Access another set of new folders is created and files put into them.

One important folder that is set up automatically is **My Documents**. This is where Windows expects you to create your own subfolders to store your work (however you can create folders outside My Documents if you wish). The important thing is to plan how you are going to organise the work you do and set up folders and subfolders accordingly. The figure below shows a small part of a directory structure.

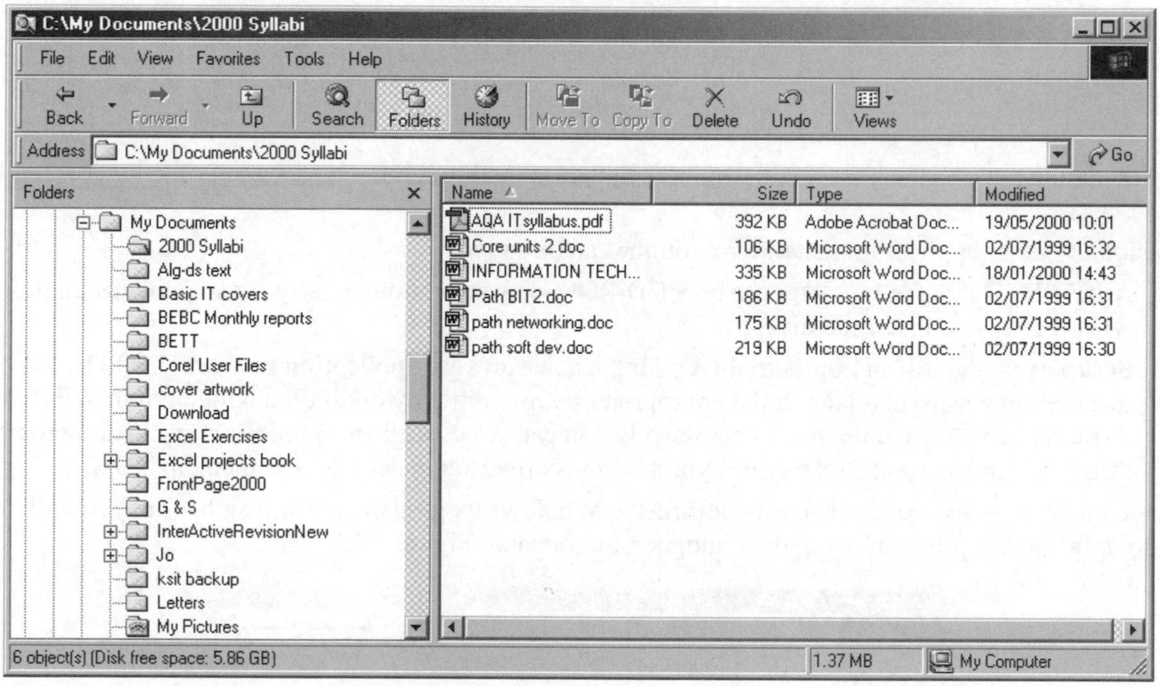

Figure 7.9: Windows Explorer

Some types of network offer students different ways to manage their files. For example RM Connect networks also provide each new user with a **MyWork** folder in which to store their documents.

7.19. Installing new software

Software is usually supplied nowadays on CD-ROM and is very simple to install on a Windows system. However, being able to uninstall software is also very important – it is not sufficient to just delete program files, they must be correctly uninstalled or some files will be left behind.

The **Add/Remove programs** facility is available from the Control Panel.

- From the **Start** menu select **Settings**, **Control Panel**.
- Click on the **Add/Remove Programs** icon.
- Click the **Add New Programs** button in the following dialogue box:

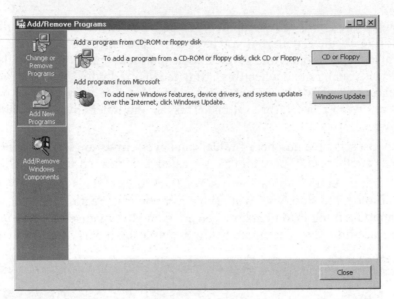

Figure 7.10: Adding new programs

As with adding new hardware, a wizard interface guides you through the installation of software step-by-step.

Occasionally other application installation routines are required:

❑ **Auto-Play** – this feature detects a new CD-ROM disk and automatically fires up the installation wizard after you insert the disk.

❑ **Setup.exe** – the instructions supplied with the new software application may tell you to bypass the installation wizard and launch the appropriate *setup.exe* file by double-clicking on it in Windows Explorer or in My Computer. Alternatively you can select **Run** from the **Start** menu and browse through your files and folders until you find the correct *setup.exe* file and then click **OK**.

Provided that the software application conforms to Windows 9x guidelines for installation, you will be able to uninstall the program using the dialogue box shown in Figure 7.12.

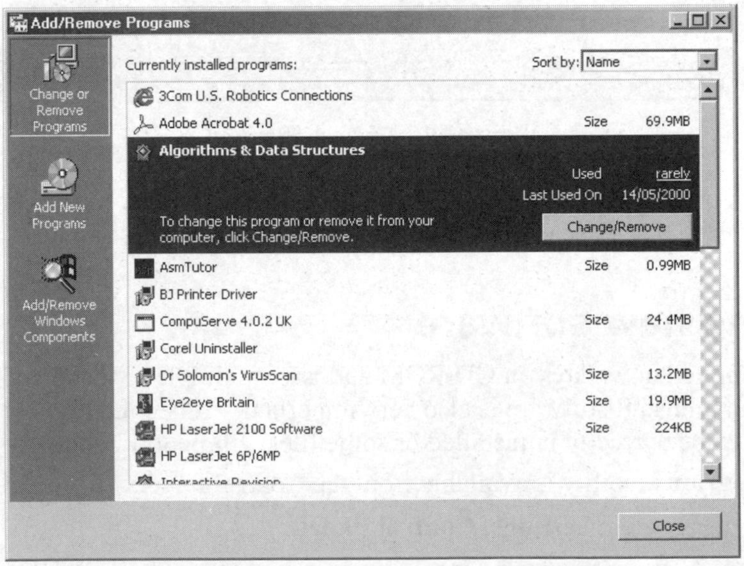

Figure 7.11: Changing or removing programs

7.20. Configuring the ROM-BIOS

The BIOS has been referred to many times. It is the most basic software within the PC and is responsible for the low-level functions required to make the hardware operate properly. The BIOS records basic information about the PC such as the type and characteristics of the hard disk drive(s) installed, the amount of memory, date and time etc. As such, it must be correctly configured or the PC simply will not operate as intended.

When a hardware change is made to the PC you need to inform the BIOS what the change is. This is particularly true for older PCs – more modern PCs will update the BIOS automatically. However it is still a good idea, even under these circumstances, to know how to view the BIOS settings.

Every PC has a SETUP utility program which may be entered on powering up the PC. The means to invoke this program varies from PC to PC – details will be in the PC user guide. Often you will have to press the DELETE key or one of the function keys in a specific time interval during power up. The screen will usually carry a message giving the instruction on how to invoke the program.

For example the SETUP utility on an HP Vectra machine gives the following BIOS information:

- ❑ Main – which deals with Operating System issues (PnP), reset configuration data, time and date and low-level hardware issues (key repeat speed, NUMLOCK on at power on etc).
- ❑ Advanced – which deals with Memory and Cache, Video, Floppy Drives, IDE Devices, NIC, I/O Ports, USB, PCI Configuration and ISA Resource Exclusion.
- ❑ Security – which deals with passwords etc.
- ❑ Boot – which deals with boot device priority (which order to scan possible boot devices) etc
- ❑ Power – which deals with the delays etc before the PC goes into sleep mode.
- ❑ Exit – where you can choose to either save or discard the configuration changes which you may have made.

7.21. Modifying OS files

Operating system files are extremely complex and should be modified only if you are confident with what it is you are trying to achieve and aware of how to do it.

If you are about to edit a system file, you must first copy the file in its unedited state and then rename it. Thus if you edit the file incorrectly and the system no longer works then you can restore the original file and put yourself back to square one.

The files which you are most likely to want to edit are:

autoexec.nt (**autoexec.bat** in previous versions of Windows)
This file can be used to customise a computer for a particular purpose at system startup. Thus, for example, a computer which is used for one particular package can be automated to load that package at startup. The obvious example of this is the automatic starting of windows on PCs. Autoexec.bat files can contain many complicated command sequences, but a simple extract is shown below:

```
echo off
rem loads UK keyboard driver
keyb uk
rem provides path to DOS commands and programs
path c:\dos;c:\word
```

config.sys

This file is also automatically executed when the system is switched on. It contains commands which configure the computer system for particular installation requirements.

system.ini

win.ini (the two initialisation files).

In order to modify these files, you must first open them with an appropriate editor. If you are in Windows you can open these files using **Notepad** or **WordPad** found under the **Accessories** menu in **Start/Programs**. You use these programs as elementary word processors and edit the appropriate lines. When you have finished you save the changes.

If you are working in DOS, then you use the **edit** command at the DOS prompt, carry out the edit in the same way and save the changes.

Bear in mind that, depending upon the file you have edited, the change may not be apparent until you reboot the machine.

Chapter 8 – Customising a GUI System Interface

Objectives

✓ Setting the time and date
✓ Setting passwords
✓ Customising the desktop
✓ Learning about the Office shortcut toolbar

Most of the Windows Graphical User Interface (GUI) features can be customised from the Control Panel. This has been used in previous chapters for adjusting hardware settings, adding and removing peripherals etc.

8.1. Setting the time and date

Most monitors are capable of displaying the current date and time. This can be modified as follows:

- From the **Start** menu, select **Settings**, **Control Panel** and click on the **Date/Time** icon.
- Change any settings necessary in the dialogue box:

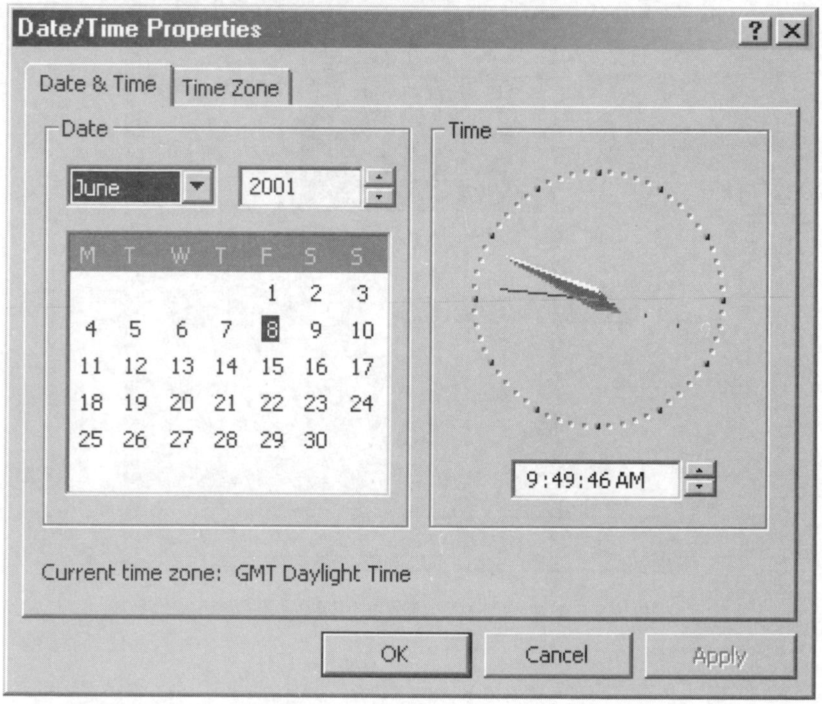

Figure 8.1: Setting the date and time

8.2. Setting passwords

In Windows there are several different levels of password that can be set to prevent unauthorised access to your system.

When you first log on to Windows you need to enter your Windows password. In Windows 2000 you can no longer change this from the Control Panel. You can change it as follows:

- From anywhere in Windows 2000 press **Ctrl-Alt-Del** to display the Windows Security dialog box.
- Click **Change Password**.
- Type your current password in the Old Password box and then type your new password twice to ensure you have typed it accurately.
- Click **OK** and then click Cancel to close the Windows Security dialogue box.

When you create a password, write it down and keep it in a secure place. If you lose the password, you cannot gain access to Windows.

A password can contain any combination of letters, numerals, spaces, and symbols, and it can be up to 15 characters long. Passwords are case-sensitive, so if you vary the capitalisation when you assign the password, you must type the same capitalisation when you enter the password.

You can also password-protect your computer if you have to leave it for a while unattended. For example you can protect your files by assigning a screen saver password.

- From the **Start** menu select **Settings**, **Control Panel** and click on the **Display** icon.
- Select the **Screen Saver** tab and select the screen saver you want to use.
- Selecting the **Password protected** check box will lock your workstation when the screen saver is activated. When you begin working again you will be prompted to type your password to unlock it (your screen saver password is the same as your logon password).

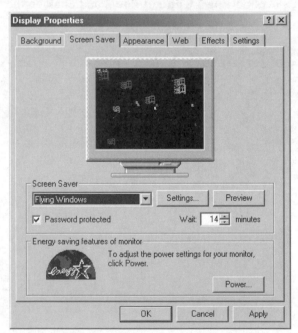

Figure 8.2: Password protecting the screen saver

In a similar way you can password-protect your computer during standby, so that a password has to be entered to leave standby mode.

- From the **Start** menu select **Settings**, **Control Panel** and click on the **Power Options** icon.
- Click on **Advanced** and make sure the **Prompt for password when computer goes off standby** check box is selected (your standby password is the same as your logon password).

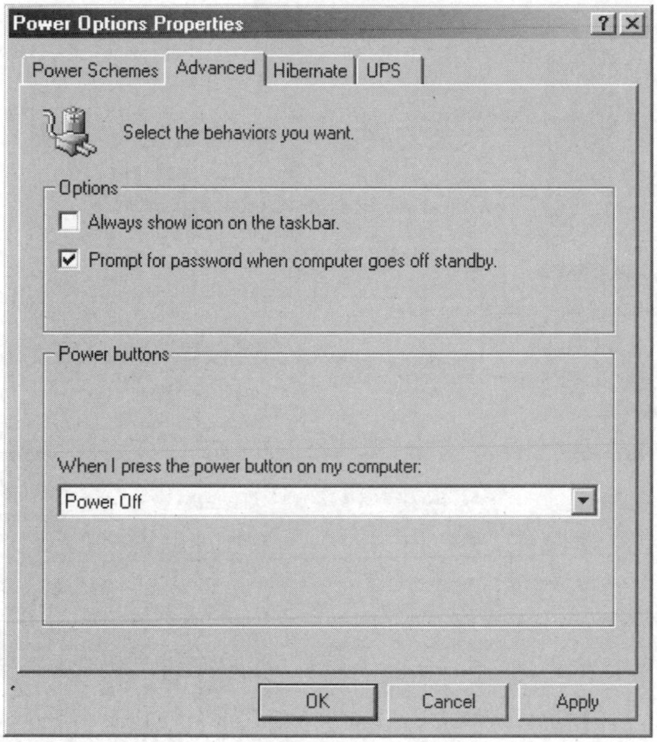

Figure 8.3: Password protecting a PC in standby mode

8.3. GUI desktop setup

The standard Windows desktop can be customised in several different ways: the colour scheme can be changed from the **Appearance** tab, a screen saver set up from the **Screen Saver** tab, different types of icon displayed from the **Effects** tab or a pattern or picture introduced as the standard background from the **Background** tab.

- From the **Start** menu select **Display**.

The Display Settings dialogue box will be displayed.

- Try clicking on the different tabs to see the options that are available.

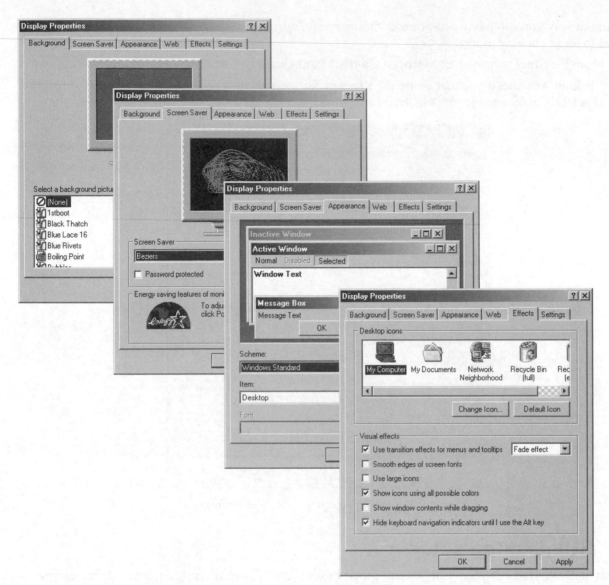

Figure 8.4: Options for customising the Windows desktop

In Windows 98 and 2000 a number of these customisations have been combined into desktop themes. You can choose to apply one of these from the **Control Panel**.

- From the **Start** menu select **Settings**, **Control Panel** and click on the **Desktop Themes** icon.

- Use the dialogue box shown below to choose a theme for your desktop.

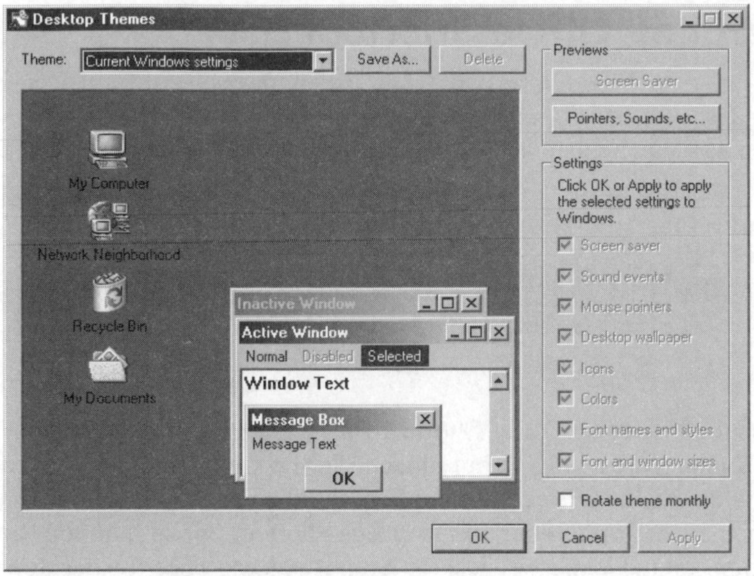

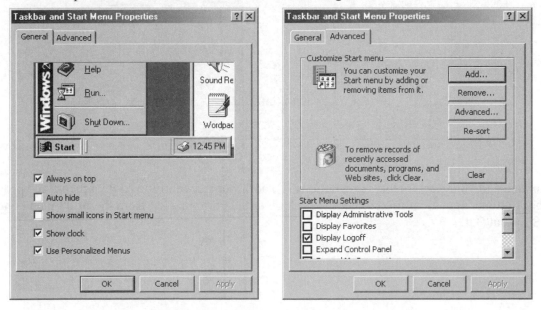

Figure 8.5: Choosing a desktop theme

The bar at the very bottom of the Windows desktop is referred to as the Taskbar. This shows which tasks are currently running. The System Tray is located to the right: graphics card settings, sound card volume and the PC's system clock can generally be accessed from here.

Figure 8.6: The Windows Taskbar

The System Tray

The appearance of the Taskbar can be changed together with the contents of the **Start** menu.

- From the **Start** menu select **Settings**, **Taskbar & Start Menu**.
- Look at the options available on the two tabs of this dialogue box.

Figure 8.7: Changing the properties of the taskbar and the Start menu

8.4. The Microsoft Office Shortcut Bar

Another optional feature of a Windows desktop is to display the Microsoft Office Shortcut Bar. This provides single-click access to the resources you need most often in Microsoft Office. It is not strictly part of the Active Desktop as it can be displayed even when the desktop is hidden by application programs.

You can drag the Shortcut Bar to any location on screen, or you can put it out of sight until you need it by right-clicking it and selecting **Auto Hide** from the menu.

Figure 8.8: The Microsoft Office shortcut bar

The first time you use the Microsoft Office Shortcut Bar, it displays only the Office toolbar. Additional shortcut buttons and toolbars are available but hidden. To show hidden buttons or toolbars, right-click the background of any toolbar on the Office Shortcut Bar, and then click **Customize** on the shortcut menu. For example, to show the Desktop toolbar on the Office Shortcut Bar so that you can easily access documents and programs on the Windows desktop even if you can't see the desktop:

- Right-click the background of the Office Shortcut Bar, and then click **Customize** on the shortcut menu.

- Select the **Toolbars** tab and then click the **Desktop toolbar** icon.

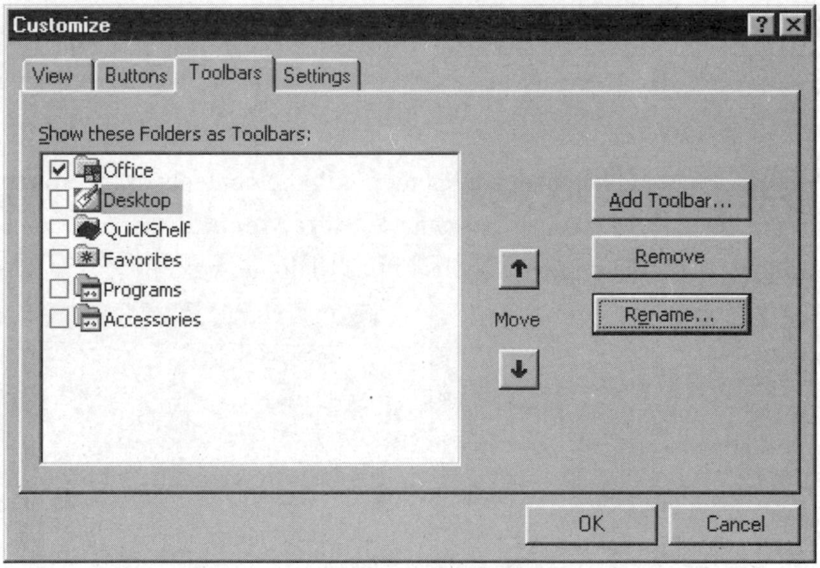

Figure 8.9: Customising the Office shortcut bar

You can also add your own toolbars and buttons. To add your frequently-used documents and programs as toolbar buttons, drag them from either the desktop or the Programs list from the **Start** menu onto the Office Shortcut Bar.

Chapter 9 – Customising Application Software

Objectives

✓ To customise toolbars and buttons

✓ To change the default printer

✓ To create and use templates

✓ To consider saving and backup security

✓ To automate tasks using macros

9.1. Toolbars and buttons

In most of the Microsoft Office applications it is possible to customise the toolbars that are displayed. Remember that you can display a particular toolbar by clicking **View**, **Toolbars** and selecting the toolbar. A quicker way is to right-click on any toolbar and select from the shortcut menu displayed. In Office 2000, adaptive toolbars were introduced. This means that on a smaller screen only the most recent toolbar buttons you have used will be displayed. To display the remaining buttons click on the small downward pointing arrow at the end of the toolbar. You can also choose which buttons to display on a toolbar by clicking on the arrow and selecting **Add or Remove Buttons**.

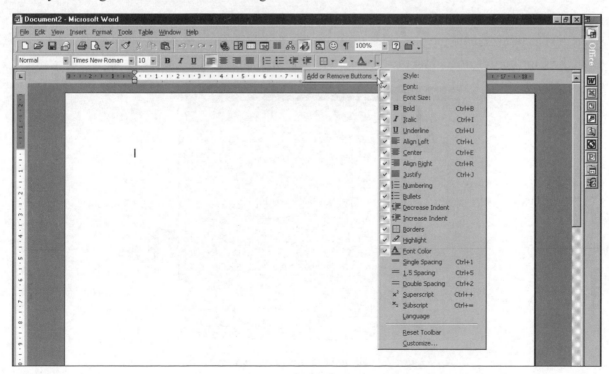

Figure 9.1: Displaying toolbar buttons

If you only use a word processor for specific work such as preparing e-mails, you may want to create a new toolbar with just those buttons you use and not display the other toolbars.

- In Word, click on **View, Toolbars, Customize**.
- Click the **Toolbars** tab.
- Click **New**.
- In the **Toolbar** Name box, type *My Toolbar* and click **OK**.

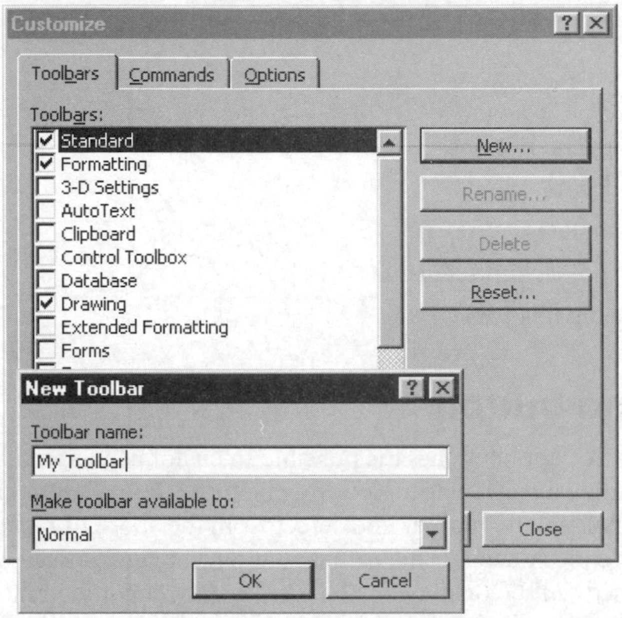

Figure 9.2: Creating a new toolbar

A small toolbar appears in the document.

- In the Customize dialogue box, click the **Commands** tab.
- In the **Commands** area, drag the **New E-mail Message** button to the new toolbar.

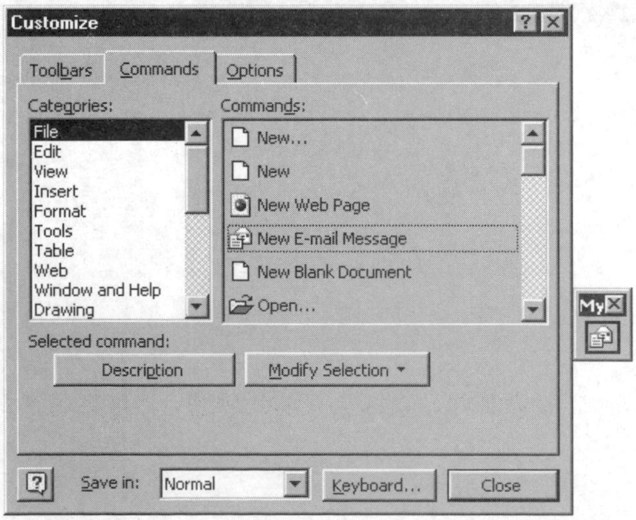

Figure 9.3: Adding buttons to the new toolbar

- In the **Categories** area, click **Insert** and then in the **Commands** area, drag the **Date** button to the new toolbar.
- Finish the toolbar by adding any other buttons you want.
- In the **Customise** dialogue box, click **Close**,
- From the **View** menu, deselect all of the other toolbars.
- Drag the new toolbar below the menus.
- Press **Ctrl-Home** to move the insertion point to the top of the document.
- Try out the new toolbar by clicking the **Insert Date** button.

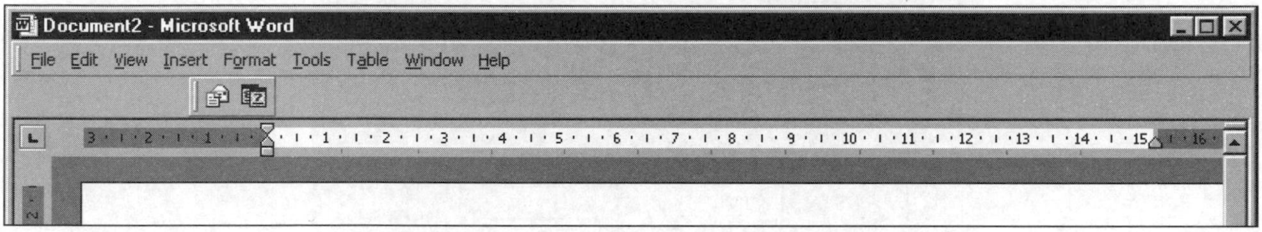

Figure 9.4: The new toolbar ready for use

To change the position of the buttons:

- Select **View**, **Toolbars**, **Customize**.
- Drag the **Date** button in front of the **E-mail** button.

To delete the new toolbar:

- Select **View, Toolbars, Customize**.
- In the **Customize** dialogue box, click the **Toolbars** tab.
- In the **Toolbars** list, select **My Toolbar**.
- Click **Delete**, **OK** and then **Close**.

Discussion: Describe some other circumstances in which a user may want a customised toolbar.

9.2. Menu layout and content

Only the items that you use most often are automatically displayed on the new adaptive menus in Office 2000. You can easily view the whole menu by clicking on the arrow beneath the menu commands. However, as with toolbars, as you use a menu command it will become one of those automatically displayed.

You can create a new menu in a similar way to creating a new toolbar.

- In Word, click on **View**, **Toolbars**, **Customize** (see Figure 9.3).
- Click on the **Commands** tab and select **New Menu** from the **Categories**.
- Drag **New Menu** from the **Commands** box up to the main menu line.

Figure 9.5: The New Menu in place

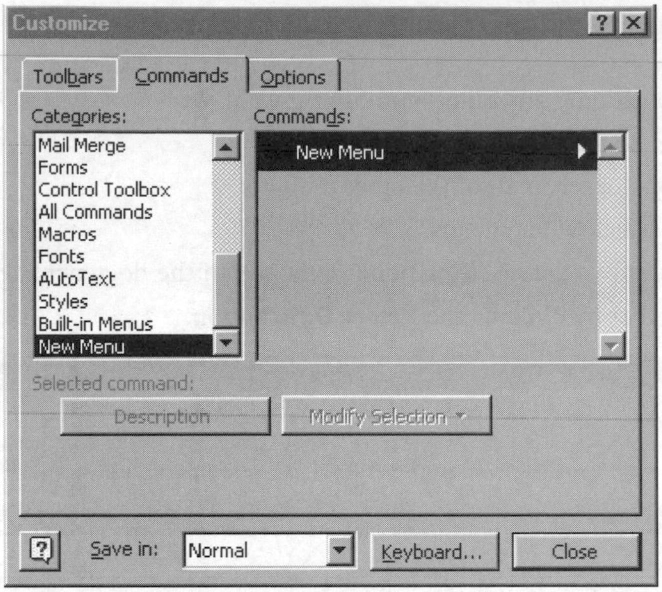

Figure 9.6: Creating a new menu

- Click on a category and select a command.
- Drag the command into the list beneath the new menu.

9.3. Selecting correct/default printer

When you print from a Microsoft Office application the default printer should be displayed in the Print dialogue box. You can select a different printer from the drop-down list.

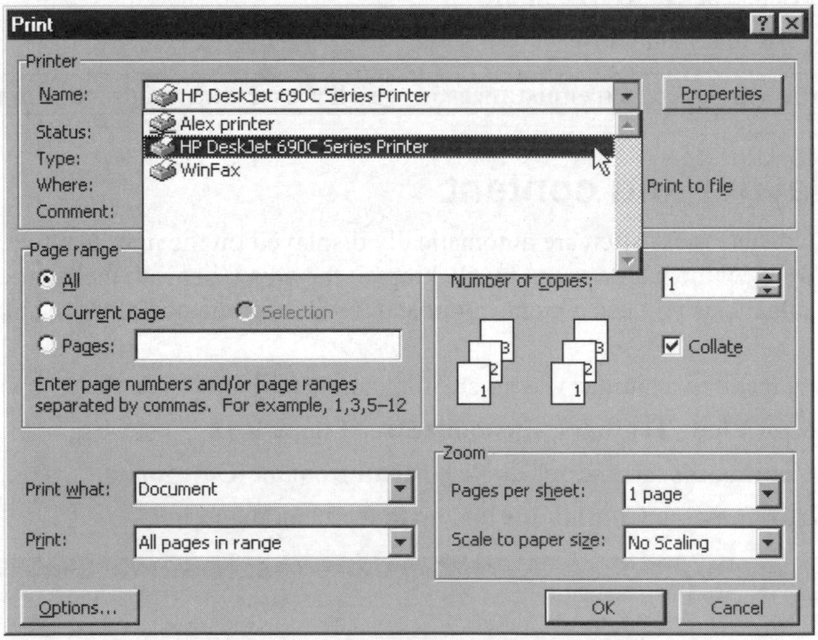

Figure 9.7: Selecting a printer in Word

You can change the default printer, but clearly the new printer must already have been set up on the system.

- On the Windows **Start** menu, point to **Settings**, and then click **Printers**.
- Right-click the icon for the printer you want to use as the default printer, and then click **Set As Default** on the shortcut menu.
- If there is a check mark next to this command, the printer is already set as the default printer.

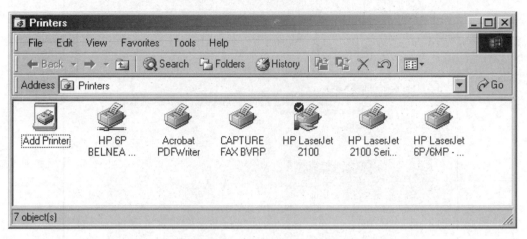

Figure 9.8: Changing the default printer

9.4. Standard templates

All documents created in applications such as Microsoft Word or Excel are based on templates. Templates can contain text, styles, macros (see section 9.6) and other layout features. A template saves the user time by providing a basic format to start with. You can then use the same template to create as many documents as you wish. Microsoft Word includes a variety of pre-prepared templates and you can modify these if required.

To use an existing Word template to create a letter:

- Select **File**, **New** and click on the **Letters & Faxes** tab.
- Click the **Contemporary Letter** icon.
- Ensure that the **Create New Document** option is selected and click **OK**.

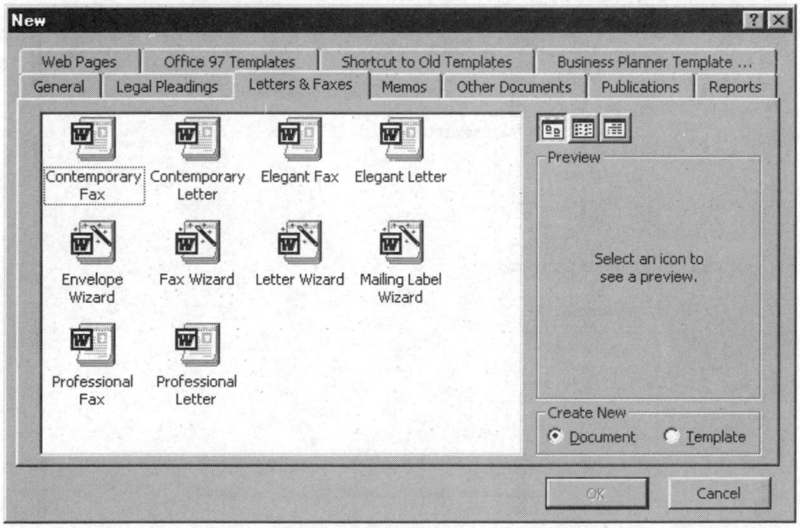

Figure 9.9: Selecting a letter template

The following new document will be displayed together with instructions on how to complete it:

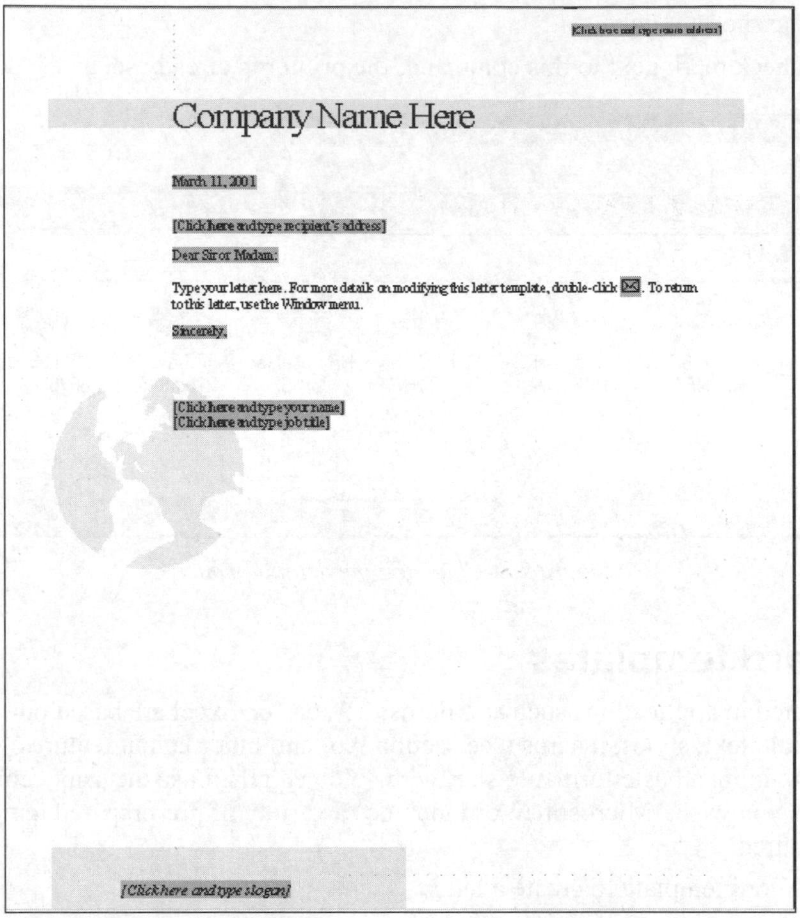

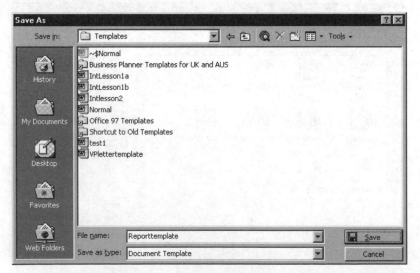

Figure 9.10: The Contemporary Letter template

If you create a document and wish to save it as a template you must specify this in the **Save** or **Save As** dialogue box.

Figure 9.11: Saving as a document template

You will be forced to save it in the system's **Templates** folder so that it will be available when you choose to create a new document.

If, however, you are working on a network you may find that you do not have access to the Templates folder and so you will have to save it on a floppy disk. To create a new document based on this template you right-click on the drive **A:** icon in **My Computer**, click **Open** and then click on the name of the template. Enter the text for the letter and this time save it as a document.

9.5. Saving and backup security

You can change the options for saving documents in some applications such as Microsoft Word. There are different settings that can be selected to work best with the size of your documents and the amount of disk space and memory your computer has.

- To see these options select **Tools**, **Options** and click the **Save** tab.

You can use this dialogue to request that Word saves a backup copy of your files, which is a sensible policy for important documents that may get corrupted or accidentally deleted.

If you select the **Save AutoRecover info every** check box you can specify the interval (in the **minutes** box) for how often you want Microsoft Word to automatically save documents. The more frequently Word saves documents, the more information is recovered if there is a power failure or similar problem while a document is open in Word. However **AutoRecover** is not a replacement for regularly saving your documents. If you choose not to save the recovery file after Word opens it, the file is deleted and your unsaved changes are lost. If you save the recovery file, it replaces the original document (unless you specify a new file name).

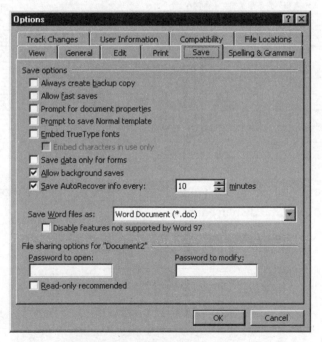

Figure 9.12: Setting Save options

Clear the **Allow fast saves** check box if you want Word to perform a full save (save the complete document). To best protect your work, it is important to have Word perform a full save instead of a fast save at these times. If you do select the **Allow fast saves** check box Word will save a list of changes separately from your stored work (you cannot view the list). If you have Word perform fast saves, it is good practice to periodically clear the **Allow fast saves** check box so that Word can integrate the list of changes with your stored work.

If you select the **Allow background saves** check box you can continue working in Word while you save a document (a pulsing disk icon appears on the status bar while Word saves your work). This setting works best when you are not using Word on a system that has low memory.

You can also use this dialogue box to set a password in order to restrict access to the document. You can choose to prevent others from opening the document or just to restrict others from modifying the document (read-only).

9.6. Macros

If you perform a task repeatedly in Word, you can automate the task by using a *macro*. A macro is a series of Word commands and instructions that you group together as a single command to accomplish a task automatically. Instead of manually performing a series of time-consuming, repetitive actions in Word, you can create and run a single macro – in effect, a custom command – that accomplishes the task for you.

Word offers two ways for you to create a macro: the **macro recorder** and the **Visual Basic Editor**. We will record a macro to sort a table of information and apply a different font colour. The end result will be that by pressing a particular key sequence the table will automatically be sorted and some text displayed in red.

- In a new Word document enter the table shown below and save it as **macrotest**.

Ref	Salesman	Type	Price
F1	AH	Flat	18,000
H6	AH	House	45,000
H4	AH	House	89,000
B1	BR	Bungalow	25,000
B3	BR	Bungalow	50,000
H7	BR	House	56,000
H3	BR	House	99,000
H1	TY	House	28,000
B2	TY	Bungalow	35,000
F2	TY	Flat	35,000
H2	TY	House	67,000

- Start the macro recorder by selecting **Tools**, **Macro**, **Record New Macro**.

The following dialogue box will be displayed:

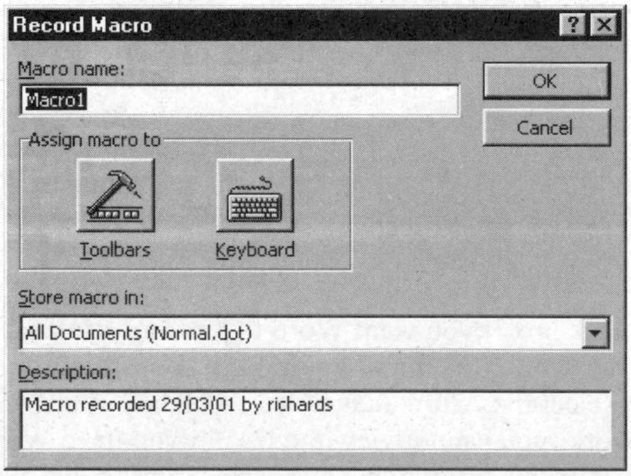

Figure 9.13: Creating a macro

- In the **Macro Name** Box type **SortAndShade**.
- In the **Assign Macro To** area, click **Keyboard**.
- Assign the key sequence **Ctrl-Shift-H** to this macro. Click **Close**.

The mouse pointer now has a cassette tape image attached and the **Stop Recording** toolbar appears.
You're now ready to start recording.

- Select **Table**, **Sort**. Choose to sort on **Price** and click **OK**.
- With the table still selected change the font colour to red.
- On the **Recording** toolbar, click the **Stop Recording** button.
- Close **macrotest** without saving the changes.
- Reopen **macrotest**.
- Press **Ctrl-Shift-H**.

The **Price** column should be sorted in ascending order and the column text should turn red.

- Delete the macro by selecting **Tools**, **Macro**, clicking **SortAndShade** and then **Delete**.

It is also possible to assign a macro to a new toolbar button.

- Repeat the exercise above but in the dialogue box shown in Figure 9.13 click on **Toolbars**.

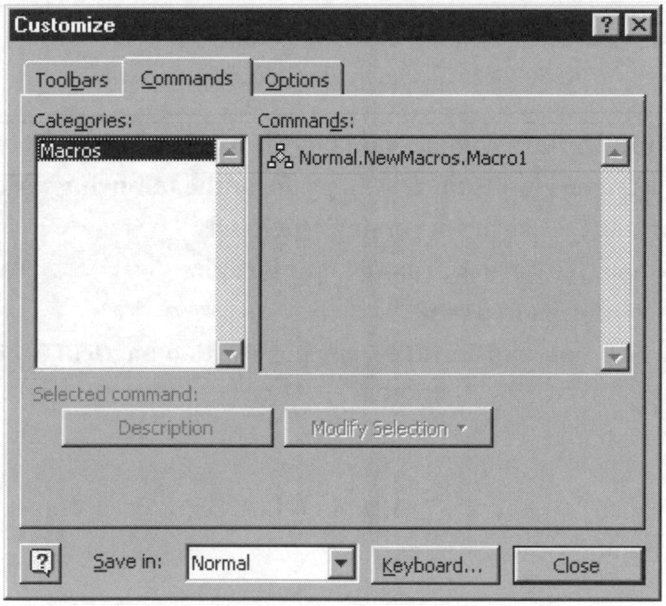

Figure 9.14: Assigning a macro to a new toolbar button

The macro will automatically be named (**Normal.NewMacros.Macro4** in the example shown above).

- Drag the name up onto a toolbar.
- Right-click the new toolbar button and select **Change Button Image**.
- A selection of images will be displayed (see Figure 9.15). Select one for your new button.
- Continue to record the macro as described above.

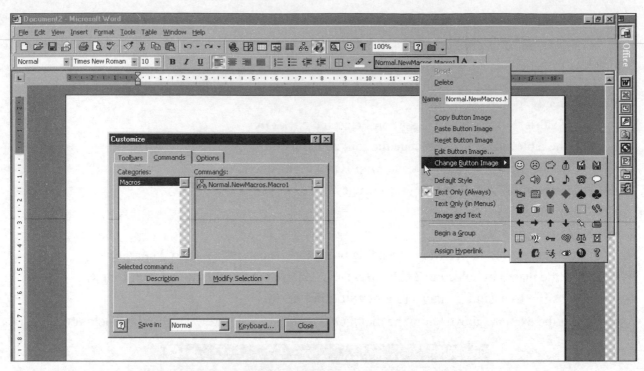

Figure 9.15: Changing the toolbar button image

Discussion: What other applications can you think of for macros in Word?

Try recording some simple macros to perform the following tasks:

- **Insert your address at the beginning of a letter.**

- **Insert a decorative border around a paragraph.**

- **Merge a row of cells in a table.**

- **Insert a page break and start the new page with a particular heading.**

Chapter 10 – System Diagnostics

Objectives:

- ✓ To investigate the POST
- ✓ To look at Windows system tools
- ✓ To consider virus checking
- ✓ To look at other diagnostic programs

Before attempting to investigate problems from inside the PC case it is recommended that you run some form of software diagnostics.

10.1. Power On Self Test (POST)

Whenever you switch on a machine it performs a short test to make sure that everything is reasonably OK. This test is called the Power On Self Test or POST.

If a machine is so faulty that it does not have a working display, the POST often beeps to inform you of what is wrong. The beeps are produced through the small loudspeaker that every PC has and not via the sound card. The beep codes are not completely standard – every manufacturer adds their own set – but normally if you hear more than one beep when the machine is starting up, then something is wrong. You need to refer to the manufacturer's documentation to discover what the different sequences of beeps mean. Even if you don't hear extra beeps, the POST can still halt the machine and display an error message on the screen.

Most machines default to a Quick POST which simply tests the hardware once. A full POST repeats the tests more than once, but it does make the start up sequence slower. You can select a full POST in the BIOS setup (see Chapter 7). If you want to supplement the POST test then there are other software diagnostics available, some of which are discussed in later sections.

10.2. Safe Mode

Safe Mode is a special way of running Windows which more or less guarantees that it will work even if there is a problem that stops it working in normal mode. To start a machine in Safe Mode, hold down the **F8** key while it is starting and select **Safe Mode** from the menu. You will know that you are in Safe Mode because the screen colour will be muted and it says Safe Mode in the corner of the screen.

Safe Mode uses only the very minimum of hardware that is available on the PC. It makes use of the video hardware in standard 16-colour VGA mode rather than high resolution. It doesn't make use of a sound card, network card or any additional hardware.

While in Safe Mode you can make changes to the configuration of the machine but you will not see the effects of the changes until you restart in normal mode. One common use of Safe Mode is to recover documents from a hard disk in a machine that is otherwise refusing to start up.

10.3. Task Manager

The Task Manager gives you some control over the applications running on a PC. It displays the applications that are running and allows you to close down any that are causing problems.

If a machine appears to 'freeze' do not panic and start pressing keys at random or immediately switch it off. Instead try these:

- See if the mouse still moves the cursor. If it does wait for up to ten minutes.

- Try **Alt-Tab** to switch to another application. If this works, save your work and close the application.

- Right-click an unoccupied area of the taskbar and choose Task Manager from the shortcut menu. End any tasks that might be blocking the machine or any marked 'not responding'.

If all of this fails, then you will have to switch off and on again. Once off, always wait a few seconds before switching on – this allows capacitors to discharge, ensuring that all voltages fall to zero otherwise some components may not reset.

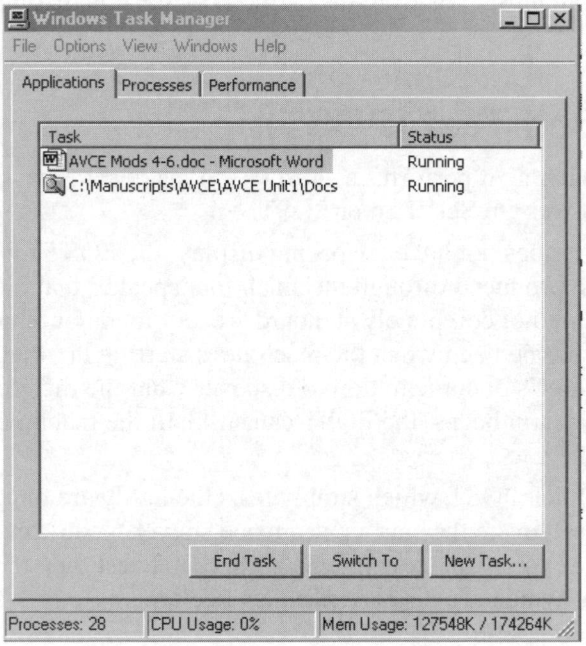

Figure 10.1: Task Manager

10.4. Windows system tools

Windows provides some system tools to assist with diagnosing system problems and these are available from the **Accessories** group of programs. Some of the most useful tools are described below.

Disk Cleanup

This utility is useful if you are running short of disk space. The program lists several categories of disk files that you could delete and shows you how much space this would release.

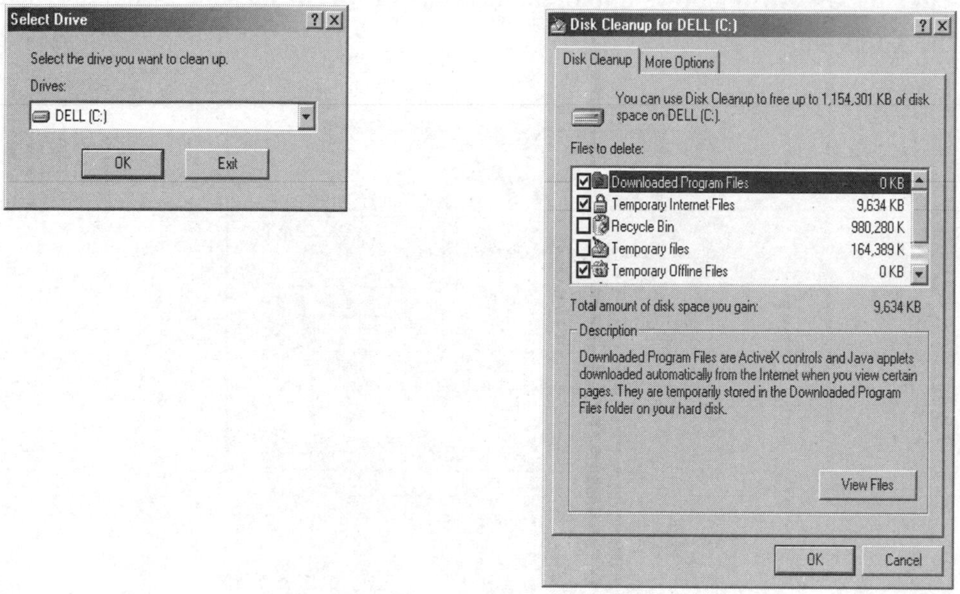

Figure 10.2: Disk Cleanup

System Information

This utility collects and displays your system configuration information. Support technicians may require specific information about your computer when they are sorting out problems. You can use System Information to quickly find the data they need.

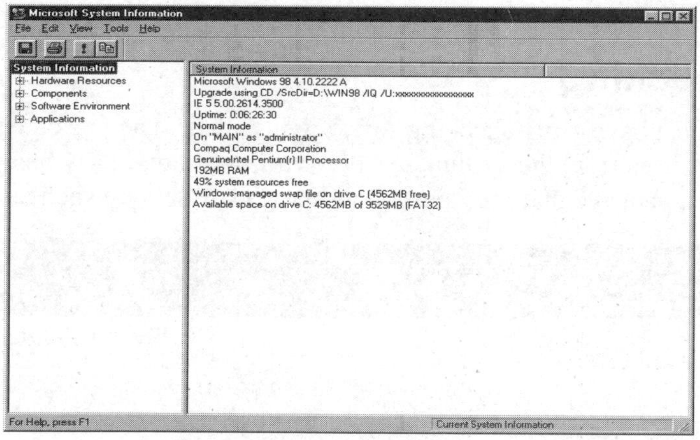

Figure 10.3: The System Information utility

It also includes a number of tools for checking and verifying various parts of your computer. They can be used to scan files, report problems and check the registry. Information about these tools can be found in the System Information Help in the usual way.

Check Disk

Windows 2000 also includes a tool that checks your disks for errors in the logical file system and problems involving the physical disks.

Discussion: What is meant by the 'logical file system'?

To use this utility:

- Right-click the disk in Windows Explorer and select **Properties** from the shortcut menu.
- Click the **Tools** tab.
- Click **Check Now**.

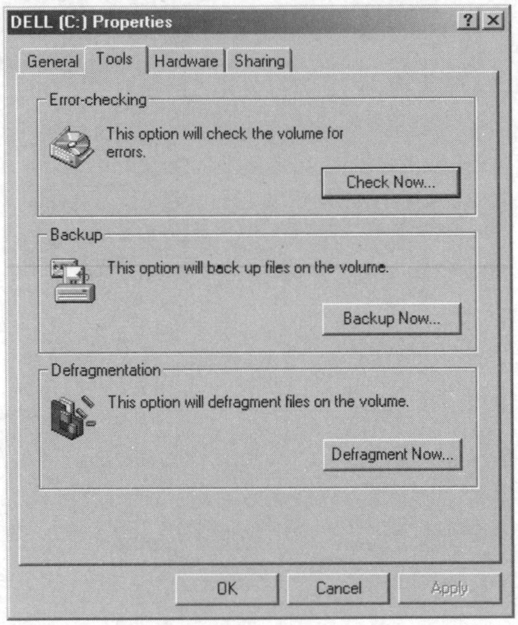

Figure 10.4: Using Check disk

If you click on **Defragment Now** the Disk Defragmenter will rearrange your files in order to optimise disk space.

10.5. Virus checking

All computer systems must have virus-checking software installed. The package should be capable of scanning and clearing viruses from the system. As new viruses are regularly being discovered it is recommended to install a package that provides an on-line update service such as Norton AntiVirus.

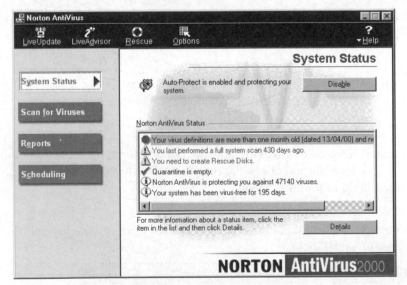

Figure 10.5: The Norton AntiVirus utility

The proliferation of viruses has increased dramatically over recent years, due in part to e-mail communication. There were 23,290 viruses recorded in May 2000 rising to 30,678 by October of the same year.

Discussion: What other safeguards can be put in place to protect a computer system from viruses?

10.6. Other diagnostic packages

Some free diagnostics software can be downloaded from the Internet (e.g. AMIDiag) or alternative diagnostics packages purchased (e.g. Checkit-Pro and Norton Utility Diagnostics). Some hardware manufacturers, such as Compaq, also supply their own diagnostics packages.

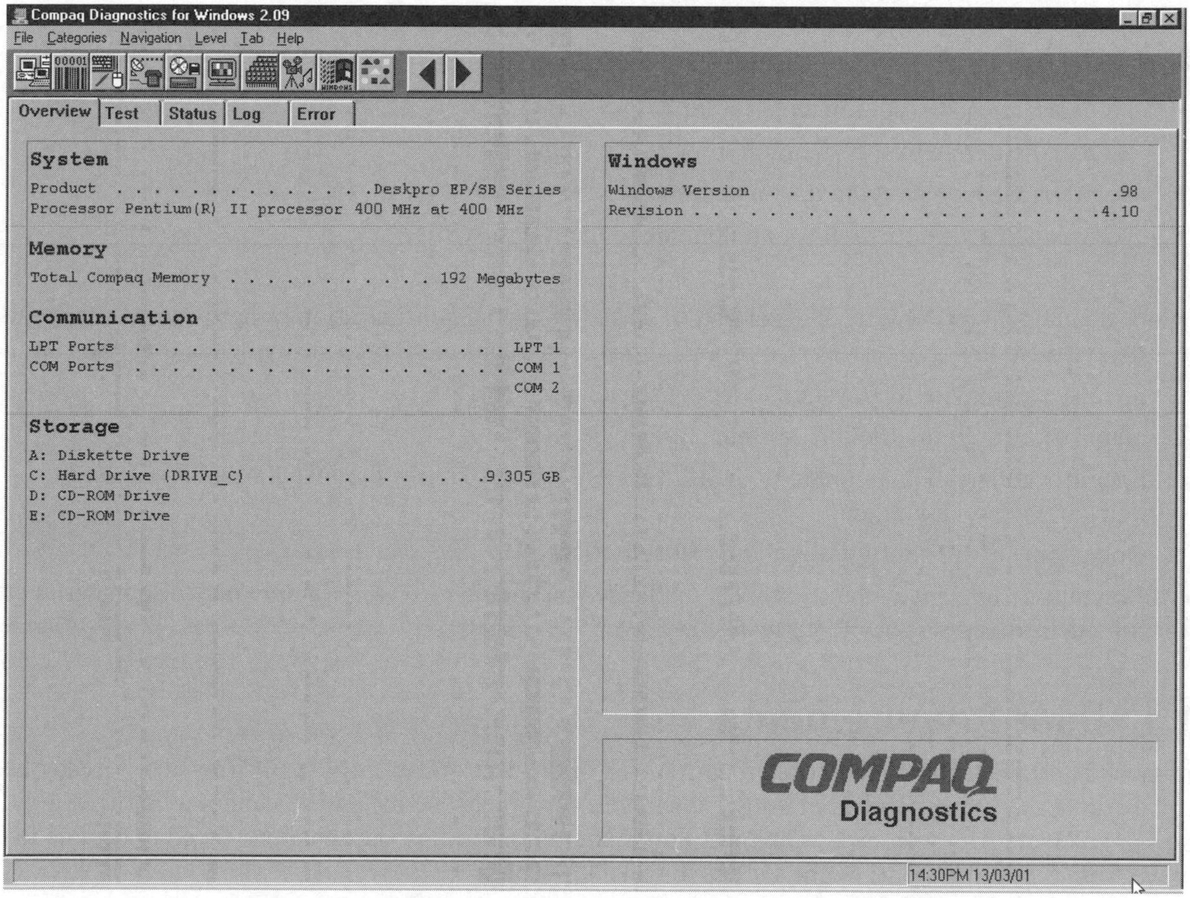

Figure 10.6: Running Compaq diagnostics

Software of this type is very useful because in addition to providing system information it also shows the status of system components and provides test facilities. A log is developed of the tests and an error report produced.

Discussion: Draw up a regular 'maintenance' procedure that could be followed to improve the performance of a room of networked PCs.

Chapter 11 – System Specification and Documentation

Objectives

✓ To determine user requirements for an ICT system

✓ To prepare a system specification to meet user requirements

✓ To prepare accompanying documentation

✓ To produce a specification for an upgrade to the ICT system

Previous chapters in this unit have described the installation and configuration of hardware components and software in an ICT system. For your portfolio you are required to provide evidence that you can:

❑ Specify a complete ICT system to meet user requirements.

❑ Install and configure the ICT system.

❑ Specify and install an upgrade to the ICT system which requires the installation of at least two items in the processing unit.

❑ Document set up, configuration and test activities.

The following sections give advice on what evidence you should provide. Sample portfolio material can be downloaded from www.payne-gallway.co.uk/avce.

11.1. User Requirements

You must determine and document the requirements of the user of the proposed ICT system. It may be that they do not have a great deal of knowledge about computer systems and so cannot tell you exactly what kind of system they require. The most important thing is to find out what they need to be able to achieve from the ICT system. Some factors to consider include:

• Cost – there is little point in you specifying an all-singing all-dancing system if it is outside the budget available.

• The physical space available for the system may also be an important point – it could for example mean that a tower unit that can be located on the floor would be more suitable than a desktop unit.

• Any special needs that the user may have – poor eyesight or a physical handicap might influence the type of monitor or input device that you recommend.

• Backup facilities for the system – this may not be something the user has considered and it is up to you to advise them on the most suitable method.

• The likely requirements for future upgrades – does the user foresee a change in their work specification that could mean more or different equipment. It is up to you to either build in the capacity in the initial configuration or to ensure that the capability to upgrade at a later date exists.

You could include records of an interview held with the user and the notes you made (you might also find this useful evidence for communication key skills) in addition to writing up the requirements in a report.

11.2. Hardware specification

Having decided on what the user needs to achieve with their ICT system it is up to you to translate this into a hardware requirement based on your knowledge of PC systems and their components. You may need to refer to books such as this one, look in computer magazines for up-to-date system specifications, research on the Internet, visit retail outlets and discuss your thoughts with other people.

Your hardware specification should not just be a shopping list: it should be accompanied by a written justification as to why you decided on this configuration (e.g. 128Mb of RAM instead of 64Mb or why you have included a Zip drive in the specification) and relate back to the user requirements.

11.3. Software specification

You must document which operating system is to be installed together with which application packages and some justification as to why these have been chosen. Again relate back to your discussions with the user and show that you are satisfying their requirements. Specify any particular configurations of the operating system that will be required such as passwords (see Chapter 8). You should also specify any customisation of the application software that will be required and why – for example, custom toolbars, menus, templates and macros (see Chapter 9).

11.4. Installation and configuration of the ICT system

Hardware tasks may be undertaken in a group if resources are limited. This is fine, but you must ensure that each member of the group participates fully. If a digital camera is available take photographs of each other installing hardware components. Evidence is also required that you can uninstall these components, so you can then restore the machine to its original state and let the next member of the group repeat the task.

The easiest way to document the system configuration is to produce a printout from either the Setup utility that runs when the machine starts up (see Chapters 3 and 10), or from the Windows Device Manager (Chapter 1), or from a diagnostics utility package such as Windows System Information or Compaq diagnostics (both discussed in Chapter 10).

Take printouts of the ROM-BIOS settings from Setup by pressing **Shift-PrintScreen**.

Take screenshots (see section 11.7) of hardware and software installation wizards in progress and any device driver software that you need to run.

When you are setting configuration options in Windows, such as time and date, passwords, customising the desktop or setting up the Office toolbar (see Chapter 8) take screenshots for your portfolio.

Also remember to record the specification and installation of the hardware upgrade that you make, take photographs again if possible and screenshots of installation wizards for both the software and hardware.

You will be able to print out a copy of the template that you produce in the application software, but you will probably need to produce screenshots of customised toolbars and menus. Depending on what your macro does, you may be able to provide printouts of the screen, printouts of the Visual Basic code produced by the macro or screenshots of the macro working.

11.5. Diagnostics

It is also important to record any faults and problems experienced and how you solved them. You should keep a fault log as discussed in the following section together with screenshots of diagnostic software in use. Chapter 10 discussed several software diagnostic programs and you should investigate what else is available on your ICT system. Even if no problems occur you should run some form of diagnostics to prove everything is working well!

11.6. Fault log

This can be quite a simple form but, when completed over a period of time, very useful evidence for your portfolio. It does not matter if it was not you who fixed the fault so long as you reported it promptly, with supporting evidence to the appropriate person. The log can be useful to help inform others of the problem and to identify a recurring problem and how it has been fixed in the past. A suggested layout for a fault log is shown below.

Date	Equipment ID & location	Person reporting fault	Description of problem	How the problem was resolved

11.7. Taking screenshots

As suggested in previous sections you should reinforce your portfolio evidence with screenshots where appropriate.

One way of doing this is to press the **PrintScreen** key on the keyboard which will take a screen dump and save it in the clipboard so that you can later paste it into another document. This will only give you a copy of the complete screen, but there are other utilities available which offer more options. For example later releases of CorelDraw are supplied with a utility called Corel Capture which allows you to select which part of the screen you want to capture and to save it in various file formats. You can also download a free copy of Screen Print Gold from Software labs (www.softwarelabs.com). This user-friendly program also allows you to specify exactly which area of the screen you wish to capture. You can then edit the images and print the result, send it to the clipboard or save it as a graphics file.

Figure 11.1: The ScreenPrint utility

Unit 5

Systems Analysis

In this unit you will be learning how to set about finding out how an existing system works. A system could be anything from how a Club keeps in touch with its members to a Sales Order Processing system or a Library Loans system. You will also be learning how to record your findings using both text and diagrams in a way that other systems analysts will be able to understand. Finally, you will need to learn how to design new systems that are going to do exactly what the user wants.

As you can imagine, these are difficult tasks and, if you master them, you will be in line for an extremely well-paid job!

Chapter 12 – The Systems Life Cycle

Objectives

✓ To learn the stages in the systems life cycle
✓ To understand the role of the systems analyst

12.1. The systems life cycle

Most organisations, such as large or small businesses, schools, hospitals, government departments and so on, have a continuous program of updating and improving the way they do things. Installing new computer systems and information systems is often a very important part of this program, and can involve dozens of people over a period of months or even years, at enormous cost.

Obviously it is essential to have a systematic approach to investigating requirements, proposing and implementing solutions and appraising their success. The stages in the development of a new system are sometimes represented graphically as shown below. The diagram gets across the idea that no system lasts for ever – sooner or later the need for a new or improved system will be recognised and the process will start over again.

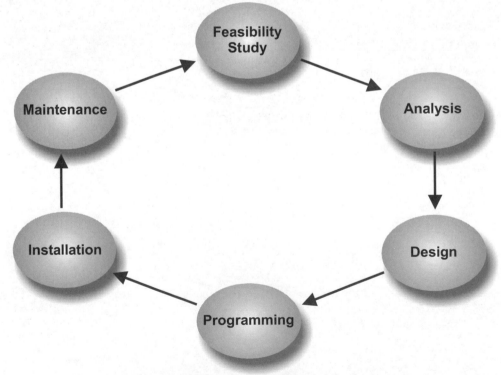

Figure 12.1: The systems life cycle

12.2. Why introduce a new system?

Businesses must adapt to remain competitive, and every business strives to be as efficient as possible. This often means introducing new and better information systems.

Some of the reasons for introducing a new system may be:

1. **The current system may no longer be suitable for its purpose.** Changes in work processes, expansion of the business, changes in business requirements or the environment in which the organisation operates may all lead to a reassessment of information system requirements.

2. **Technological developments may have made the current system redundant or outdated.** Advances in hardware, software and telecommunications bring new opportunities which an organisation cannot ignore if it is to keep ahead of its rivals.

3. **The current system may be too inflexible or expensive to maintain**, or may reduce the organisation's ability to respond quickly enough to customer's demands.

4. **Better management information is required for decision-making.** The ability of computers to provide information quickly and accurately means that management can use this information to make better decisions.

5. **The provision of better customer service.** This could mean producing clearer, itemised invoices or a faster service when a customer orders goods, for example.

12.3. The role of the systems analyst

This unit is all about systems analysis, which basically covers the first three stages shown in the Systems Life Cycle diagram shown in Figure 12.1 – feasibility study, analysis and design. These stages will be carried out by a **systems analyst**. The other major participants in the development of a new system are the **users** and the **programmers**.

The users will provide information about the current system, and they will be able to say, in their own words, what they want the new system to be able to do. The programmers will be responsible for turning these requirements into programs. They will be computer specialists who do not necessarily have much understanding of how the business runs or how to translate the user's requirements into the required programs.

The systems analyst acts as a go-between to communicate with both the users and the programmers. The analyst has to have a good understanding both of the business requirements and how these can be implemented using a computer system.

Users communicate their requirements to the systems analyst...

The systems analyst designs a new system and specifies programs etc to be written

The programmers write and test the new system as designed by the analyst

Figure 12.2: The role of the systems analyst

Good communication skills, a diplomatic way of handling conflicts of interest, and a confident, enthusiastic personality are invaluable assets to a systems analyst for a range of responsibilities:

- ❑ investigating and analysing the existing system to establish how things work currently;
- ❑ performing a feasibility study to judge whether a new computer system is feasible;
- ❑ designing the new system, specifying programs, hardware, and procedures to be followed;
- ❑ testing and overseeing the installation of the new system;
- ❑ making sure that all user and technical documentation is complete;
- ❑ evaluating the performance of the new system to make sure it fulfils the requirements.

12.4. The feasibility study

This is the first stage of the systems life cycle. The **scope** and **objectives** of the proposed system must be written down. The aim of the feasibility study is to understand the problem and to determine whether it is worth proceeding. There are five main factors to be considered:

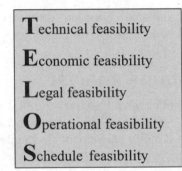

Technical feasibility

Economic feasibility

Legal feasibility

Operational feasibility

Schedule feasibility

Figure 12.3: TELOS – a mnemonic for the five feasibility factors

- ❑ **Technical feasibility** means investigating whether the technology exists to implement the proposed system, or whether this is a practical proposition.
- ❑ **Economic feasibility** has to do with establishing the cost-effectiveness of the proposed system – if the benefits do not outweigh the costs, then it is not worth going ahead.
- ❑ **Legal feasibility** determines whether there is any conflict between the proposed system and legal requirements – for example, will the system contravene the Data Protection Act?
- ❑ **Operational feasibility** is concerned with whether the current work practices and procedures are adequate to support the new system. It is also concerned with social factors – how the organisational change will affect the working lives of those affected by the system.
- ❑ **Schedule feasibility** looks at how long the system will take to develop, or whether it can be done in a desired time-frame.

The completion of this stage is marked by the production of a feasibility report produced by the systems analyst. If the report concludes that the project should go ahead, and this is agreed by senior managers, detailed requirements analysis will proceed.

12.5. Investigating the current system

There are several ways of finding out about how the current system works, many of which will be used both before the feasibility study and in producing a more detailed systems specification.

- ❑ Interviewing staff at different levels of the organisation from the end-users to senior management.
- ❑ Examining current business and systems documents and output. These may include current order documents, computer systems procedures and reports used by operations and senior management.
- ❑ Sending out questionnaires and analysing responses. The questions have to be carefully constructed to elicit unambiguous answers.
- ❑ Observation of current procedures, by spending time in various departments. A time and motion study can be carried out to see where procedures could be made more efficient, or to detect where bottlenecks occur.

The systems analyst's report will examine how data and information flow around the organisation, and may use **data flow diagrams** to document the flow. It will also establish precisely and in considerable detail exactly what the proposed system will do (as opposed to how it will do it). It will include an in-depth analysis of the costs and benefits, and outline the process of system implementation, including the organisational change required. It must establish who the end-users are, what information they should get and in what form and how it will be obtained.

Alternative options for the implementation of the project will be suggested. These could include suggestions for:

- ❑ Whether development should be done in-house or using consultants;
- ❑ What hardware configurations could be considered;
- ❑ What the software options are.

The report will conclude with a recommendation to either proceed or abandon the project.

12.6. Design

The design specifies the following aspects of a system:

- ❑ The hardware platform – which type of computer, network capabilities, input, storage and output devices;
- ❑ The software – programming language, package or database;
- ❑ The outputs – report layouts and screen designs;
- ❑ The inputs – documents, screen layouts and validation procedures;
- ❑ The user interface – how users will interact with the computer system;
- ❑ The modular design of each program in the application;
- ❑ The test plan and test data;
- ❑ Conversion plan – how the new system is to be implemented;
- ❑ Documentation including systems and operations documentation. Later, a user manual will be produced.

12.7. Programming, installation and maintenance

During the implementation (or programming) phase of the systems life cycle the programs are written and tested, and documentation is completed. When the system is fully tested and ready to be installed, data is loaded from the old system to the new one, staff are trained in the operation of the new system, and the changeover to the new system is made. This may involve a period of parallel running when both systems run side-by-side to ensure that the new system works smoothly.

More than one company has gone out of business as a direct result of installing a new computer system which fails to live up to expectations and indeed leads to such chaos that the business cannot continue to function normally. Failure of the systems analyst to cater for 'exceptional cases', poor staff training, inadequate hardware for the volume of data and inaccurate data entry are among the many factors that can cause systems to fail. The effect on staff morale and level of customer service must be carefully considered during the changeover process.

Maintenance involves writing new programs where required, ironing out any 'bugs' and keeping the system up-to-date. Eventually a new system will be required and the life cycle starts over again.

12.8. Case study

In Appendix A of AVCE ICT (Units 1-3) you will find a full case study about Victory Publishing Ltd. All the parts of the case study that you need for this module are given within the text, but if you want to look up extra background information you can download the case study from our web site www.payne-gallway.co.uk/avce.

Victory Publishing Ltd publishes a range of textbooks for schools and Colleges. They have expanded their list of titles enormously over the past two years, and the Managing Director feels that the current method of calculating authors' royalties is too time-consuming. She would like the Systems Analyst to investigate the possibility of developing a new system for calculating royalties and producing the necessary reports.

> **Discussion:** **Imagine that you are the Systems Analyst and this request has been handed to you in a memo from the Managing Director. What method(s) would you use to find out how the current system works, and what the requirements of the new system are?**
>
> **Make a list of the questions that you would ask. Who would they be addressed to?**

12.9. Exercises

1. Show in a diagram the main stages in the systems life cycle.   (5 marks)

2. Name 5 items that should be considered in the design of a new system.   (5 marks)

3. Suggest 3 reasons why a company may want to change their existing stock control system. (3 marks)

4. Look up some advertisements for systems analysts. Name four skills or qualities that are desirable in a systems analyst.   (4 marks)

5. After a new computer system has been installed, it has to be maintained. Name three tasks that *maintenance* may involve.   (3 marks)

6. Describe briefly **four** risks associated with changing to a new system.   (4 marks)

Chapter 13 – Initial Systems Investigation

Objectives

- ✓ To write a statement of purpose for a new system
- ✓ To write a definition of the scope of a proposed new system
- ✓ To learn about methods of fact-finding
- ✓ To plan an interview to ascertain user requirements

13.1. Case study: KOC Ltd

In this chapter a case study will be introduced so that the various stages of systems analysis and design can be practised. Of course, being presented with a case study is no substitute for going out and investigating the requirements of a business for yourself, as the information given has already been carefully sifted and presented in a logical way. However, it provides a useful starting point!

KOC Ltd

Introduction

KOC Ltd has been in business for just over 30 years, supplying a range of bags and rucksacks to retail outlets all over the country. The company was started by two young Business Studies graduates who married shortly after leaving University and after a few years of working for other companies, started the business in their rented house. Since then the business has grown to the point where they now have a turnover of £5 million per annum and a workforce of 36 employed in an office building and warehouse on a small industrial estate.

Patrick Carson, the Managing Director, dictates the policy and strategy for the Company. His wife Gina is the Sales Director and is in charge of Sales and Marketing. The Personnel Manager, who is in charge of recruitment, staff training and the day-to-day smooth running of the business, reports to Gina. (She often fills in for employees who are sick or on holiday in other departments or helps where necessary during particularly busy periods.) Richard Handford is the Finance Director and is in overall charge of the Accounts and Payroll Departments. Paul Sheldon, the Production Manager, is in charge of Production and Stock Control.

Trading Information

The company has approximately 1000 credit customers (retail stores) and a number of cash customers who ring up and place orders for individual items. They receive on average about 100 orders each day, with up to 250 in peak periods. An order may typically be for 6 different items. The company sends an invoice and delivery note with each order, and a statement at the end of the month. Payment is due within 30 days of the statement date. If payment is not received within 60 days, the Credit Control Department takes action to remind the customer that payment is due, and their account will be put on stop (no further goods to be supplied) until payment is received.

When a new customer rings up to place an order for which credit is requested, a credit check is carried out and if this is satisfactory a credit limit is allocated. This credit limit can be exceeded only at the discretion of Richard Handford. Credit customers receive a discount, which varies between 10% and 40%. Cash customers pay by credit card and do not get any discount. On all types of order, carriage charges are made on orders valued at under £100.

The company uses about 35 major suppliers who supply approximately 120 different items including different types of cloth, thread, fasteners, frames etc. The Company normally pays for all goods within 60 days of being invoiced.

The company produces 30 different lines of finished goods, all attracting VAT at the standard rate.

Production information

A sales catalogue is produced once a year that lists the range of goods currently produced. When a particular line is no longer to be produced, it may nevertheless appear in the catalogue if there are existing stocks to be sold. Some new items may be put in the catalogue on a 'trial' basis to see whether orders are received before making them up.

Some customers have expressed dissatisfaction at the length of time between placing an order and receiving the goods. The delay may occur for a number of reasons:

❑ sometimes the person taking the order over the telephone may not know how many items are in stock and promise unrealistic delivery times;

❑ existing stock may not be available;

❑ if stock has to be made up, sometimes there are insufficient raw materials in stock;

❑ it can take considerable time to obtain stocks of certain raw materials.

The company has a standard accounting package and a network of computers which are used to enter customer and supplier orders, print invoices, record payments and log movement of finished goods into and out of stock.

There is no computerised system for controlling the stock of raw materials and it is the responsibility of Mr Sheldon to ensure that there are sufficient supplies to make up the required quantities of finished goods.

Mr and Mrs Carson's son Robert has recently joined the business as Systems Analyst and has been asked to carry out an initial investigation into streamlining some aspects of the business, in particular the order processing and stock control systems.

13.2. Statement of scope and objectives

The systems analyst may initially be given a verbal summary of the perceived problems of an organisation and some idea of what the requirements are. It may not be entirely clear either to the analyst or the management exactly what is expected or what the scope of the proposed project is. The first task for the analyst, therefore, is to carry out a preliminary investigation, which may take one or two days, and then put in writing the perceived problems, scope and objectives, together with a rough estimate of costs. This document, if agreed, will then form the starting point for the feasibility study which will follow.

Figure 13.1: Initial stages of systems analysis

The **scope** of a business system means the specific set of activities that it includes. For example, if a systems analyst is designing a new system for recording books and loans for the school library, the activities that are included in the system need to be defined. Will the system be capable of creating mailing labels for all people whose books are overdue and calculating fines on overdue books or are those activities outside the scope of the system? If you are designing a system for the local Scout group, what activities are included in the proposed system?

The system described in the example below is a comprehensive one which includes sales order processing, invoicing and stock control of both raw materials and finished goods. A system with a more limited scope could for example handle the sales order processing and invoicing but not the stock control.

Statement of scope and objectives

Project title:	Order Processing at KOC Ltd
Date:	01/02/2001
Current problems:	The following problems are currently causing concern at KOC.

1. The sales catalogue which is produced once a year is not accurate as it frequently features items which are no longer stocked or which are not available. New lines, on the other hand, are sometimes not put in the catalogue.

2. When a customer rings up to order goods, the sales clerk often does not know whether there is sufficient stock to fill the order and so cannot deal with enquiries efficiently.

3. If orders cannot be filled from current stock, back orders can take several weeks to be processed.

4. At peak periods when up to 250 daily orders are received, orders may not be despatched for up to two weeks even if the goods are in stock.

5. The system of deciding what raw materials need to be reordered is sometimes haphazard and relies heavily on the knowledge and expertise of Mr Sheldon, the Production Manager, who has a 'feel' for what stock is required and checks periodically on what raw materials are due for replenishment.

6. There are overstocks of some raw materials which are used in making up items which are no longer in great demand.

Objectives:	To investigate the development and installation of a new system for sales order processing, invoicing and stock control of both raw materials and finished goods.
Constraints:	The system is to be completed within 9 months with a budget of no more than £100,000.
Plan of Action:	Investigate fully the existing sales order processing, invoicing and stock control systems.
	Investigate the feasibility of purchasing or designing and implementing a new computer system.
	Produce a feasibility report within the next two weeks.

Figure 13.2: A statement of scope and objectives

13.3. Systems investigation

The analyst now has to conduct a more comprehensive investigation to gather facts for the feasibility report. First of all, it will be necessary to establish:

- ❑ how the existing systems work;
- ❑ what personnel are involved;
- ❑ the organisational, social and economic environment within the organisation.

Why study the existing system if it is to be changed? The answer is that even if is not a perfect system, it must function at some level and it will give valuable clues as to what is required, and what problems need to be solved to improve things. Studying the organisational and social environment is important in order to take into consideration how this might be affected by a new system. No system will succeed if the personnel who are expected to operate it are against it or resentful of the changes to their work patterns that it brings.

13.4. Methods of finding out about the current system

The main ways of finding out how current systems work are:

1. Interviews
2. Studying documentation
3. Questionnaires
4. Observation

We will look at each of these methods in turn.

Interviews

Interviews with key personnel are an important way for the analyst to obtain a clear picture of how a current system works and what each person's role is in an organisation. Before holding an interview, it is essential for the analyst to prepare carefully by:

- ❑ establishing in advance the purpose of the interview;
- ❑ becoming familiar with as much background information as possible about the role and responsibilities of the interviewee;
- ❑ preparing a list of questions to which answers are needed.

The following tips will help to ensure a successful interview.

- ❑ Try to organise the interview somewhere free of interruptions.
- ❑ Try to put the interviewee at ease. Explain the purpose of the interview so that the person does not feel they are under interrogation.
- ❑ Go through the prepared questions in a logical order, but be prepared to follow up a point with questions that are not on the list if the line of enquiry appears fruitful.
- ❑ Never criticize any aspect of the way things are currently done, or any personnel involved. The job of the interviewer is to find out information, not offer opinions.
- ❑ Summarise the points that the interviewee makes from time to time to make sure you have understood them correctly, and especially at the end of the interview.
- ❑ Make notes or use a tape recorder, and explain the purpose of these to the interviewee.
- ❑ Keep the interview short – about 20 or 30 minutes should be plenty.
- ❑ Don't forget to write up your notes of the interview after you have finished while the main points are still fresh in your mind.

Interviews, although a very good way of finding out information, can have drawbacks. These include the following:

- ❑ Some employees may be reluctant to answer questions fully if they feel that their jobs are under threat or that they are somehow being 'spied upon'. They may give the analyst a description of how they think they should be doing the job rather than how they are actually doing it, even if their way is more efficient.

- ❑ Some workers may not be very articulate about why they perform certain tasks, or what difficulties they may have in some circumstances.

- ❑ The analyst may have preconceptions about the way things work which result in misunderstandings.

Studying documentation

It may be helpful to the analyst to study various documents such as:

- ❑ instruction manuals and procedures manuals which specify how various tasks are carried out;

- ❑ blank forms such as order forms filled in by sales personnel when a customer places an order;

- ❑ examples of invoices, despatch notes, etc. already completed;

- ❑ reports produced by the current system.

The disadvantage of studying documentation is that it may be out of date if, for example, a procedure has changed and the documentation has not been updated. In spite of this the study of documents is a useful tool for gathering information.

Observation

Spending time in a department, watching how people perform their jobs and noting the problems which arise from time to time is a very useful way of gathering information. However it suffers from some drawbacks, notably:

- ❑ it is extremely time-consuming for the analyst;

- ❑ employees may feel uncomfortable being observed and may change the way they normally do things, thus giving a distorted picture of how things usually work;

- ❑ observation may not reveal problems that arise only occasionally but which can be an important factor in the weakness of an existing system;

Questionnaires

Questionnaires are of limited use in obtaining information about an existing system, and are most useful in situations where information is required from a large number of people spread over a wide geographical area and a low response rate is acceptable. Questionnaires may be used to confirm evidence that has been gathered in other ways. In designing a questionnaire it is important to:

- ❑ have a clear idea of what information you are aiming to collect;

- ❑ keep the questions short, simple and unambiguous;

- ❑ use multiple-choice questions if possible, as these are easier to answer and to analyse;

- ❑ make clear the deadline by which you need the completed questionnaire, and enclose a stamped self-addressed envelope.

Discussion: Which method(s) of fact-finding would you use to investigate the current systems used by KOC Ltd?

13.5. Portfolio work

Investigate an information processing system for a real end-user and write a statement of scope and objectives.

In subsequent chapters you will be asked to write a feasibility study and a detailed system specification to meet the requirements. In Unit 6 (Database Design) you will implement your design.

13.6. Exercises

1. A major concern at KOC is that they do not always have the correct quantity of raw materials in stock. The systems analyst has interviewed Mr Sheldon, the Production Manager, and has discovered that he uses the following system to decide when stock needs to be replenished.

    Each item is described in a stock list. This includes the following details:

    Product code

    Product description

    Supplier code

    Price

    Quantity in stock

    Average units used per week

    Lead time (i.e. the time it takes from ordering new stock to actually receiving it)

    Reorder level (i.e. the minimum level of stock allowed before more is reordered)

    Reorder quantity

    The reorder level and reorder quantity are calculated manually by Paul Sheldon. For each item he multiplies the average units used per week by the lead time to arrive at the reorder level. When the quantity in stock falls to this level, stock needs to be reordered. The reorder quantity is usually 2 months supply.

    (i)   Calculate the reorder level for an item that has an average weekly usage of 20 units and a lead time of 4 weeks. If there are 130 units currently in stock, when will it become necessary to order more? (2 marks)

    (ii) What weaknesses do you see in the current system of ordering raw materials? (3 marks)

    (iii) Suggest ways in which these weaknesses can be overcome. (2 marks)

2. Suggest two ways of solving the problem of the catalogue being out-of-date during its current life. What are the advantages and disadvantages of each of the solutions you propose? (4 marks)

3. What is the purpose of a feasibility study? (2 marks)

4. Describe briefly four methods of gathering information about a current system. (4 marks)

5. Describe briefly three things you might try and find out about an existing stock control system. (3 marks)

Chapter 14 – Data Flow Diagrams

Objectives

✓ To define what is meant by structured analysis

✓ To define the symbols used in a Data Flow Diagram (DFD)

✓ To draw a context diagram (Level 0 DFD) for a given scenario

✓ To refine a DFD to a more detailed (lower-level) view

14.1. Structured analysis

Structured analysis is a widely-used top-down method for defining system inputs, processes and outputs. It shows how information flows through a system, using several diagrams showing progressively more and more detail at each level. The primary tool of structured analysis is the Data Flow Diagram (DFD).

14.2. Data Flow Diagrams

A data flow diagram shows how data moves through a system and what data stores are used. It does not specify what type of data storage is used or how the data is stored.

The following four symbols are used in data flow diagrams:

External entity – data source or data destination, for example people who generate data such as a customer order, or receive information such as an invoice. Data sources and destinations are also known as sources and sinks.

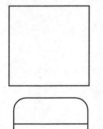

Process – an operation performed on the data. The two lines are optional; the top section of the box can be used to label or number the process, the middle to give a brief explanation, the bottom to say where the process takes place. An alternative convention is to use a circle for a Process.
Make the first word an active verb – e.g. **validate** data, **adjust** stock level.

Data store – such as a file held on disk, a table in a database. It can also represent a batch of documents held, for example, in a filing cabinet.

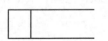

Data flow – the arrow represents movement into or out of a process. The arrow should be labelled to describe what data is involved. In the early stages of analysis, the analyst may be concerned with physical data flows such as an invoice or report. At a more detailed level, the data flows describe the actual data, e.g. customer name and address, items ordered.

Figure 14.1: Symbols used in Data Flow Diagrams

To see how these diagrams are used, we'll look at several examples. Note that each symbol in a DFD should be labelled to show what it represents.

Example 1.

A customer goes to a Travel Agent to book a flight. The travel agent looks up the flights using an on-line system, and books the flight.

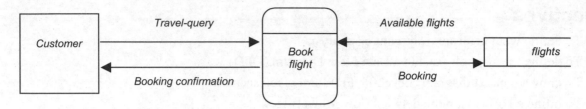

Figure 14.2: Data Flow Diagram of Travel Agent Booking system

Example 2.

Gas meter readings are read using a hand-held device which stores the reading. Later the reading is transferred to the customer's record on the main computer system.

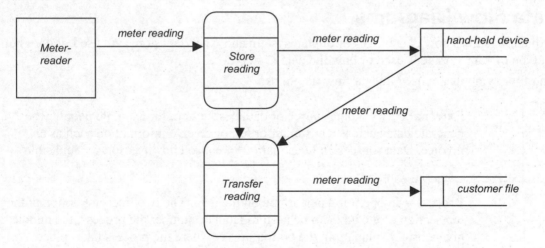

Figure 14.3: Data Flow Diagram of gas meter reading and storage

In the above diagram, the actual process of reading the meter is not shown. Note that it would not be correct to miss out the Process box "Transfer Reading", and show the data flowing directly from the data store "hand-held device" to "customer file".

> ## A data flow can only go to or come from a process.

Example 3.

Gas meter readings are read using a hand-held device which stores the reading. Later the reading is validated from the customer record on the main computer system to make sure that it is greater than the previous reading for that customer. Valid readings are stored on the customer file. Invalid readings are printed on a report.

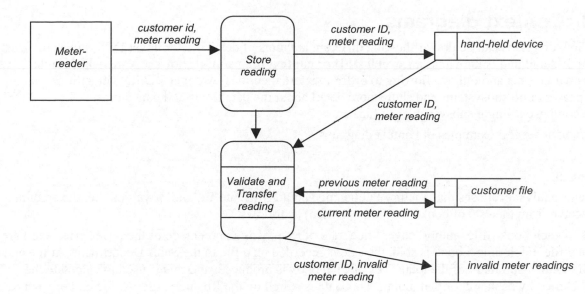

Figure 14.4: Data Flow Diagram of gas meter reading, validation and storage

Note that more detail has been added to this DFD, as the written description was more detailed than before. 'Customer-id' would have been part of the data in Figure 3.3 and you can exercise judgement as to whether it should have been included. There are two data flows from the Process box 'Validate and transfer reading'. You could use two process boxes, one for Validate and one for Transfer data. Try redrawing the DFD differently. There is often more than one 'right answer' to how a DFD should be drawn. The main thing is that the meaning should be clear.

Example 4.

A customer places an order with a mail-order company for some goods. The order is accepted by the Sales Order Processing Department. The stock file is checked and if there is sufficient stock, an invoice is printed and sent to the customer. If there is insufficient stock to fill the whole order, the customer is invoiced for any part of the order that can be filled, and the rest of the order is put on a Backorders file. A despatch note is sent to the warehouse. If any part of the order cannot be filled, an 'out-of-stock' notice is sent to the customer.

(This is only part of what happens – at some point the goods are also sent to the customer!)

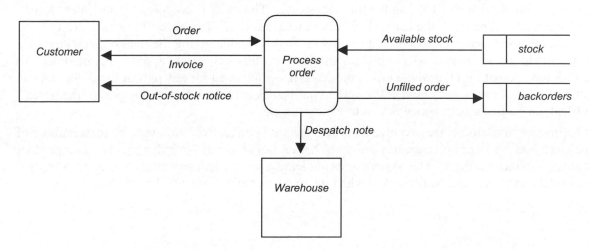

Figure 14.5: Data Flow Diagram of part of an order processing system

14.3. Context diagrams

Data Flow diagrams can be drawn showing different amounts of detail – a top-level DFD shows the least amount of detail and is known as a **Level 0 DFD** or **context diagram**. It shows a system as a single process with inputs and outputs flowing to or from external entities. A Level 1 DFD will split up that single process into subsystems and show more detail about the data flows and data stores. A Level 2 DFD may decompose a single subsystem even further.

We'll look at several examples of context diagrams.

Example 5.

A systems analyst proposes that Victory Publishing should calculate authors' royalties (i.e. the amount they receive from the sale of books they have written) as follows.

Details of each book (title, author, cover price, rate of royalty as a percentage of the cover price, etc.) are held on a file. Each time a book is sold, the sale is recorded on a file in the Sales Department. At the end of each month a summary of the total sales of each book is produced, and this is used to calculate the royalty earned by each author that month. This data is stored on the Royalties file. At the end of each 6-month period the total royalty is calculated and a statement and cheque is sent to each author.

The Level 0 DFD will show the system as a single process box with the relevant inputs and outputs. In this case, the input to the Royalties system comes from the Sales Department, and the royalty goes to the author. These are the external entities. No data stores are shown in a Level 0 DFD.

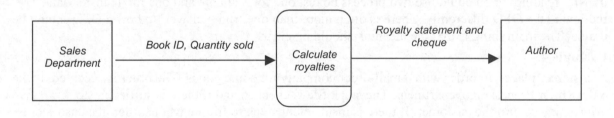

Figure 14.6: High-level DFD (Level 0) of proposed Royalties system

Example 6.

A customer places an order with KOC Ltd for some rucksacks. The order is accepted by the Sales Order Processing Department. The stock file is checked and if there is sufficient stock, an invoice is printed and sent to the customer. A picking list is sent to the warehouse (this is a list giving the total of each item to be despatched to aid the warehouse staff in picking the stock off the shelves and assembling the order). If there is insufficient stock to fill the whole order, the customer is invoiced for any part of the order that can be filled, and the rest of the order is held in the system until stock is replenished. If any part of the order cannot be filled, an 'out-of-stock' notice is sent to the customer.

Instead of an invoice, a customer may receive an order-rejection notice. Rejection may be for a number of reasons such as a bad credit rating, customer on 'stop' because of an unpaid overdue invoice, or a product ordered that is no longer available. This system does not handle backorders separately – they are simply held on the system until they can be processed when the required stock is received in the warehouse.

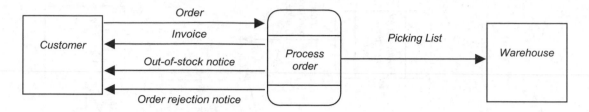

Figure 14.7: High-level DFD (Level 0) of KOC Ltd's Sales Order Processing system

The Level 0 DFD shown in Figure 14.7 shows that the SOP system accepts customer orders and produces the invoices sent to customers; it also prints a picking list which is sent to the warehouse.

14.4. Refining a data flow diagram

To draw a Level 1 DFD diagram of the Sales Order Processing system described above, the analyst would need to find out more detail about how the system works. Suppose that the analyst has established the following facts:

1. The customer order is received and the customer's credit rating is checked. New customers or those on 'stop' are put in a suspense file and referred to the Credit Control Manager. If the order is rejected, an order-rejection notice is printed and sent to the customer.

2. For orders which are accepted, stock availability is checked. Stock is allocated where possible and the stock file updated. The order is priced using the price held on the stock file.

3. If the order cannot be filled (there is insufficient stock to allocate to the order), it is left on the Orders file as an unfilled order. An out-of-stock notice is sent to the customer.

4. For completed orders, a picking list is produced and sent to the warehouse. This shows the location (Bin number) and quantity of each product needed to fill the batch of orders.

5. An invoice is produced and sent to the customer.

The Level 1 DFD is shown on the next page. It is shown in two stages so that you can see how it is built up.

Note that:

- ❑ Generally you should draw a DFD with the main flow going from left to right to make it as easy as possible to follow. You will probably need several tries before you produce a correct, complete, easy-to-follow DFD of your own.

- ❑ You can repeat an external entity or a data store at different points in the DFD to make the diagram easier to read – for example the entity Customer appears at both ends of the DFD.

- ❑ Note that a data store does not imply any particular type of storage – for example the Suspense-file may simply be a pile of paper orders in the Credit Control Manager's In-tray.

- ❑ No more than 10 processes should be shown on a DFD – use levelling where necessary to show further levels of detail. (Levelling means going from Level 1 to Level 2, or Level 2 to Level 3, etc.)

- ❑ Each process in the Level 1 DFD is numbered 1, 2, 3 etc.

- ❑ Subsequent levels are obtained by progressively decomposing individual processes into separate DFDs. The processes in a Level 2 DFD should be numbered 1.1, 1.2, 1.3 etc if the DFD is a decomposition of Process 1, or 2.1, 2.2 etc if it is a decomposition of Process 2.

First of all start by putting in the main processes and data flows, and label them. Then you can add in the data stores and more detail of what happens, for example, when there is insufficient stock to fill the order.

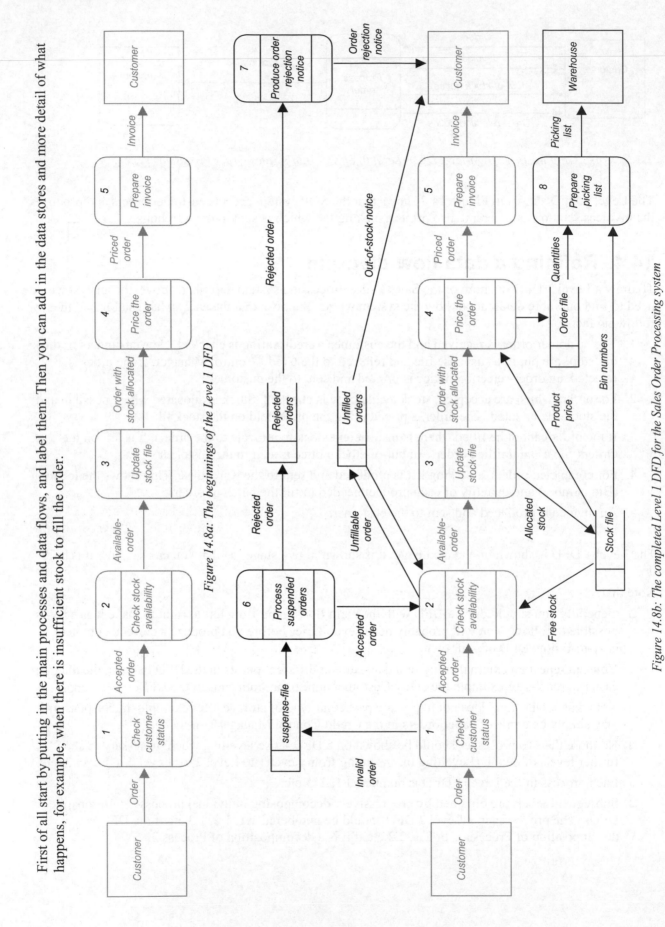

Figure 14.8a: The beginnings of the Level 1 DFD

Figure 14.8b: The completed Level 1 DFD for the Sales Order Processing system

14.5. Exercises

1. Read the following description of a system and look at the Level 1 DFD which an inexperienced trainee analyst has drawn to represent it. What is wrong with it? Redraw it correctly.

   A customer places an order with Victory Publishing for some books. The order is accepted by the Sales Order Processing Department. An invoice is printed and sent to the customer. A despatch note is printed and sent to the warehouse. The goods and the despatch note are sent to the customer from the warehouse. A second copy of the invoice is sent to the Accounts Department.

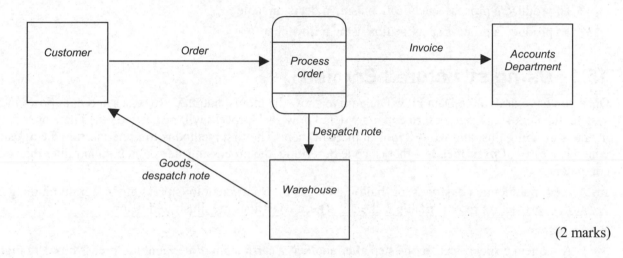

   (2 marks)

2. A student can register by mail for a college course by submitting a registration form with their name, ID number and the numbers of the courses they wish to take. The system verifies that the course is not full and enrols the student on each course for which a place is still free. The course file and student master files are updated and a confirmation letter is sent to the student to notify them of their acceptance or rejection for each requested course.

   Draw (i) a Level 0 DFD   (3 marks)

           (ii) a Level 1 DFD of the above system.   (5 marks)

3. A payroll system works as follows:

   At the end of each month, the Payroll Department is informed of any holidays, unpaid leave, maternity leave or sick days taken by any employees. Payroll data is entered and validated, valid transactions are stored on a transaction file and invalid transactions are printed in an error report. Payroll calculations are carried out using the transaction file and the employee master file, which is updated with year-to-date figures. Payslips are sent to the employees, funds transferred electronically to the employees' bank accounts and the Accounts system is sent the data necessary to update the ledgers.

   (i) Identify the external entities in the above description.   (3 marks)

   (ii) Draw (a) a Level 0 DFD   (3 marks)

                (b) a Level 1 DFD of the above system.   (5 marks)

4. What is the purpose of a Level 0 DFD?   (2 marks)

Chapter 15 – Process Specifications

Objectives

✓ To produce a process specification using structured English

✓ To produce a process specification using a decision table

✓ To produce a process specification using a flow chart

15.1. Using structured English

Once you have drawn the Data Flow Diagram to show the inputs, outputs, processes and data flows in a system, the next stage is to describe in more detail how each process will be carried out. There are several methods of doing this, and we will look at three of them. The first method is to use **structured English**, which is a form of **pseudocode** – that is, code describing the processing steps to a human rather than a computer.

Just three fundamental constructs, or 'building blocks', are sufficient to express any programming logic. A fourth construct represents multiple choice. These constructs are illustrated below.

1. Sequence

A sequence specifies that one step after another is carried out. For example Process box 3 in Figure 14.8b in the last chapter specifies the process 'Update stock file'. This can be broken down into the steps:

        Read stock record
        Add quantity to Stock Allocated
        Subtract Quantity from Free Stock
        Write stock record back to Stock file

Note that *structured English* consists of clear, imperative statements that are easily understandable, and which are quite close to program code. (For example multiplication is represented by *.)

> **Discussion: The process description given below describes how to calculate the total price of a quantity of items on an order line. Translate it into 'structured English'.**
>
> **'Look up the unit price of the item on the stock file. Multiply this by the quantity required to get the net price. Calculate the VAT by multiplying this figure by 17.5%, and add the VAT to the net price to get the Total price.'**

Sequence may be represented in a flowchart as follows:

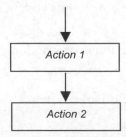

Figure 15.1: Sequence

For calculating the total price of an order line you should have written something like this:

```
Read stock record
Compute NetPrice = UnitPrice * Quantity
Compute VAT = NetPrice * 17.5/100
Compute TotalPrice = NetPrice + VAT
```

2. Iteration or 'loop'

Iteration specifies that a group of actions is to be carried out repeatedly while or until a given condition is true. There are several different variations of iterative statements in a typical programming language. The most important are **While...Do** and **Repeat...Until**.

With the **While...Do** loop, the condition that stops the loop is tested at the beginning of the loop. Therefore, if the condition is already true, the loop will not be executed at all.

For example,

```
WHILE there are more unfilled orders on the Order file DO
        Read the next order
        Read customer file
        Look up customer name and address
        Print out-of-stock notice
END WHILE
```

If there are no unfilled orders, the loop will not be performed. This can be flowcharted as follows:

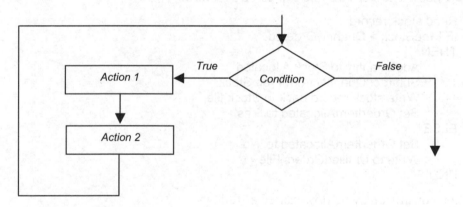

Figure 15.2: The While...Do loop (Iteration)

In the **Repeat...Until** loop, the condition is tested at the end of the loop, so the loop is always performed at least once. For example, there will always be at least one, and there may be several lines to be priced on an order.

```
REPEAT
        Read stock record
        Compute NetPrice = UnitPrice * Quantity
        Compute VAT = NetPrice * 17.5/100
        Compute TotalPrice = NetPrice + VAT
UNTIL no more order lines
```

Note the indentation used when writing structured English. This is important as it shows clearly which statements are included in a loop.

A **Repeat...Until** loop may be flowcharted as shown in Figure 15.3.

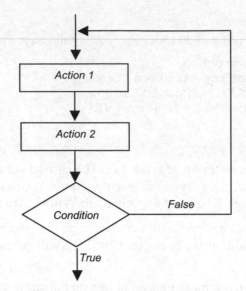

Figure 15.3: The Repeat...Until loop (Iteration)

3. Selection

There are two selection constructs, namely **If...Then...Else** and **Case**. Sometimes an **If** statement has no **Else** clause.

Consider the procedure for checking stock availability and updating the stock file (Processes 2 and 3 in Figure 14.8b). The steps may be expressed as follows:

```
Read stock record
IF FreeStock > QuantityOrdered
THEN
        Add quantity to Stock Allocated
        Subtract Quantity from Free Stock
        Write stock record back to Stock file
        Set OrderItemAllocated to 'Yes'
ELSE
        Set OrderItemAllocated to 'No'
        Write to UnfilledOrders File
ENDIF
```

A Selection construct may be flowcharted as follows:

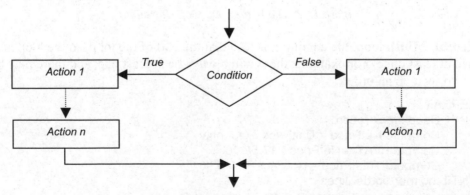

Figure 15.4: If...Then...Else (Selection)

The **Case** construct is used when there are several alternative courses of action. For example, suppose a discount is applied to an order depending on the value of the order, according to the following rules.

For order value £0 - £99.99	No discount
For order value £100 - £249.99	5% discount
For order value £250 - £499.99	10% discount
For order value > £500	12.5% discount

The procedure to calculate the discount may be written in structured English as follows:

```
CASE OrderValue
    <100.00:                Compute Discount = 0.00
    >=100 and <250.00:      Compute Discount = 5% * OrderValue
    >=250 and <500.00:      Compute Discount = 10% * OrderValue
    >=500.00:               Compute Discount = 12.5% * OrderValue
ENDCASE
```

A CASE statement can be flowcharted as in Figure 15.5.

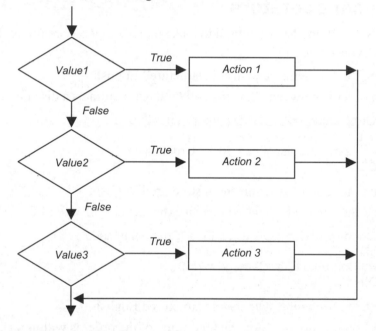

Figure 15.5: The CASE construct (Selection)

Question 1: Write structured English and draw a flowchart to represent the following procedure for checking a customer status:

For each order in a batch, examine the order and if the customer is new, put the order in the suspense file. If the customer is already on the customer file, check whether they are on 'stop', and if so, put the order in the suspense file. Otherwise, accept the order.

Question 2: Write structured English and draw a flowchart to represent the following procedure for adding a carriage charge to an order:

If the customer is a wholesaler, there is no carriage charge. Otherwise, a carriage charge of £5.50 is applied on orders up to a value of £100. No carriage is charged on orders with a value greater than or equal to £100.

15.2. Relational operators

The following relational operators are used in structured English constructs, as well as in most programming languages.

=	equal to
<	less than
>	greater than
<=	less than or equal to
>=	greater than or equal to
<>	not equal to

For example you might write

```
IF StopCode <> 'Yes' THEN Action1 ELSE Action2
```

15.3. Logical operators

The operators AND, OR and NOT are used to make more complex conditions. Take care not to confuse AND and OR in a condition.

Example 1: Write the following statement in structured English:

If the value of an order is between £250 and £499.99 then it attracts a discount of 10%.

```
IF (OrderValue>=250) AND (OrderValue<500.00)
THEN
        Compute Discount = 10% * OrderValue
ENDIF
```

Example 2: Write the following statement in structured English:

Orders to Eire and the Channel Islands attract an extra carriage charge of £7.50.

```
IF (Country = "Eire") OR (Country = "Channel Islands")
THEN
        Compute ExtraCarriage = 7.50
ENDIF
```

Example 3: Write the following statement in structured English:

If a customer's account is not on 'Stop' and the value of the order is within than the customer's credit limit, then write the order to the Orders file.

```
IF (NOT StopCode = "Yes")  AND (OrderValue <= CreditLimit)
THEN
        Write Order to Orders file
ENDIF
```

This could be written without the use of NOT. There are nearly always several correct ways of writing statements using logical operators.

Question 3:	**Write the following statement in structured English:**
	For each line of each order to be processed, the price is looked up in the catalogue. If the item is found, the price is added to the order. If the item is not in the catalogue, a supplementary list is consulted and if the item is found the price is added to the order. Otherwise, the order is rejected.

15.4. Decision tables

A decision table specifies in tabular form the actions to be carried out under a given set of conditions. It has the general format shown below.

Heading

Condition stub	Condition Entries
Action Stub	Action Entries

Figure 15.6: The format of a decision table

A decision table for student grades is shown below.

Example 4: A student who passes their exams and completes all coursework is awarded a Pass grade. Students who pass the exam but do not complete the coursework are referred, as are those who complete the coursework but do not pass the exam. Students who fail the exam and do not complete the coursework are given a Fail grade.

Carriage Charges

Pass Exam	Y	Y	N	N
Complete coursework	Y	N	Y	N
Pass	X			
Refer		X	X	
Fail				X

Figure 15.7: A decision table for student grades

The procedure for designing a decision table is as follows:

1. Specify the name of the table as its heading. You can insert a reference to it in the process description where the table applies.

2. List all possible conditions in the condition stub.

3. List all possible actions in the action stub. Fill in the conditions with Y and N alternately in the bottom row of conditions. In the next row up, fill in Y, Y, N, N. If there are three condition rows, there will be 8 columns and you fill in the top row with Y, Y, Y, Y, N, N, N, N. This gives all possible combinations of Y and N.

4. For every condition entry, mark an X in the appropriate Action entry box.

Example 5: The following carriage charges are proposed by Victory Publishing Sales Manager.

For UK orders a carriage charge of 10% of the order value is applied on orders for 1-19 books, to a maximum of £7.50. No charge is made on orders for 20 books or more.

Carriage Charges (1)

Order < 20 books	Y	Y	N	N
Order value >£75	Y	N	Y	N
10% carriage charge		X		
£7.50 carriage charge	X			
No carriage charge			X	X

Figure 15.8: A decision table for carriage charges (1)

111

Notice that the number of columns doubles with each extra condition inserted. For example, if we add a further condition to the example above, the number of columns doubles to 8. However, some of the columns are superfluous and the table can be 'collapsed'.

Example 6: The following amended carriage charges are proposed by Victory Publishing Sales Manager, who has noted the high cost of shipping books to Northern Ireland.

For UK orders (except Northern Ireland) a carriage charge of 10% of the order value is applied on orders for 1-19 books, to a maximum of £7.50. No charge is made on orders for 20 books or more. For orders to Northern Ireland, an additional charge of £3.00 is applied to orders of 1-19 books regardless of the order value.

Carriage Charges (2)

Order < 20 books	Y	Y	Y	Y	N	N	N	N
Order value >£75.00	Y	Y	N	N	Y	Y	N	N
Northern Ireland?	Y	N	Y	N	Y	N	Y	N
10% carriage charge			X	X				
£7.50 carriage charge	X	X						
No carriage charge					X	X	X	X
Additional £3.00 carriage charge	X		X					

Figure 15.9: A decision table for carriage charges (2)

Now note that if the order is for 20 books or more (i.e. not <20 books) there is no carriage charge regardless of the order value or whether or not it goes to Northern Ireland. Therefore, the last 4 columns can be replaced by one column as follows. The dash (-) means that the condition is irrelevant in that particular column.

Carriage Charges (2)

Order < 20 books	Y	Y	Y	Y	N
Order value >£75.00	Y	Y	N	N	-
Northern Ireland?	Y	N	Y	N	-
10% carriage charge			X	X	
£7.50 carriage charge	X	X			
No carriage charge					X
Additional £3.00 carriage charge	X		X		

Figure 15.10: The reduced decision table

15.5. Exercises

1. Write structured English to represent the following process for calculating an employee's weekly pay:

    To compute the weekly pay, apply the standard rate for thirty-five or fewer hours worked on weekdays. Overtime rates are paid for hours worked on a weekend and work beyond thirty-five hours on weekdays. Print out the names of employees who only worked overtime.   (8 marks)

2. A program reads a file of student marks and calculates the number of students who have obtained a Distinction, Merit, Pass or Fail. It also prints a report showing the name of each student and the grade they obtained. Underneath the marks is printed the total number of students obtaining each grade.

    (i)   Write structured English to describe this process.   (8 marks)

    (ii) Draw a flowchart to represent the processing of a single record.   (4 marks)

3. Victory Publishing uses certain criteria to decide which printer to use for a specific book. The rules are as follows:

    If the book is to be printed in colour, then it goes to printer A unless it is a rush job in which case it goes to printer B. If it is to be printed in black and white only, and fewer than 5000 copies are required it goes to printer B. If 5000 copies or more are required then it will go to printer C unless it is a rush job, when it goes to printer B however many copies are required.

    Draw up a decision table to express these rules.   (8 marks)

4. The following procedure is used to select customers from a file who will be sent a mailshot.

    First of all, the user is asked to enter a date, which is input to the computer. The program then reads each customer record and if their last purchase was on or after that date, and the total amount spent was £50 or more, they are selected for the mailshot by writing the record to a temporary file.

    (i)   Write structured English to describe this procedure.   (6 marks)

    (ii) Draw a flowchart to represent this process.   (6 marks)

5. Write a process specification for producing a reorder report from a stock file. Each stock record shows the stock ID and description, quantity in stock, reorder level, (i.e. the level at which stock should be reordered), reorder quantity and the supplier ID. The names and addresses of suppliers are held on a separate file.   (6 marks)

Chapter 16 – Logical Data Modelling Techniques

Objectives

✓ To define data modelling terms including entity, attribute, primary key, foreign key, relationship

✓ To represent the relationship between entities using an entity-relationship diagram (ERD)

✓ To normalise data to first, second and third normal form

✓ To produce a data dictionary comprising the entities in a system, their attributes and the relationship between them

16.1. Entity-relationship modelling

In Chapter 14 you saw how data flow diagrams may be used to show the flow of data around a system or organisation. In Chapter 15 you looked at different ways of describing the processes that need to take place. In this chapter we look at another important aspect of system design – the contents of the datastores and how they are related to each other. Entity-relationship modelling is the name given to this process, and the aim is to provide a model of the data that leads to effective database design.

Just three distinct sorts of object are used in entity-relationship modelling. These are:

1. An **entity** is a thing of interest to an organisation about which data is to be held. Examples of entities include Customer, Employee, Stock Item, Supplier.

2. An **attribute** is a property or characteristic of an entity. Examples of attributes associated with a Customer include Customer ID, Surname, Initials, Title, Address, Credit Limit.

3. A **relationship** is a link or association between entities. An example is the link between Owner and Car; one owner may have many cars, but each car is registered to only one owner.

There are only three different 'degrees' of relationship between two attributes. A relationship may be

One-to-one	Examples include the relationship between Husband and Wife, or between Householder and Main Residence.
One-to-many	Examples include the relationship between Mother and Child, between Customer and Order, between Publisher and Book.
Many-to-many	Examples include the relationship between Student and Course, between Stock Item and Supplier, between Film and Film Star.

These relationships may be represented diagrammatically as shown below. A line is drawn between two related entities shown in boxes, and the 'many' end of a relationship is shown by a forked ending called a *crow's foot*.

16.2. Entity-relationship diagrams

An entity-relationship diagram is a diagrammatic way of representing the relationships between the entities in a database. To show the relationship between two entities, both the **degree** and the **name** of the relationship need to be specified. For example in the first relationship shown below, the **degree** is *One-to-one*, the **name** of the relationship is *Drives*:

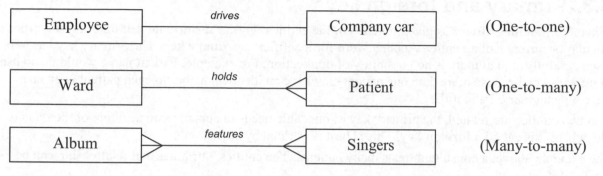

Figure 16.1: Simple entity-relationships

Sometimes it can be tricky to establish the degree of the relationship. For example, several employees may use the same company car at different times. A single employee may change the company car that he uses. The relationship will depend upon whether the data held refers to the current situation, or whether it is a historical record. The assumption has been made above that the database is to record the current car driven by an employee.

Example 1

The data requirements for a hospital in-patient system are defined as follows:

A hospital is organised into a number of wards. Each ward has a ward number and a name recorded, along with a number of beds in that ward. Each ward is staffed by nurses. Nurses have their staff number and name recorded, and are assigned to a single ward.

Each patient in the hospital has a patient identification number, and their name, address and date of birth are recorded. Each patient is under the care of a single consultant and is assigned to a single ward. Each consultant is responsible for a number of patients. Consultants have their staff number, name and specialism recorded.

State four entities for the hospital in-patient system and suggest an identifier for each of these entities.

Draw an entity-relationship diagram to show the relationship between the entities.

Answer:

Entity	Identifier	
WARD	Ward number	(WardID)
NURSE	Staff number	(StaffID)
PATIENT	Patient identification number	(PatientID)
CONSULTANT	Staff number	(StaffID)

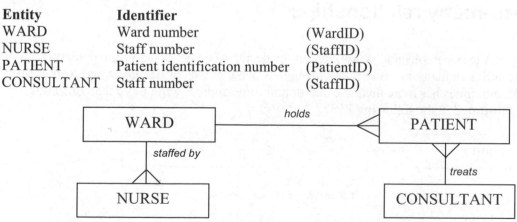

Figure 16.2: More complex entity-relationships

Note that a one-to-many relationship does not necessarily imply that **every** ward, for example, has many patients, merely that is possible that at least one ward has more than one patient. It is possible that some wards have no patients at all.

16.3. Primary and foreign keys

In Example 1 an **identifier** was given for each of the entities. This is an attribute that uniquely identifies a particular occurrence of an entity. Another word for identifier is **primary key**. The primary key has to be chosen carefully so that there is no possibility of duplication. For example, Patient name would be no use as a primary key because more than one patient may have an identical name, so each patient is given a unique alphanumeric Patient ID.

When two entities are related, the primary key of one table needs to appear as an attribute of the related table, where it is called a **foreign key**. This is best illustrated by an example.

In the example above, a consultant treats many patients. The entities, attributes and relationship can be shown as follows:

Consultant

| StaffID |
| Title |
| Surname |
| FirstName |

Primary Key

Patient

PatientID	Primary Key
Title	
Surname	
FirstName	
DateOfAdmission	
StaffID	Foreign key

Figure 16.3: Primary and foreign keys

A standard notation is commonly used to show entities, attributes, primary and foreign keys. The entity name is shown in uppercase letters, and the attributes are shown in parentheses with the primary key underlined and any foreign keys in italics or with an asterisk. Thus the two entities above can be represented as follows:

CONSULTANT (StaffID, Title, Surname, FirstName)

PATIENT (PatientID, Title, Surname, FirstName, DateOfAdmission, *StaffID*)

16.4. Many-to-many relationships

Example 2

The systems analyst at Victory Publishing is working on the design of a new system for calculating royalties. She has identified a many-to-many relationship between the two entities Book and Author. In other words, a book sometimes has more than one author and some authors write more than one book. The relationship is illustrated in the following ERD.

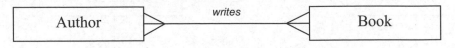

Figure 16.4: A many-to-many relationship

It is impossible to assign a fixed number of attributes to either of these entities. The entity AUTHOR could have attributes Book1, Book2, Book3, but what if an author writes 4 books? Likewise, BOOK could have attributes Author1, Author2 – but suppose a book was published that had 3, 4 or even more authors?

When an entity has a **repeating attribute**, e.g. a book has several authors, the repeating attribute is shown with a line over it.

BOOK (<u>ISBN</u>, Title, AuthorID, DatePublished, Price)

The ISBN (International Standard Book Number, found on the back of every published book) is unique and is used as the primary key.

The Author entity can be represented in a similar manner. There are two repeating attributes shown below, because the royalty rate will depend on the particular book. If there is only one author, the royalty might be 10%, for example. If there are two authors, each may receive a royalty of 5%.

AUTHOR (<u>AuthorID</u>, Surname, Initials, ISBN, RoyaltyRate)

Many-to-many relationships cannot be represented in a relational database.

An additional entity has to be introduced that has a one-to-many (or more accurately, a many-to-one) relationship with each of the others.

To get rid of the many-to-many relationship such as the one shown in Figure 16.4, a new entity (named Book/Author or some other suitable name) needs to be introduced 'in the middle'.

Figure 16.5: Transforming a many-to-many relationship into two one-to-many relationships

> **Note:** When an extra entity is introduced to get rid of a many-to-many relationship, the "crow's feet" representing the 'many' side of the relationship always point to the newly introduced entity and away from the original entities.

16.5. Normalisation

Normalisation is the process of ensuring that the database is designed in the best possible way, so that:

- ❑ there is a minimum of data duplicated in different tables.
- ❑ inconsistencies between data items are eliminated (for example, a person's surname is not spelt *Humphreys* in one place and *Humphries* somewhere else in the database).
- ❑ it is as easy as possible to extract information from the database.

There are several stages in normalisation, the first three of which are enough for nearly all databases, including any that you will come across or design on this course. These stages are known as first, second and third normal form.

In this unit you are required to normalise only to first normal form, but in Unit 6 you have to be able to normalise to third normal form so all three stages are covered here.

Normalisation is sometimes perceived as baffling and difficult, but is really a question of common sense – avoid repeating attributes, put all the attributes in the table where they obviously belong and you will end up with correctly normalised tables. Two different approaches to normalisation are shown below.

First Normal Form

Definition: A database in first normal form must not contain repeating attributes.

Normalising to first normal form ensures that no entity has any repeating attributes, and that there are no many-to-many relationships in the model.

To put an entity into first normal form, all repeating attributes must be removed from it.

Thus BOOK and AUTHOR need to be rewritten as follows:

AUTHOR (AuthorID, Surname, Initials)

BOOK (ISBN, Title, DatePublished, Price)

The third entity, BOOK/AUTHOR, links to each of the original tables by holding their primary keys as foreign keys. It also needs to hold any other repeating attribute from the original tables.

The Primary key of this table needs to identify any occurrence of the entity. In our example, it will be a composite key consisting of two attributes:

BOOK/AUTHOR (*ISBN, AuthorID*, RoyaltyRate)

This table shows which book(s) were written by which author(s) and what royalty rate is received by each author for each title. The database is now in first normal form.

Example 3

A database is to be created to hold details of students, courses, lecturers and the relationships between these three entities.

We will approach the problem of normalisation from a different starting point. The ERD is shown in Figure 16.6, but as you work through the example you will see that a fourth entity has to be introduced because of the many-to-many relationship between STUDENT and COURSE.

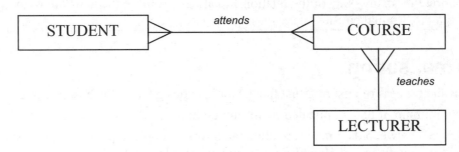

Figure 16.6: ERD showing relationships between Student, Course and Lecturer

Sample data to be held in the database is shown in the table below:

STUDENT

Student Number	Student Name	DateOf Birth	Sex	Course Number	CourseName	Lecturer Number	Lecturer Name
12345	Heathcote,R	20-08-85	M	EC6654	A-Level Computing	T345267	Glover,T
22433	Head,J	13-02-85	F	EC6654	A-Level Computing	T345267	Glover,T
				HM7756	A-Level Music	T773351	Reader,B
				AD1121	Pottery	T876541	Day,S
66688	Hargrave,R	13-09-54	M	BM3390	HNC Business	T666758	Newman,P
				HM7756	A-Level Music	T773351	Reader,B

Each of the entities STUDENT, COURSE and LECTURER will need their own table, each with a unique primary key and holding the attributes that belong to the entity. As a first try, we will start with the two tables STUDENT and COURSE, represented in standard notation as

STUDENT (StudentNumber, StudentName, DateOfBirth, Sex)

COURSE (CourseNumber, CourseName, LecturerNumber, LecturerName)

The question now is, how can the relationship between these two tables be shown? How can we hold the information about which students are doing which courses?

The two tables need to be linked by means of a common field, but the problem is that because this is a many-to-many relationship, whichever table we put the link field into, there needs to be *more than one field*.

e.g.   STUDENT (StudentNumber, StudentName, DateOfBirth, Sex, CourseNumber)

is no good because the student is doing several courses, so which one would be mentioned?

Similarly,   COURSE (CourseNumber, CourseName, LecturerNumber, LecturerName, StudentNumber)

is no good either because each course has a number of students taking it.

One obvious solution (and unfortunately a bad one) springs to mind. How about allowing space for 3 courses on each student record?

STUDENT (StudentNumber, StudentName, DateOfBirth, Sex, Course1, Course2, Course3)

You can probably see the weakness in this solution. Sooner or later a student will come along who wants to do four courses.

What we have engineered is a repeating attribute – not permitted in 1st normal form. In other words, the field **CourseNumber** is repeated 3 times. The table is therefore NOT in first normal form.

It would be represented in standard notation with a line over the repeating attribute:

STUDENT (StudentNumber, StudentName, DateOfBirth, Sex, CourseNumber)

To put the data into first normal form, the repeating attribute must be removed. In its place, the field CourseNumber becomes part of the primary key in the student table. The tables are now as follows:

STUDENT (StudentNumber, StudentName, DateOfBirth, Sex, CourseNumber)

COURSE (CourseNumber, CourseName, LecturerNumber, LecturerName)

Can you see why CourseNumber has to be part of the primary key? Remember that the primary key is the field or combination of fields that uniquely identifies each row in a table.

The two tables STUDENT and COURSE, now in first normal form, look like this:

STUDENT

Student Number	Student Name	DateOf Birth	Sex	Course Number
12345	Heathcote,R	20-08-85	M	EC6654
22433	Head,J	13-02-85	F	EC6654
22433	Head,J	13-02-85	F	HM7756
22433	Head,J	13-02-85	F	AD1121
66688	Hargrave,R	13-09-54	M	BM3390
66688	Hargrave,R	13-09-54	M	HM7756

COURSE

Course Number	CourseName	Lecturer Number	Lecturer Name
EC6654	A-Level Computing	T345267	Glover,T
HM7756	A-Level Music	T773351	Reader,B
AD1121	Pottery	T876541	Day,S
BM3390	HNC Business	T666758	Newman,P

Note that in database terminology, a *table* is also known as a *relation*. This type of database, consisting of many relations, is called a *relational database*.

Second normal form

Definition: A table is in second normal form if it is in first normal form and no column that is not part of a primary key is dependent on only a portion of the primary key.

This is sometimes expressed by saying that *a table in second normal form contains no partial dependencies*.

The tables above are not in second normal form. For example, StudentName is dependent only on StudentNumber and not on CourseNumber. To put the tables into second normal form, we need to introduce a third table (relation) that acts as a link between the entities Student and Course.

The tables are now as follows:

> STUDENT (<u>StudentNumber</u>, StudentName, DateOfBirth, Sex)
>
> STUDENT_TAKES(<u>StudentNumber</u>, <u>CourseNumber</u>)
>
> COURSE (<u>CourseNumber</u>, CourseName, LecturerNumber, LecturerName)

As in the Book/Author example, a new entity has had to be introduced to link the two original entities STUDENT and COURSE.

As you get more practice in database design, you will see that *whenever* two entities have a many-to-many relationship, you will *always* need a link table 'in the middle'. Thus

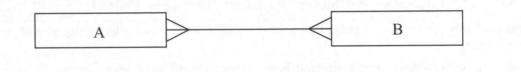

will become

Figure 16.7: A 'link' table is needed in a many-to-many relationship

Third normal form – Non-key dependence test

Definition: A table in third normal form contains no 'non-key dependencies'.

Looking at the COURSE table, the lecturer name is dependent on the lecturer number, not on the course number. It therefore needs to be removed from this relation and a new relation created:

> LECTURER (<u>LecturerNumber</u>, LecturerName)

The database, now in third normal form, consists of the following tables:

> STUDENT (<u>StudentNumber</u>, StudentName, DateOfBirth, Sex)
>
> STUDENT_TAKES (<u>StudentNumber</u>, <u>CourseNumber</u>)
>
> COURSE (<u>CourseNumber</u>, CourseName, LecturerNumber)
>
> LECTURER (<u>LecturerNumber</u>, LecturerName)

The tables are now correctly normalised to third normal form.

16.6. The data dictionary

A data dictionary describes all the data components in a system. It will show, for example:

- ❏ the entities in a system
- ❏ the name and description of each attribute
- ❏ the relationship between the entities

One possible layout for a data dictionary is shown below. A different layout is shown in the Systems Specification in Chapter 9. There are many ways of documenting the data dictionary and you must choose the one that you consider most suitable for your particular project.

Data dictionary for the Student database

Primary keys are shown underlined

Foreign keys are shown in italics

Entity List

Name	Description	Attributes	Relationships
tblStudent	Table of data relating to each student	StudentNumber, StudentName, DateOfBirth, Sex	One-to-many with tblStudent_Takes
tblCourse	Table of data relating to each course	CourseNumber, CourseName, *LecturerNumber*, LecturerName	One-to-many with tblStudent_Takes
tblStudent_Takes	Table of data showing which student takes which course	*StudentNumber*, *CourseNumber*	
tblLecturer	Table of data relating to each lecturer	LecturerNumber, LecturerName	One-to-many with tblCourse

Attribute list

Name	Description	Type	Range	Where Used
CourseNumber	Unique course code	Text (7)		Primary key in tblCourse foreign key in tblStudent_Takes
CourseName	Name of course	Text (50)		tblCourse
LecturerNumber	Unique Lecturer ID	Text (7)		Primary key in tblLecturer foreign key in tblCourse
etc.				

16.7. Atomic attributes

The attribute *Name* used above holds data in the format **Head,J**. However this is not satisfactory because there may be occasions when you want to separate the initials from the surname, for example if you were using the data in a mail merge latter starting 'Dear Miss Head'. The attribute Name should be split into 3 atomic attributes *Title*, *FirstName*, *Surname*. An atomic attribute is one which cannot be broken down any further.

16.8. Exercises

1. Making sure that all attributes are atomic, amend and complete the data dictionary started above.

    (10 marks)

2. The Author/Book database in Example 2 of this chapter has been put into first normal form. Does anything more need to be done to it to put it into third normal form? Justify your answer.   (2 marks)

3. A company proposes to have three entities in its order processing system. Sample contents of three proposed tables are shown below.

Customer

Surname	Firstname	Address1	Address2	Town	Postcode
Wilson	James	35 Maple Road	Bredfield	Woodbridge	IP12 4RE
McLay	Angus	The Studio	Bridge Road	Woodbridge	IP12 6GH

Order

Surname	Firstname	Postcode	OrderDate	ItemOrdered	Qty	Price	TotalCost
Wilson	James	IP12 4RE	15/03/2001	Garden Bench	1	35.95	35.95
Wilson	James	IP12 4RE	15/03/2001	Garden Chair	2	15.00	30.00
McLay	Angus	IP12 6GH	17/03/2001	Hanging Basket	2	8.00	16.00
McLay	Angus	IP12 6GH	17/03/2001	Water Butt	1	17.50	17.50
McLay	Angus	IP12 6GH	17/03/2001	Bag compost	4	5.00	20.00
Wilson	James	IP12 4RE	31/03/2001	Hanging Basket	4	8.00	32.00
McLay	Angus	IP12 6GH	18/04/2001	Garden Chair	4	15.00	60.00

Stock

StockItem	Price	QtyInStock
Garden Bench	35.95	6
Garden Chair	15.00	22
Water Butt	17.50	4
Bag compost	5.00	67
Hanging Basket	8.00	33

(i) Explain why this design is unsatisfactory. Draw an entity-relationship diagram to show the relationship between the entities.   (5 marks)

(ii) Normalise the tables to third normal form.   (5 marks)

Chapter 17 – The Input Specification

Objectives

- ✓ To define the data sources and methods of data capture for an application
- ✓ To define the verification and validation methods used on the input data
- ✓ To design a data input form
- ✓ To design an input screen layout
- ✓ To describe different methods of data capture

17.1. The source of data

An important consideration in system design is the question of where the data comes from, what form it is in, how it is to be entered into the new system and what steps will be taken to ensure that it is entered accurately. Several different kinds of data will be entered into a system. In a Sales Order Processing system, data about new customers and new products will be entered onto master files. On a daily basis, new orders from customers will be entered as they arrive. Some orders may arrive in the post, some may be telephoned or faxed and some may be submitted via the Internet.

In the case of Victory Publishing, suppose that orders may be made either by phone, fax or mail. The systems analyst needs to consider the following points:

- ❑ When a customer orders by post, do they normally use a standard order form taken, for example, from Victory's catalogue? Are the product codes pre-printed on the order form to eliminate the possibility of error? Or does each customer use their own standard order form?
- ❑ What information needs to be entered into the system from a customer order?
- ❑ When orders are telephoned, does the person answering the telephone have a pad of standard order forms on which they record the order? If so, what form does the order form take?
- ❑ Alternatively, are they typed into the computer system immediately by the person taking the order without the need for a paper form?
- ❑ Or, are all (telephoned and mailed) orders collected into a batch and entered later?

17.2. Data items for a Sales Order Processing system

Suppose that a new customer telephones to place an order. Details about the new customer must first be entered onto the system, and then details of the order. The following data will probably be entered:

Customer data

Different categories of data will be entered, probably using several input screens. Shown on the next page are typical data entry screens for a new customer.

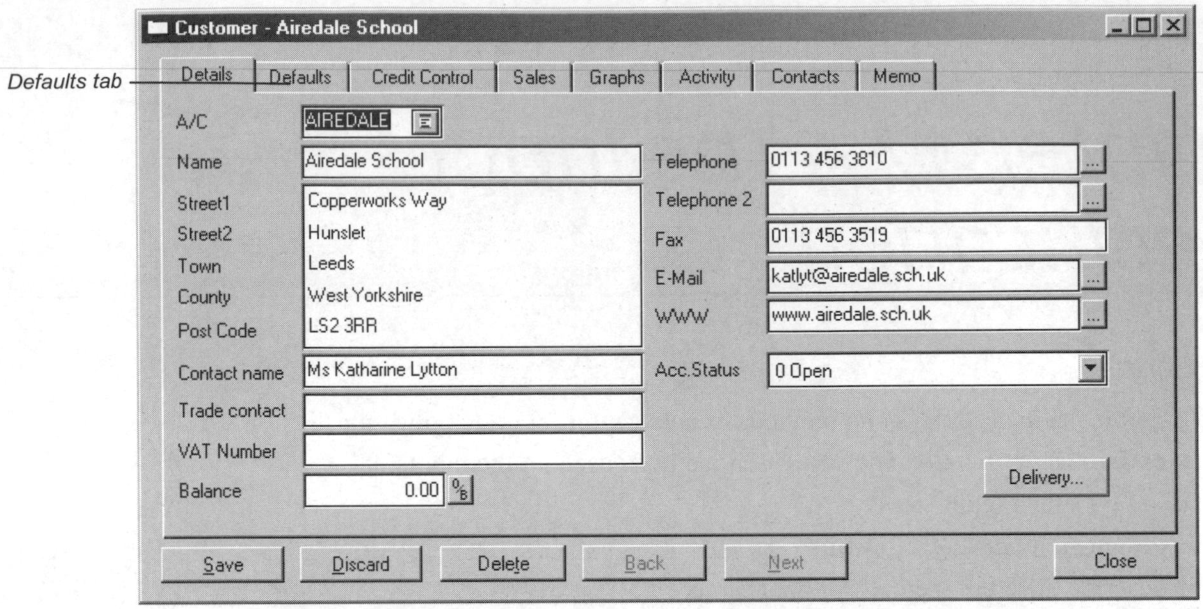

Figure 17.1: The first data entry screen for entering a new customer

By clicking the Defaults tab, a further screen is brought up for entry of discount and analysis codes.

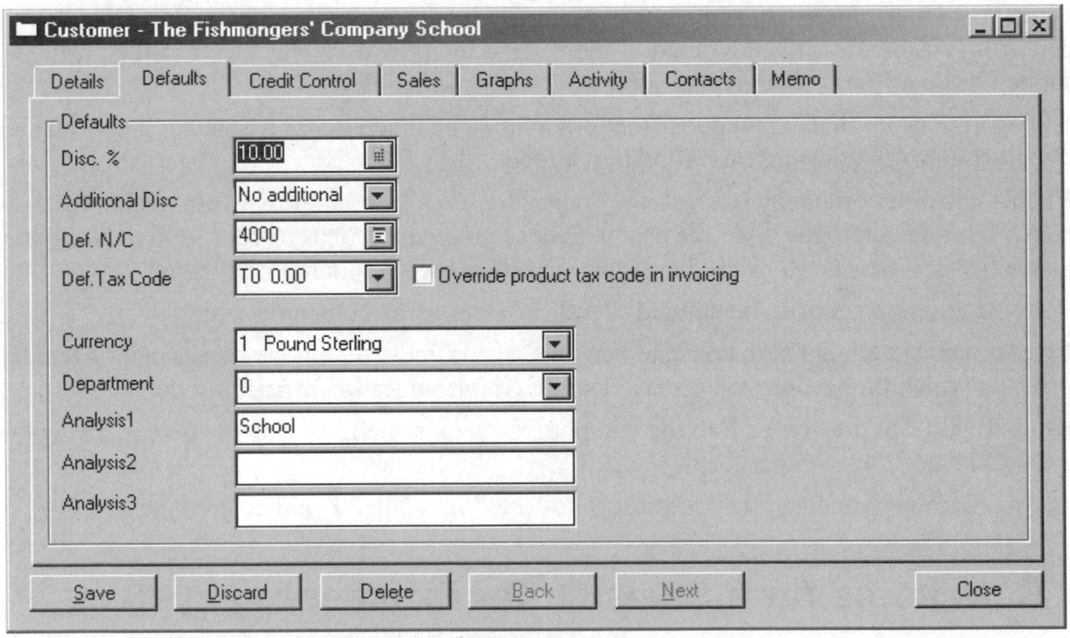

Figure 17.2: The second data entry screen for entering a new customer

Credit control information can now be entered:

124

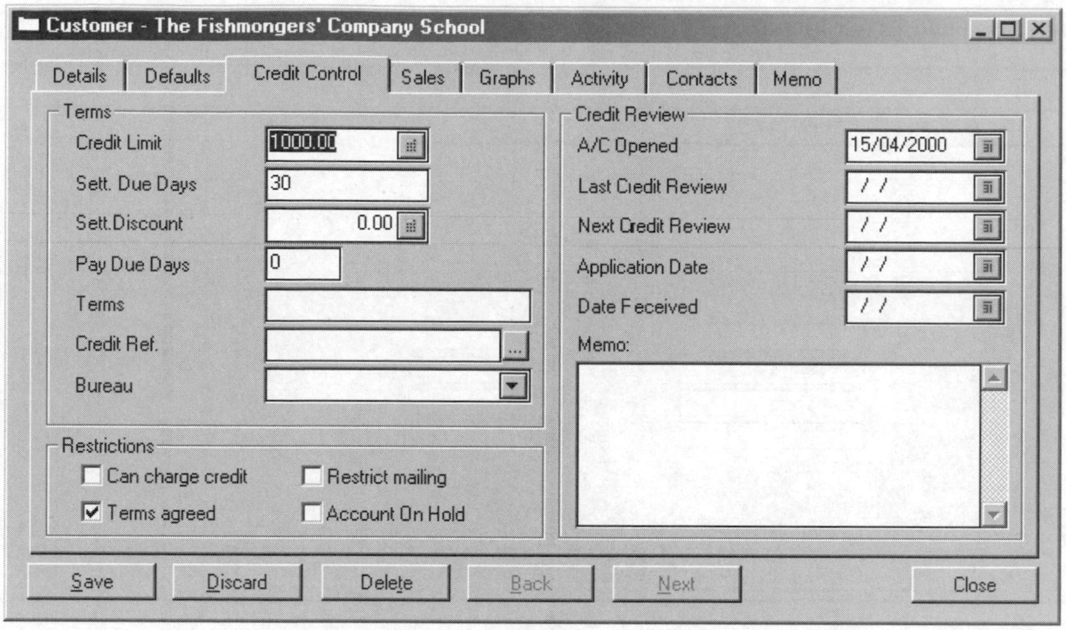

Figure 17.3: The third data entry screen for entering a new customer

Make a list of the most important fields required when entering a new customer record.

Describe a possible source of this data.

Which screen would you go to in order to put a customer's account on 'stop' or 'hold'?

Sales order data

A typical sales order screen is shown below:

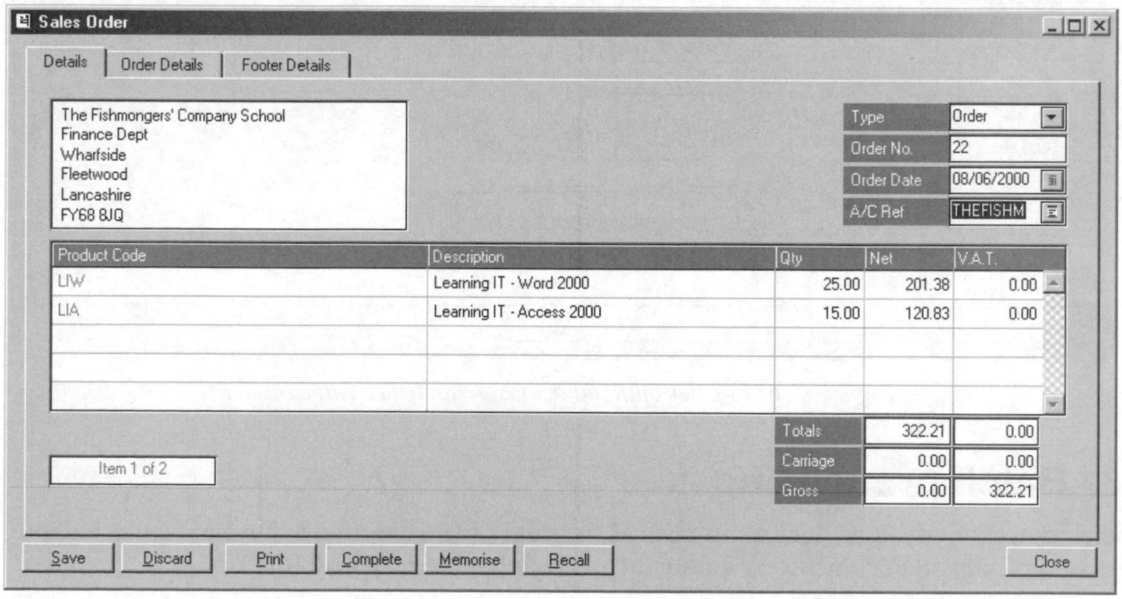

Figure 17.4: Entering a sales order

When the Customer code is entered, the customer name and address automatically appear. Likewise, when the Product code is entered, the product description appears. As soon as the quantity is entered, the price is calculated.

A second screen allows additional order details to be entered:

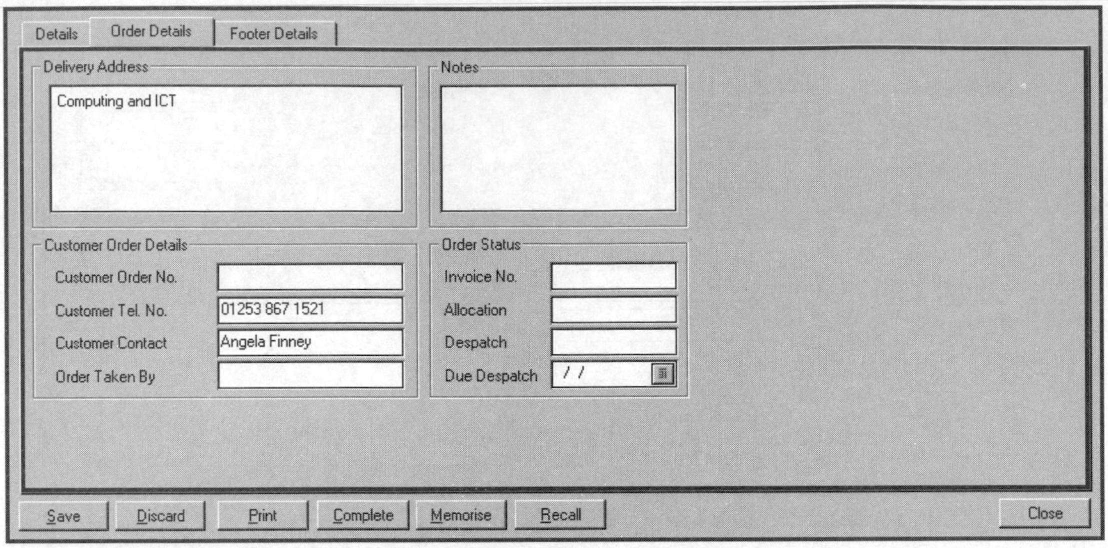

Figure 17.5: Order details screen

A third screen allows default values to be altered and any carriage charges to be added:

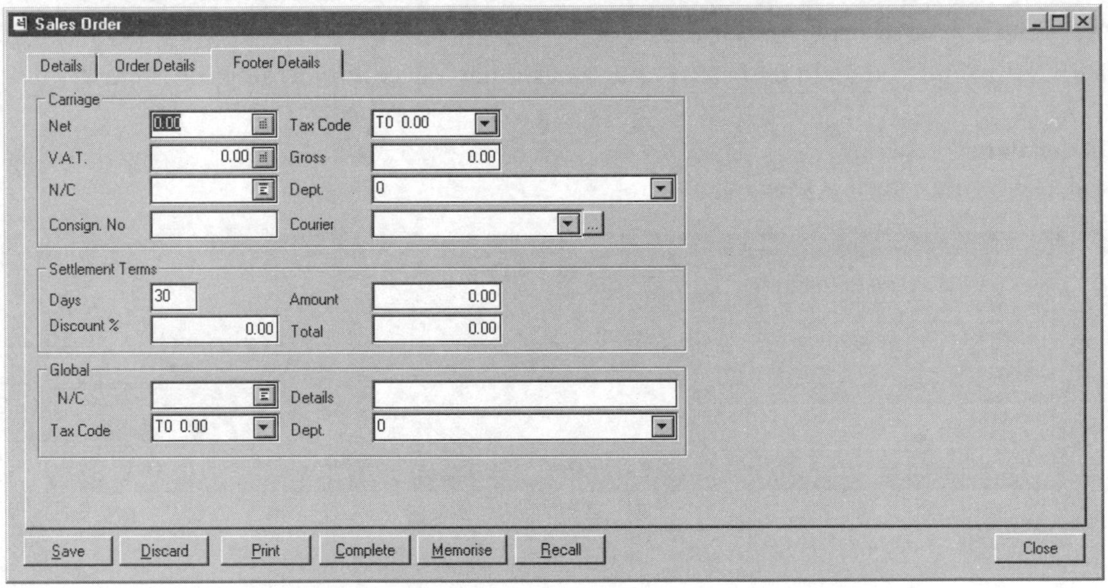

Figure 17.6: Further optional details on an order entry screen

17.3. Batch processing

In a batch processing system, documents such as the sales orders described above are collected into batches of typically 50 documents. A **data control clerk** has the responsibility of:

- ❏ counting the documents;
- ❏ checking each one visually to see that the customer has entered essential details such as their name and address, and card details if that is the payment method;
- ❏ calculating a **control total** of some crucial field such as Total Quantity, for the entire batch of 50 documents;

❏ filling in a batch header document which will show, for example:
- batch number
- number of documents in batch
- date received
- control total

❏ logging the batch in a book kept for this purpose.

The data from the batch header is keyed in as well as the contents of all the documents in the batch, and the computer performs the same summing calculations that the data entry clerk made manually. If there is any discrepancy, then an error is reported and the batch is rechecked.

17.4. Verification

Data verification is the process of double-checking that data entry is correct. This is sometimes done by typing in the data twice, as for example when you are asked to enter and then re-enter a new password. In large-volume data-entry, a batch of data is sometimes entered by one operator and saved on disk, and then the same batch is re-keyed by a second operator and the data compared with the data held on the disk.

In an online system where an order is taken over the telephone and typed straight into the computer without the need for writing the order on paper, verification may be verbal. The customer will identify themselves as, say, ABC Ltd, and the sales order clerk will type the A/C Reference ABC into the data entry screen form. The address will then appear and she will verify with the customer:

"Is that ABC at 136 Henley Road, Ipswich?"

The required product codes and quantities will then be entered and she can tell the customer

"That comes to £98 and £5.50 carriage. Is that all right?"

The customer will know if the price is different from what they expected or if a discount has not been applied.

17.5. Validation

Validation is done by a computer program, and checks as far as possible that the data is accurate. Many items can only be checked for 'reasonableness' – that is, the computer can check that a particular product exists, or that the quantity ordered is within a certain range, but this does not eliminate the possibility of errors being made in data entry. Typical validation checks include the following:

1. **Presence check.** Certain fields such as customer number, item code, quantity etc must be present. The data control clerk may have visually checked this but the program can perform a second check. Also, if this is a new customer, a number could be automatically assigned.

2. **Format check** (also called **picture check**). For example the code perhaps has a pattern of 2 letters followed by 4 numbers. The quantity and price must be numeric.

3. **Range check.** The expiry date of a credit card must have a month number between 1 and 12, and the date must be later than today's date.

4. **File lookup check.** The computer can look up the customer account number on the customer file and display the name and address. The data entry operator can check that it tallies.

5. **Check digit check.** This is an extra digit on the end of a number such as the ISBN. (See exercise in Chapter 2.)

6. **Batch header checks.** The total number of records in the batch should be calculated by the computer and compared with the figure on the batch header. The control totals are also calculated and compared.

Discussion: What validation checks can the computer perform when data is entered using the input screens shown in Figure 17.4?

17.6. Designing an input screen

When an analyst designs a system from scratch, rather than using a package, input screens have to be specially designed. Some basic rules of screen design include the following:

- ❑ the form should be given a title to identify it;
- ❑ the form should not be too cluttered – spaces and blanks are important;
- ❑ it should give some indication of how many characters can be entered in each field of data;
- ❑ the user should be given a chance to go back and correct any field before the data is accepted;
- ❑ items should appear in a logical sequence to assist the user;
- ❑ default values should wherever possible be prewritten onto the form so that a minimum of data entry is required;
- ❑ lower case in a display is neater and easier to read than all upper-case;
- ❑ colours should be carefully chosen to be legible and easy on the eyes;

Screens can be designed using paper and pencil initially, and then refined within, say, the database package that is being used to implement the system. You need to know what the possibilities are before you can come up with the best design. For example, in Access you can place different types of object on an input form including list boxes, radio buttons, check boxes and so on. You can also design a form that incorporates data from more than one table.

An initial paper and pencil design for the data entry form used to input a new author and the books they have written is shown below.

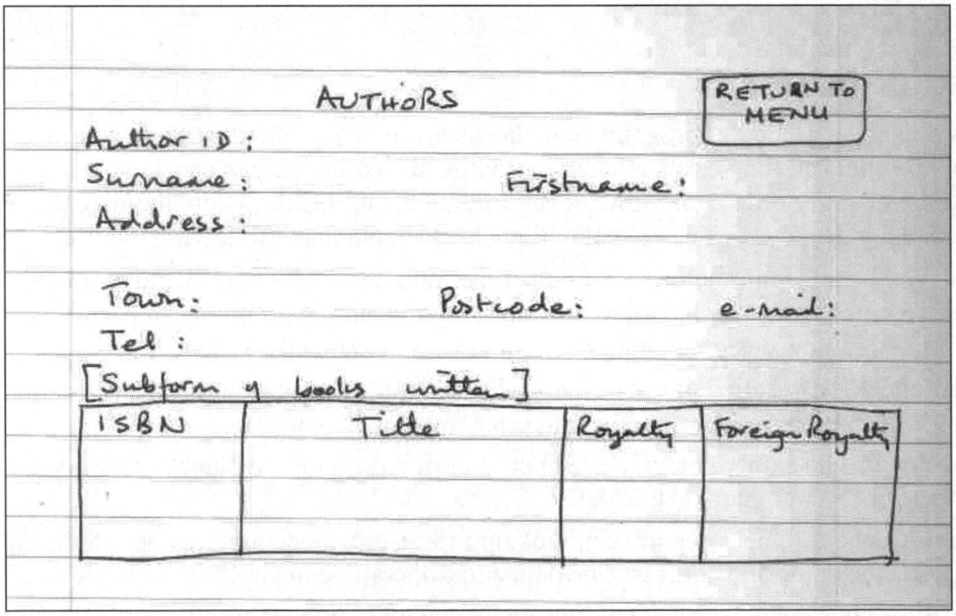

Figure 17.7: Rough plan for a data entry form for entering a new author

17.7. Methods of data capture

In the above examples the data has been 'captured' by entering it at a keyboard. The keyboard is the most common input device, suitable for a wide range of applications from entering programs to typing all kinds of documents using a word processor, or entering personal details of customers or patients at a hospital, etc. Data entered at a keyboard is commonly copied from a source document, and as such has disadvantages:

❑ it is easy to make **transcription** errors – that is, copy the data wrongly from the document;

❑ it is time-consuming;

❑ data entry operators who enter data all day every day are prone to **repetitive strain injury** (RSI), a condition which renders them unable to do any further data entry or even perform everyday tasks such as pouring a cup of tea.

There are many other methods of data capture which are more suitable in different circumstances.

Voice data entry

The user speaks the text into a microphone and special software such as IBM's VoicePad or Dragon's Naturally Speaking interprets the text and displays it on a screen, where it may be edited using the keyboard and exported to a word processing package such as Word. The accuracy of the voice recognition system is improved by 'training' it to a particular user's voice – an embarrassing process of speaking a given set of a few hundred short sentences to your computer, repeating any that are not accurately interpreted.

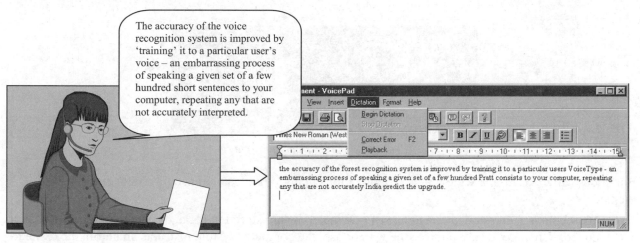

Figure 17.8: Voice recognition: not always 100% accurate!

Scanners and OCR

An optical scanner can be used to scan graphical images and photographs, and software can then be used to edit or touch up the images. Scanners can also be used to read typed or even hand-written documents and OCR (Optical Character Recognition) software can then be used to interpret the text and export it to a word processor or data file. Scanners are also used to input large volumes of data on pre-printed forms such as credit card payments, where the customer's account number and amount paid are printed at the bottom of the payment slip.

Magnetic Ink Character Recognition (MICR)

All banks use MICR for processing cheques. Along the bottom of a cheque the bank's sort code, customer account number and cheque number are encoded in special characters in magnetic ink. The amount of the cheque is encoded in magnetic ink when it is handed in at a bank. The cheques can then be processed extremely fast by high-speed MICR devices that read, sort and store the data on disk. MICR has several advantages for processing cheques:

- ❑ it is hard to forge the characters;
- ❑ the characters can be read even if the cheque is crumpled, dirty or smudged;
- ❑ the characters are readable by humans, unlike bar codes.

Optical Mark Recognition (OMR)

An optical mark reader can detect marks in preset positions on a form. It is widely used for marking multiple-choice exams and market research questionnaires.

Magnetic stripe

Cards with magnetic stripes are used as credit cards, debit cards, railway tickets, phone cards and many other applications such as customer loyalty cards. The magnetic strip can be encoded with up to 220 characters of data, and there are over 2.4 billion plastic card transactions every year in Britain, with 83% of adults owning at least one card. The information provided when someone signs up for a loyalty card with Sainsbury, Tesco, Boots or W.H.Smith, for example, plus a few months of shopping records, can provide a detailed portrait of customers' habits.

Bar code reader or scanner

Bar codes appear on almost everything we buy. The pattern of thick and thin bars represents the 13-digit number underneath the bar code.

Figure 17.9: A product bar code

Bar codes can be used in a wide range of applications that require fast and accurate data entry. These include:

- ❑ Warehousing. Bar-coded containers of raw materials are stored in racks of bins which are also bar coded. When goods are put into the warehouse, the computer system instructs an automatic crane to retrieve the nearest available empty bin. The filled bin is then returned to an empty location. The crane relies entirely on bar codes to move goods in and out.

- ❑ Transport and distribution. All major road freight carriers now use bar codes. Individual packages are bar-coded as are depot consignments. The exact location of any package is known at any one time together with details of the type of service used. Individual customers can be billed quickly and missing parcels traced more easily.

- ❑ Manufacturing. Very accurate data relating to work in progress can be obtained using bar codes as the data entry method. Management can obtain up-to-date data on the progress of unfinished goods, enabling bottlenecks and over-production to be reduced and production efficiency to improve.

- ❑ Marketing. Many polling companies now use bar-coded multiple-choice questionnaires to enter data quickly and accurately. Survey times can be dramatically reduced.

- ❑ Medical. Bar codes are commonly used to identify blood and other samples. Hospital patients' and outpatients' records are increasingly bar-coded for fast retrieval and better accuracy.

- ❏ Libraries. Bar codes are used to record loans and provide more information on stock.
- ❏ Banking, insurance and local government. Bar codes are used extensively for accurate document control and retrieval. Many cheque book covers, insurance claim files and council tax forms are bar coded.

Hand-held input devices

Portable keying devices are commonly used in such applications as reading gas or electricity meters, where the meter reader displays the next customer name, address and location of meter on a small screen, then reads the meter and keys in the reading. At the end of the day all the readings can be downloaded via a communications link to the main computer for processing.

Touch screen

A touch screen allows the user to touch an area of the screen rather than having to type the data on a keyboard. They are widely used in tourist centres, where tourists can look up various local facilities and entertainments, in fast food stores such as McDonald's for entering customer orders, in manufacturing and many other environments.

EDI

Electronic data interchange (EDI) is the electronic transmission of business data, such as purchase orders and invoices, from one firm's computerised information to that of another firm. Since EDI transmission is virtually instantaneous, the supplier's computer system can check for availability and respond quickly with a confirmation.

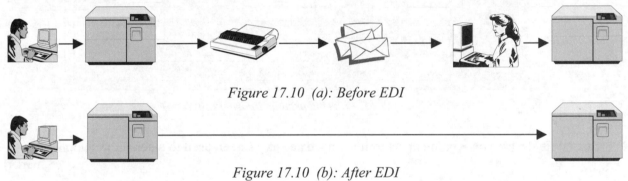

Figure 17.10 (a): Before EDI

Figure 17.10 (b): After EDI

Speed and reliability are major advantages of EDI. It does away with re-keying data, increases accuracy and eliminates delays.

17.8. Exercises

1. The figure below shows an input screen for entering a new product or editing an existing product record. List:

    (i)   Ten fields that are entered by the operator.

    (ii) Five fields that are calculated automatically by the system as a result of inputting orders, allocating and dispatching stock and entering orders for new stock.

    (iii) Three fields that are validated by looking up information from other files held on the system.

    (10 marks)

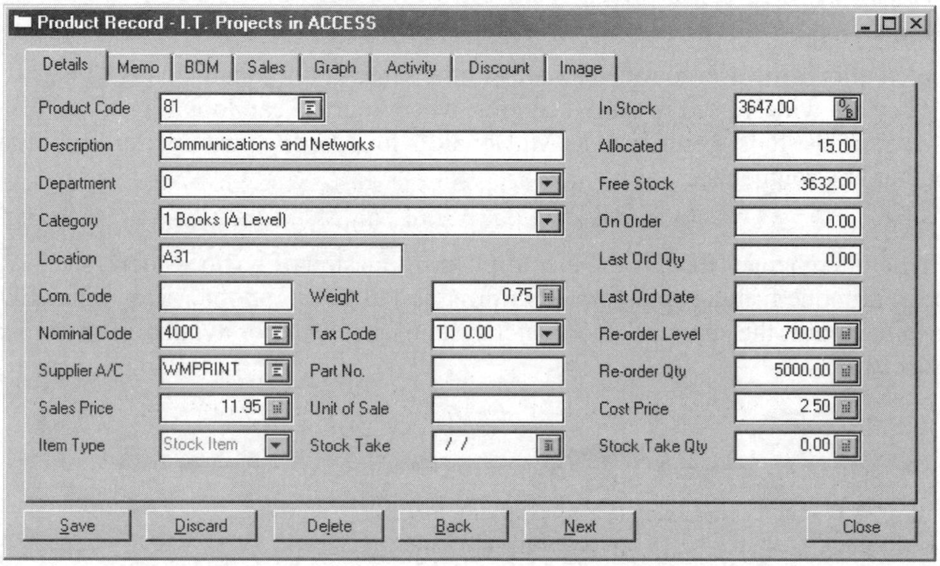

Figure 17.11: Entering product information

2. List 10 fields that you would expect to find on a data entry screen used to enter a new supplier.

    (5 marks)

3. (i)   List 10 fields that you would expect to find on a data entry screen used to enter a purchase order to a supplier, for example for new raw materials from which to manufacture stock.

    (5 marks)

    (ii) Of the 10 fields mentioned in (i), which would you expect the computer to enter or calculate automatically?

    (4 marks)

4. Design a screen input form to enter a new supplier.

    (5 marks)

5. Describe a modern method of data capture which may be used for

    (i)   stocktaking in a warehouse.

    (2 marks)

    (ii) entering details of credit card payments (by the credit card company).

    (2 marks)

6. Explain the difference between validation and verification.

    (4 marks)

Chapter 18 – Designing Output

Objectives

✓ To examine what types of output are needed from a system

✓ To distinguish between operational output and management information

✓ To design a screen report layout

✓ To design a printed report layout

18.1. Types of output

Each of the subsystems of an organisation – sales order processing, purchase order processing, stock control, payroll and so on – will need different kinds of output. Information can be categorised roughly into:

❑ operational information or output

❑ management information

Operational information is needed for the day-to-day running of an organisation or department. For example, in a Sales Order Processing system, the following printed output will be needed, either regularly or on demand:

❑ customer invoices and delivery notes

❑ stock order list showing which items of stock need reordering

❑ daily sales journal (showing all the sales for one day)

Management will need reports to help them with decision-making. They need to know, for example, which products are selling well, which are slow-moving, who their best customers are, whether increasing discounts or lowering prices has a significant impact on profits, and so on. They will need information such as:

❑ total sales analysed by month

❑ sales for a given product

❑ sales for a given customer

Some of these may be printed reports, and some may be screen-based, available on request.

18.2. Output from a Sales Order Processing (SOP) system

When a sales order has been entered and stock allocated, an invoice is produced. A typical invoice is shown on the next page.

> **Discussion: Which fields will the operator have to enter on the sales input screen in order to obtain this output? Which fields will be looked up automatically by the computer?**

Victory Publishing Ltd
Unit 4
Teelmark Business Park
Ipswich
Suffolk
Tel: 01473 888999
Fax: 01473 444555

Invoice

Settlement due days: 30

Attn: Angela Haddock

The Fishmongers' Company School
Finance Dept
Wharfside
Fleetwood
Lancashire FY68 8JQ

Invoice No.	22
Invoice/Tax Date	30/06/2000
Order No.	
Account No.	THEFISHM

Quantity	Product Description	Unit Price	Discount %	Net Amount	VAT Amount
25	Learning IT - Word 2000	8.95	10.00	201.37	0.00
15	Learning IT - Access 2000	8.95	10.00	120.82	0.00

Net Amount	322.19
VAT Amount	0.00
Carriage	0.00
Invoice Total	322.19

Registered in England 3554997
VAT Reg. No: 865 4567 49

(SS8570) © 1999 The Sage Group Plc. To re-order stationery ring 0191 255 0303 STOCK CODE 063921

Figure 18.1: A typical invoice

What sort of reports about stock can be produced? Take a look at part of the list of standard reports that can be produced by Sage Line 50, a standard accounting package – and these are just the product reports!

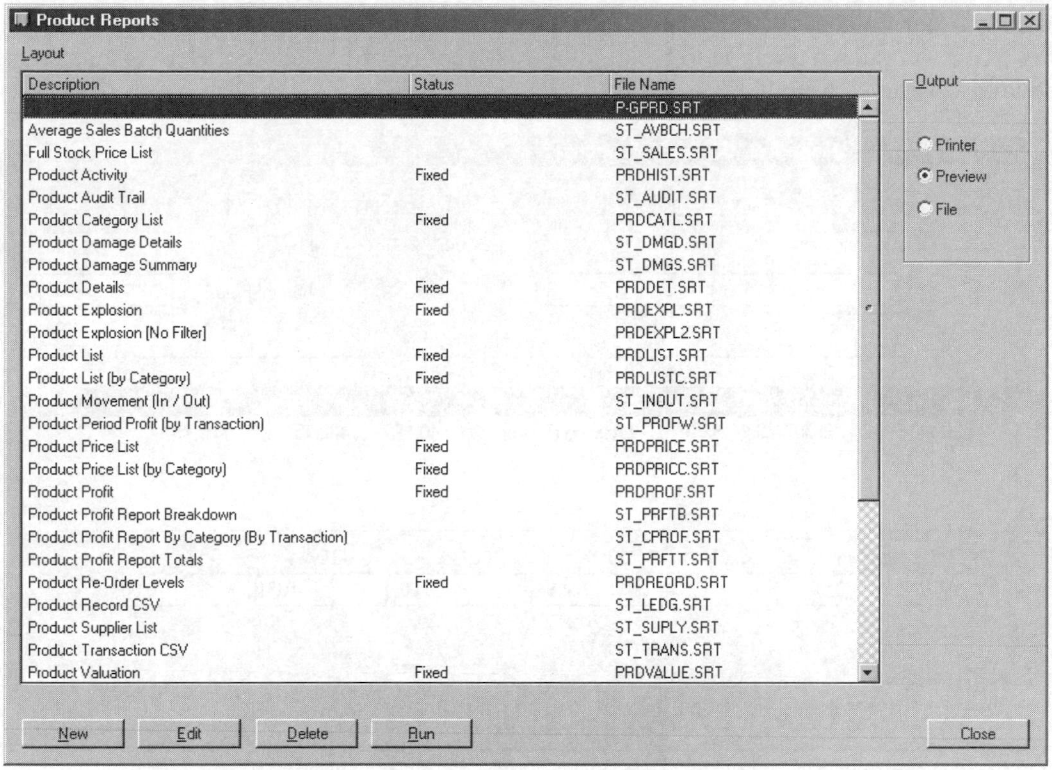

Figure 18.2: Some of the available Product reports

The full stock price list, for example, looks like this:

Date: 11/03/2001 **Victory Publishing Ltd** **Page:** 1
Time: 13:26:15 **Full Stock Price List**

Category From 1 **Stock Code From**
Category To 999 **Stock Code To** ZZZZZZZZZZZZZZZZZZZZZZZ

Stock Cat 1 **Stock Cat Name** Books (Secondary)

Stock Code	Description	Unit Of Sale	Sales Price
GFE	Going Further - Excel 2000	1	9.95
GFSA	Going Further - Sage Accounts		9.95
GFW	Going Further - Word 2000		9.95
LIA	Learning IT - Access 2000		8.95
LIAC	Learning IT - Autocad 2000		8.95
LIE	Learning IT - Excel 2000		8.95
LIFP	Learning IT - Front Page 2000		8.95
LISA	Learning IT - Sage Accounts		8.95
LIW	Learning IT - Word 2000		8.95

Figure 18.3: A product price list

18.3. Screen reports

At an operational level, a sales order clerk may have to answer telephoned customer queries such as "Did you receive the order I placed on 21st March?" or "Is there any outstanding balance on my account?" The easiest way to answer such a query is to look up the customer record on screen. Here is an example of a screen showing Customer Activity.

Customer - The Fishmongers' Company School								_ □ ×

| Details | Defaults | Credit Control | Sales | Graphs | Activity | Contacts | Memo |

A/C	THEFISHM					Balance	724.94
Name	The Fishmongers' Company School					Amount Paid	0.00
Credit Limit	1000.00					Turnover YTD	724.94

No		Tp	Date	Refn	Details	Amount	O/S		Debit	Credit
		60 SI	30/06/2000	22	Learning IT - Word 2	322.19	322.19	*	322.19	
		115 SI	26/07/2000	52	Learning IT - Access	402.75	402.75	*	402.75	

Future	Current	30 Days	60 Days	90 Days	Older
0.00	0.00	724.94	0.00	0.00	0.00

Tidy List   Range

Save	Discard	Delete	Back	Next	Close

Figure 18.4: A screen report showing customer activity

18.4. Graphical reports

Sometimes a report in the form of a graph can be very helpful in showing trends clearly. Below is a graph of last year's budget and actual monthly sales of a particular title sold by Victory Publishing:

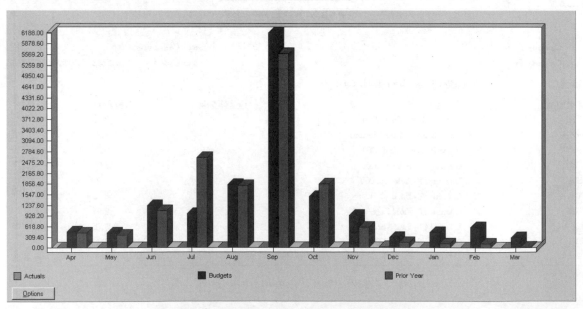

Figure 18.5: Monthly sales of a product

Discussion: What does this chart tell you? How would you set a reorder level for this product?

18.5. Designing your own reports

When you design your own reports, you have to decide on several aspects of the report including:

- the contents of the report
- whether it is to be screen-based or paper-based
- the layout of the report – in columns or an alternative format, portrait or landscape etc.
- page and/or column headings
- any grouping of data, for example all transactions relating to one product may be grouped together, before moving on to the next product
- any subtotals and final totals that are to appear on the report
- any parameters that the user will be able to specify, for example which products or customers the report will list, or the range of dates that will apply
- fonts and (on a screen report) colours used.

When a new system is designed, the analyst will need to draw up report layouts to show these features.

Example:

Produce a layout for a report showing the royalties due to each author at Victory Publishing.

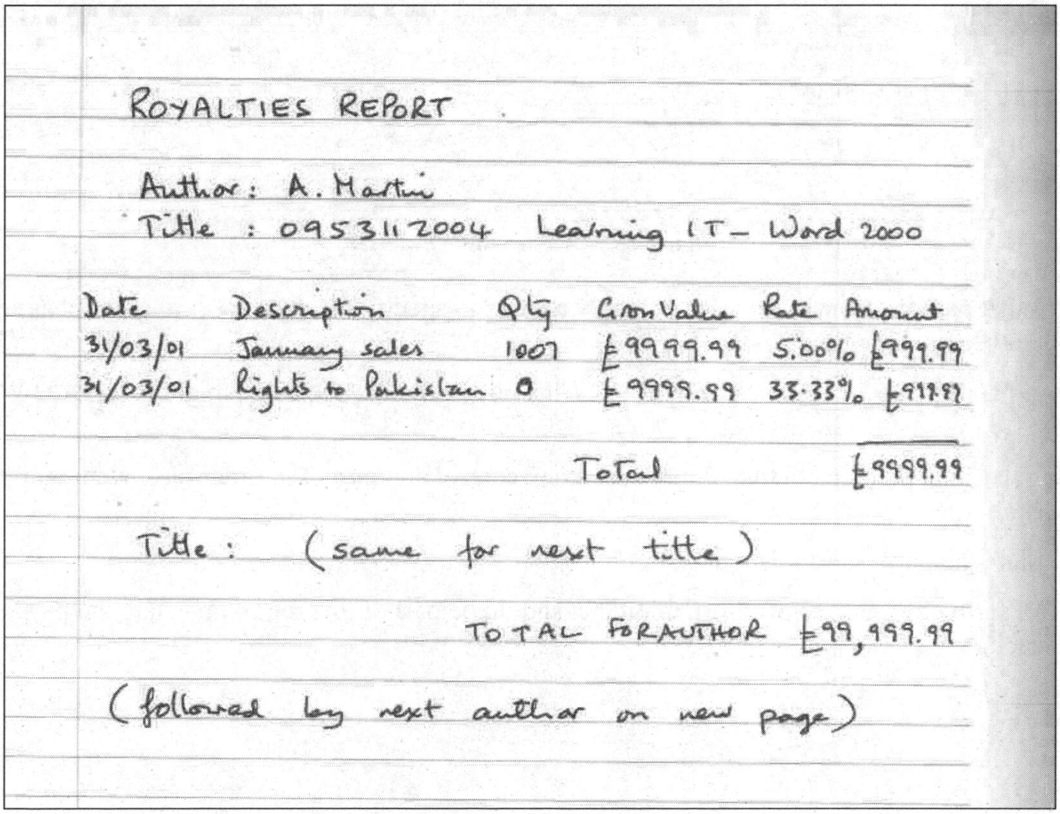

Figure 18.6: A report layout

18.6. Exercises

1. Other than a Purchase Order List, describe three reports that a Purchase Order Processing system would typically produce, stating whether they should be screen-based or paper-based. Show a report design for one of these reports. (10 marks)

2. Study the following example of a Purchase Order list.

| Date: | 07/01/2001 | **Payne-Gallway Publishers Ltd** | | | Page: | 1 |

Time: 11:30:31

Purchase Order List

| Order Number From | 1 | Order Date From | 01/01/2001 | Supplier From | | Stock Code From | |
| Order Number To | 9999999 | Order Date To | 31/01/2001 | Supplier To | ZZZZZZZZ | Stock Code To | ZZZZZZZZZZZZZZZZZZZZZ |

Order Number	1		Order Date	07/01/2001	Account Ref	WMPRINT	Name	WM Print Limited		
Stock Code	Description		Unit Of Sale	Qty Order	Discount		Net Amount	Tax Amount		Gross Amount
78	A Level IT (P.M. Heathcote)			2,000.00	0.00		4,840.00	0.00		4,840.00
				2,000.00	0.00		4,840.00	0.00		4,840.00

Order Number	2		Order Date	07/01/2001	Account Ref	NUFFIELD	Name	Nuffield Press		
Stock Code	Description		Unit Of Sale	Qty Order	Discount		Net Amount	Tax Amount		Gross Amount
80	I.T. Projects in EXCEL		1	1,000.00	0.00		1,240.00	0.00		1,240.00
81	I.T. Projects in ACCESS			3,000.00	0.00		3,930.00	0.00		3,930.00
				4,000.00	0.00		5,170.00	0.00		5,170.00

Order Number	3		Order Date	02/01/2001	Account Ref	WMPRINT	Name	WM Print Limited		
Stock Code	Description		Unit Of Sale	Qty Order	Discount		Net Amount	Tax Amount		Gross Amount
2	Basic Spreadsheets for Schools			6,000.00	0.00		2,700.00	0.00		2,700.00
2T	Basic Spreadsheets for Schools (Teache:			500.00	0.00		345.00	0.00		345.00
79	I.T. Projects in WORD			5,000.00	0.00		6,500.00	0.00		6,500.00
				11,500.00	0.00		9,545.00	0.00		9,545.00
				17,500.00	0.00		19,555.00	0.00		19,555.00

Figure 18.7: A Purchase Order list

    (i) What parameters will the user probably be able to specify for this report (e.g. Purchase orders between two given dates). (2 marks)

    (ii) What sequence is the above report in? What other possible sequence might be useful? Why? (3 marks)

3. At regular intervals the Victory Publishing stock control and purchase ordering system will produce a stock reorder report.

    (i) State the purpose of this report. (1 mark)

    (ii) Describe four pieces of information that should be part of this report and state the purpose of each. (8 marks)

Chapter 19 – The Feasibility Report

Objectives

✓ To select a suitable project for study

✓ To plan the sections of the feasibility report

✓ To write a feasibility report

19.1. Choosing a project

For some Examination Board assessments (e.g. AQA) you may have to investigate a real organisation and produce a feasibility report together with a design for a solution that could be implemented using a relational database package. Choosing an appropriate project is crucial – if you choose something too simple, involving only one database table, you will not be able to achieve a high grade. On the other hand, choosing a very complex problem involving 6 or more entities will probably be a disaster, involving far more time and work than you can possibly afford to put in.

Your solution should involve no more than say 4 or 5 tables and even 3 will be sufficient to get a good grade. If you find you need more than this, simplify the problem, cut down on the scope of the project, or choose something else. The project might be quite a small system for one department of an organisation – your school or college may be able to suggest a project, or if your parents work in a business, they may have some suggestions. Here are a few suggestions:

❑ a simple library system for books and borrowers – maybe a departmental, rather than a school, library;

❑ a booking system for holiday cottages;

❑ a system to record which personnel have been on which training courses;

❑ a vet's system for recording owners, pets and treatments;

❑ a database for a builder keeping records of customers and jobs;

❑ a stock control system for a school shop;

❑ a hairdresser's database to keep records of treatments that customers have had;

❑ a database for a garage to keep records of work done for customers;

❑ an estate agent's database to keep records of houses for sale, purchasers and sellers;

❑ an art gallery's records of paintings and artists and maybe buyers.

> **Discussion: Identify the external entities for each of the above ideas. Draw a Level 0 DFD for each one.**
>
> **Then identify the entities that would each need their own table in a database. Draw the ERD (entity-relationship diagram) for each one. If you find you have more than 3 or 4 entities then put some boundaries on the scope of the project, simplify it and try again!**

19.2. The contents of a feasibility report

The case study in this chapter will be used to illustrate the process of writing a feasibility study and a system specification (Chapter 20). The system will be implemented in Unit 6 (Database Design). The statement of scope and objectives (see Chapter 13) is incorporated into the Feasibility Report.

Typical headings for this report are shown below. You can use this as a checklist when producing your own feasibility report.

Title page:

> Name of project, report name, author and date.

Statement of purpose of the system:

> Statement of reasons for initiating the project, the background of the current system, how it is handled in the organisation.

A definition of system scope:

> The boundaries and constraints are described.

Deficiencies of the current system:

> Statement of the main features of the current system including personnel involved, its major tasks, data storage, control procedures, hardware used and the way it interfaces with other systems in the organisation. A description of the shortcomings of or problems with the current system.

Statement of user requirements:

> A detailed list of user requirements.

Costs and benefits of development:

> The proposed system (or each proposed system, if alternatives are proposed) is described in outline. A high-level data flow (contextual) diagram may be given to explain each proposal. The economic, technical and organisational feasibility of each proposal will be discussed. The risks and potential benefits, and a cost-benefit analysis to support your recommendations should be included.

Conclusion and recommendations:

> One system is recommended, with reasons given for the preferred choice, including the cost and benefits of development.

Figure 19.1: The contents of a feasibility report

19.3. A sample feasibility report

The rest of this chapter shows the feasibility report that was written for Victory Publishing by the systems analyst who was asked to look at improving the royalties system.

Feasibility Report

Authors' Royalties System

written by

J. Jennings

18/01/2001

Statement of purpose of the system

The system of calculating and reporting on authors' royalty payments, which worked well when there were only a handful of authors is no longer adequate for the current situation. It is very time-consuming to produce the royalty reports and is prone to error, and a new system is required.

The purpose of this feasibility study is therefore to investigate the development and installation of a new system for royalty calculation and reporting which will take into account foreign royalties and which will provide an easy method of clearing the previous period's figures ready for the start of the new period.

Scope of the new system

The system is confined to the calculation and reporting of royalty payments on sales in the UK and sale of rights to foreign publishers. It does not include the recording of payments actually being made to the authors. This is done within the existing accounts system.

Constraints

The system must be fully tested and installed by the end of April so that all data for the current royalty period (1 September 2000 – 31 March 2001) can be entered. The budget for the new system is £3,000 including employee time charged at £100 per day.

Present system

The information on monthly sales of each title is available from the Sage Accounts system and this is entered onto the spreadsheet on a monthly basis by the Accounts Manager. She is however reliant on the Editorial Department to inform her when a new title is commissioned, who the author(s) are and what royalty rate they are being paid. Information on the royalties payable to authors from the sale of foreign rights is available from the Foreign Rights Manager, generally in the form of an informal memo to the Accounts Manager. When a foreign publisher purchases the right to publish a particular title in another country (either in English or another language) they pay Victory Publishing a royalty of typically 10% of the cover price charged in that country for every book sold. The normal contract signed by authors entitles them to, say, 66.67% of all royalties received from a foreign publisher, with Victory keeping 33.33% as their share.

Royalties are payable within 3 months of the end of each accounting period. When the individual royalty reports are checked and passed as correct by the Chief Editor, copies of all the reports are sent to Accounts and payment is made and recorded in the Sage Accounts system.

Two backup copies are then made of the Excel spreadsheet; one is stored on the network server and the other on a zip disk stored offsite in a fireproof safe. The spreadsheet for the next 6-month period is then prepared by clearing the figures for the previous period, changing all the dates, and entering any figures to be brought forward.

The hardware used is a networked PC in the Accounts Department loaded with Microsoft Office 2000. MS Access 2000 is also loaded on the server.

The flow block diagram below illustrates the flow of data between the various business systems.

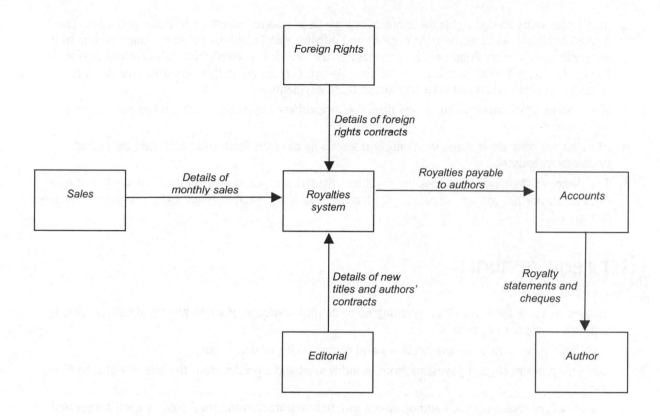

Figure 19.2: A flow block diagram showing the interface with other systems

Deficiencies of the current system

The current system of calculating and reporting authors' royalties was developed at a time when there were only a handful of authors receiving royalties, and no foreign rights sales. The calculations were done by the Chief Editor, who knew all the authors and titles written and was able to spot any errors or omissions before issuing royalty reports and authorising payments. She used a spreadsheet and although it was somewhat time-consuming, it was manageable.

As the company grew and more authors were commissioned, the Accounts Manager took over the task. There are currently approximately 120 titles written by 55 authors on which royalties are paid. Every year about 20 new titles are added.

An additional problem arose when the company started to sell foreign rights to certain titles. Information on what advance had been paid to Victory Publishing, for what title and by whom, was not automatically entered into the Royalties spreadsheet, resulting in the need for time-consuming double-checking by both the Accounts Manager, the Foreign Rights Manager and the Chief Editor (who all rely on memory to spot any omissions) before the reports were accepted and payments to authors authorised.

This situation cannot be allowed to continue as the company expands, and the Managing Director has requested that both the manual procedures and the computer system be thoroughly investigated and a new more automated system implemented.

To summarise, the following problems with the calculation of authors' royalties are currently causing concern at Victory Publishing.

1. The current system of entering sales data and calculating royalties, which uses a spreadsheet model, is extremely time-consuming.

2. In the past year, foreign rights for some titles have been sold to publishers in other countries. The foreign publisher acquires the right to print and distribute an English or other language version of a title, and pays Victory Publishers a percentage of the revenue received from sales (referred to as a foreign royalty). The authors are entitled to a portion (say 50%) of this revenue. The current spreadsheet model does not take account of these payments.

3. When an existing author writes a new title, the spreadsheet model has to be altered and formulae recalculated.

4. Mistakes are sometimes made in manually transcribing the sales figures for each title on to the Royalties spreadsheet.

5. The Accounts Manager who does the royalties calculation is not always kept informed of what new titles an author has written, what advance has been paid, and what Foreign Rights contracts have been negotiated.

User requirements

The new system must:

❑ be automated as far as possible, requiring no in-depth knowledge of spreadsheets, databases or other software in order to operate it

❑ have built-in controls to ensure accuracy and completeness of data input

❑ take into account royalty payments from monthly sales and royalties from the sale of rights to foreign publishers

❑ print royalty reports for each author, and a summary report showing total paid to each author and overall total

❑ include an option to delete royalty records prior to a given date so that the file does not expand indefinitely.

Proposed systems

Three alternative proposals have been considered. These are described below.

1. Improvement to existing spreadsheet system

The existing spreadsheet could be automated to a certain extent with macros. The communications procedures between departments and the routine of exactly when the facts about new authors' contracts and new foreign rights contracts are signed, and when payment is received from foreign publishers, can be improved.

This proposal, however, will not really satisfy the objectives of providing a system which can be operated by someone without an in-depth knowledge of spreadsheets. The spreadsheet is already large and unwieldy and has to be modified every time a new author is signed up, title published, or foreign rights contract signed. There is no practical way of automating these functions.

2. Purchase an integrated software solution

Software packages exist which are written specifically for publishers and which would provide a complete integrated system handling all the subsystems in the organisation, including the royalties application. This solution would involve a major change to every subsystem in the organisation and is beyond the scope and budget of the specified system.

3. Develop a solution using MS Access

A tailor-made solution could be written using MS Access which would provide a standalone solution to the problem. Improvements need to be made to the communications procedures between departments to ensure that all data is captured correctly.

This solution will potentially satisfy all the objectives within the allotted budget. No new software or hardware will need to be purchased. A new system of ensuring that all relevant information is entered into the Royalties system will also need to be put into place. This proposal has the added benefit that queries from staff in either the Editorial Department or the Foreign Rights Department about contracts or royalty payments may be answered by reference to the database.

Recommendation

The Access database solution is recommended as it is the only system that will satisfy the objectives within the given budget and time span. It should provide a very satisfactory solution o the current problems. In particular:

- ❏ It will be possible to develop a menu-driven system which can be operated without any technical knowledge of databases;
- ❏ It will help to solve the problem of entering correct author's royalty rates into the royalty system because this will be done in the Editorial Department;
- ❏ It will help to solve the problem of entering correct Foreign Rights royalty rates into the royalty system because this will be done in the Foreign Rights Department;
- ❏ Validation and verification procedures will be implemented which will help to ensure the accuracy of data input.

Cost, benefits and risks

Victory Publishing already has the hardware and software required to implement the proposed new system. The costs therefore will be the analyst's and programmer's time for development, and the cost of transferring data to the new system and the extra cost of parallel running. This is estimated as follows:

Systems analyst:	10 hours at £30.00 per hour.	£300
Programmer:	50 hours at £20.00 per hour	£1,000
Data entry:	4 hours at £18.00 per hour	£72
Contingencies		£200
TOTAL		£1572

The benefits will include the time saved in performing royalty calculations and the greater accuracy achieved. The time spent on updating the spreadsheet will no longer be required. The total time-saving is expected to be in the region of 10-12 hours per month by various senior members of staff. The system should therefore pay for itself within the first 6 months and thereafter will achieve a substantial cost saving.

No new system is completely risk-free as things can always go wrong. For this application the risks are low as Access is a well-tried and tested software package and no new hardware has to be purchased. The greatest risk in this system is that the clerical procedures will not be correctly followed, leading to a situation where, for example, authors are not credited with the correct amounts. Careful auditing procedures will need to be put In place to avoid this.

Chapter 20 – Systems Specification

Objectives

✓ To write a systems specification for a project.

20.1 The contents of a systems specification

In this chapter we will develop the detailed systems specification for the Royalties application for which a Feasibility report was written in Chapter 19.

There are no hard and fast rules for what should be included in a systems specification, but it will probably include the following:

❑ A description of the proposed system and its objectives. Flow block diagrams and data flow diagrams may be used to illustrate the system graphically. The roles and functions of the users of the system may be defined.

❑ Database specification including:

- database structure including entities, attributes and relationships between entities
- a data dictionary
- menu structure

❑ Input specification including

- methods of data capture
- validation methods
- data-input form or screen layouts

❑ Output specification including

- data required for output
- screen report layouts
- printed report layouts

❑ Process specifications showing details of the processes that need to be carried out on the data to generate the required output

❑ Test plan and test data with expected results

❑ Conclusion, including a discussion of

- software
- hardware
- possible constraints
- personnel

There follows a sample systems specification.

Detailed Systems Specification

Authors' Royalties System

written by

J. Jennings

26/01/2001

Description of the proposed system

Description of the problem

A new system of calculating and reporting on authors' royalties is to be designed and implemented. Authors' royalties are based on two separate sets of data:

1. Monthly sales of books written by the author;

2. Royalties received from foreign publishers who have purchased the right to publish an edition of a book in their own country or region, either in English or another language. The normal arrangement is that the publisher pays Victory Publishing a royalty of say 10% of gross sales, and this sum is divided between Victory Publishing and the author, with each receiving a percentage agreed in the author's contract.

Objectives

The new system must:

❑ be automated as far as possible, requiring no in-depth knowledge of spreadsheets, databases or other software in order to operate it;

❑ have built-in controls to ensure accuracy and completeness of data input;

❑ take into account royalty payments from monthly sales and royalties on sale of rights to foreign publishers;

❑ print royalty reports for each author, and a summary report showing total paid to each author and overall total;

❑ include an option to delete royalty records prior to a given date so that the file does not expand indefinitely.

Data flow diagram

The proposed new system may be shown in a Level 0 Data Flow Diagram as follows:

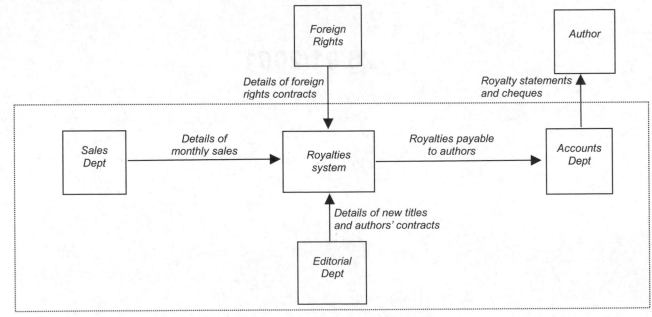

Figure 20.1: Royalties System - Level 0 DFD

The dotted line shows the scope of the proposed system. A Level 1 DFD is shown on the next page.

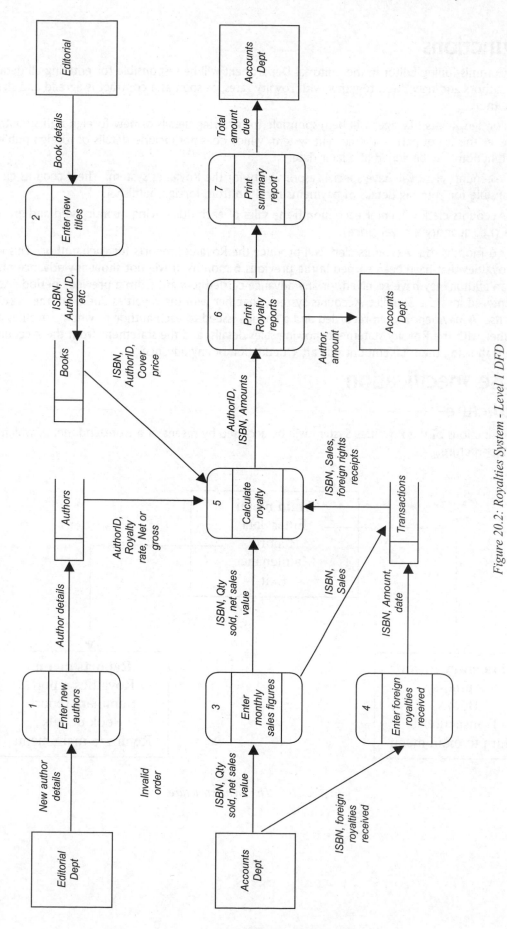

Figure 20.2: Royalties System - Level 1 DFD

User functions

1   The Commissioning Editor in the Editorial Department will be responsible for entering all details of new authors and new titles, together with royalty rates, as soon as a contract is agreed and signed by the author.

2   The Foreign Rights Manager will be responsible for entering details of new foreign rights contracts. However this is not part of the current system, which does not include details of foreign publishers. This function may be added at a later date.

3   One Accounts clerk will have special responsibility for the Royalties system. The Accounts clerk will be responsible for entering details of payments received from foreign publishers.

4   The Accounts clerk will enter each month the sales of each title, giving quantity sold and gross sales value (i.e. quantity x cover price).

5   Every 6 months, the Accounts clerk will produce the Royalties reports for each author. This will show the royalties that have been earned in the previous 6 months. It will not show any advance on royalties that an author may have received, or any advance carried forward from a previous period. Advances are entered into the Supplier Accounts system, together with the royalties due from the previous 6 months. A payment is then recorded and a cheque issued to each author to whom royalties are due, together with the Royalty statement showing sales details, and the statement from the Accounts system showing the total amount due after deduction of any advance.

Database specification

Menu structure

The various functions of the Royalties System will be accessed by means of a front-end menu, which will have the following structure.

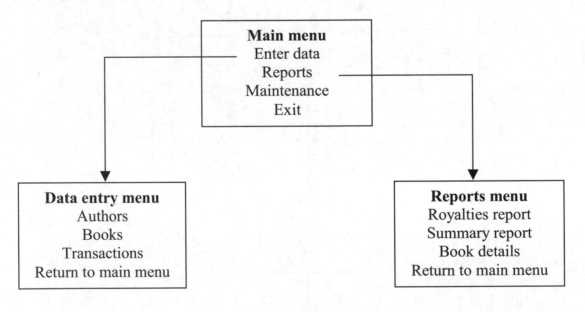

Figure 20.3: The menu structure

The data model

There are three main entities in this system related as shown in the entity-relationship diagram shown below.

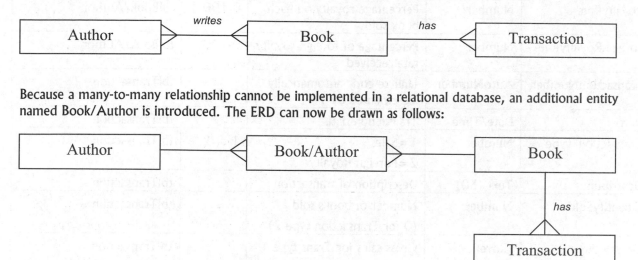

Because a many-to-many relationship cannot be implemented in a relational database, an additional entity named Book/Author is introduced. The ERD can now be drawn as follows:

Figure 20.4: Entity-relationship diagram

The database will have the following tables:

tblAuthor (<u>AuthorID</u>, Surname, FirstName)

tblBook (<u>ISBN</u>, ShortTitle, Title, Author(s), DatePublished, Price)

tblBook/Author (*<u>ISBN</u>*, *<u>AuthorID</u>*, RoyaltyRate, ForeignRoyaltyRate)

tblTransaction (<u>TransactionNumber</u>, Date, *ISBN*, TransactionType, Description, QuantitySold, GrossValue)

Data dictionary

Name	Type	Meaning	Range	Where Used
tblAuthor	Table	Author table		
tblBook	Table	Book table		
tblBook/Author	Table	Book/Author table		
tblTransaction	Table	Transaction table		
AuthorID	Text(10)	Unique ID		Primary key in tblAuthor Foreign key In tblBook/Author
Surname	Text (20)	Author's surname		tblAuthor
Firstname	Text (15)	Author's first name		tblAuthor
ISBN	Text (13)	Unique book code		Primary key in tblbook Foreign key in tblBook/Author, tblTransaction
ShortTitle	Text (10)	Abbreviated book title		tblBook
Title	Text (40)	Book title		tblBook
Author(s)	Text (40)	All authors named on book cover		tblBook

DatePublished	Date/Time	Publication date of book		tblBook
Price	Currency	Cover price		tblBook
RoyaltyRate	Number	Percentage royalty on each book sold	0-100	tblBook/Author
ForeignRoyaltyRate	Number	Percentage of foreign royalty rate received	0-100	tblBook/Author
TransactionNumber	AutoNumber	Unique code automatically incremented by 1		tblTransaction
Date	Date/Time	Transaction date		tblTransaction
Transaction Type	Number	1 = Sales 2 = Foreign Royalty	1 or 2	tblTransaction
Description	Text (50)	Description of transaction		tblTransaction
QuantitySold	Number	Number of books sold (0 for Transaction type 2)		tblTransaction
GrossValue	Currency	Gross sales for Trans type 1 Amount of foreign royalty received by publisher for Trans type2		tblTransaction

Figure 20.5: Data Dictionary

Input specification

Three input forms will be required.

frmBook

This will be used to enter book details.

Validation methods:

Only valid dates will be accepted for PublicationDate.

frmAuthor

This will be used to enter details of an author and all the books on which they receive royalties. The royalty percentages for each book will be entered in a subform of the main form.

Validation methods:

The ISBN will be selected from a drop-down list of existing ISBNs. Once an ISBN is entered, the book title will be automatically displayed.

All fields will be mandatory.

frmTransaction

This form will be used to enter transactions.

Validation methods:

Only valid dates will be accepted.

The ISBN will be selected from a drop-down list of existing ISBNs. Once an ISBN is entered, the book title will be automatically displayed.

The transaction type will be chosen by selecting a radio button so that only a valid option can be selected.

Layouts for the three forms are shown below.

Book Form

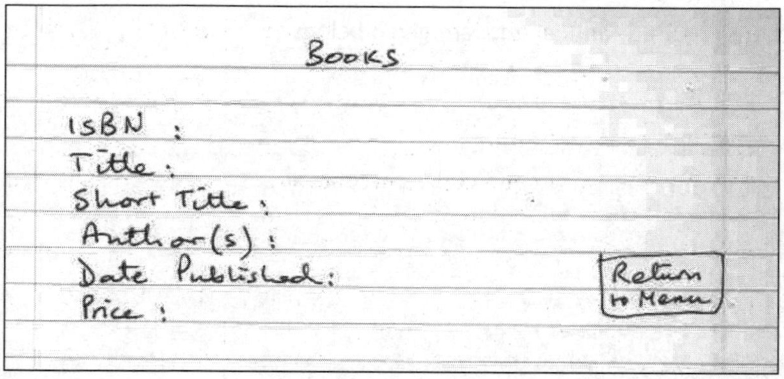

```
                    BOOKS


    ISBN :
    Title :
    Short Title :
    Author(s) :
    Date Published :          ┌──────────┐
    Price :                   │ Return   │
                              │ to Menu  │
                              └──────────┘
```

Author Form

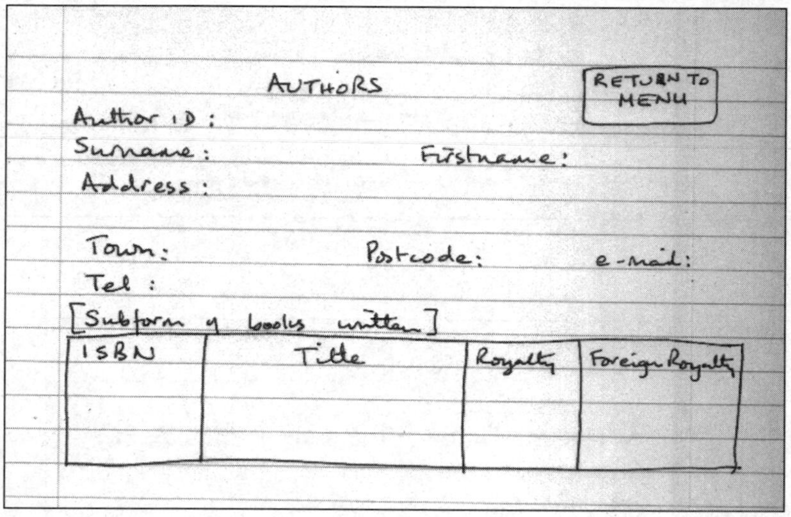

```
                                        ┌──────────┐
                AUTHORS                  │RETURN TO │
    Author ID :                          │  MENU    │
    Surname :             Firstname :    └──────────┘
    Address :


    Town :          Postcode :      e-mail :
    Tel :
    [Subform y books written]
    ┌────────┬──────────────┬────────┬─────────────────┐
    │ ISBN   │    Title     │ Royalty│ Foreign Royalty │
    │        │              │        │                 │
    │        │              │        │                 │
    └────────┴──────────────┴────────┴─────────────────┘
```

Transaction form

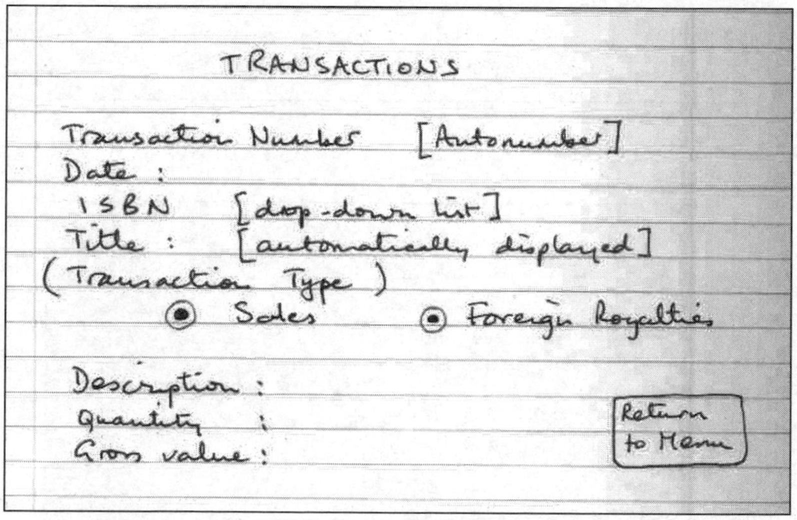

```
                TRANSACTIONS


    Transaction Number  [Autonumber]
    Date :
    ISBN    [drop-down list]
    Title :  [automatically displayed]
    (Transaction Type )
            ◉ Sales       ◉ Foreign Royalties

    Description :
    Quantity :                      ┌──────────┐
    Gross value :                   │ Return   │
                                    │ to Menu  │
                                    └──────────┘
```

Figure 20.6

Output specification

Three printed reports are required, and layouts are given below:

Royalties report:

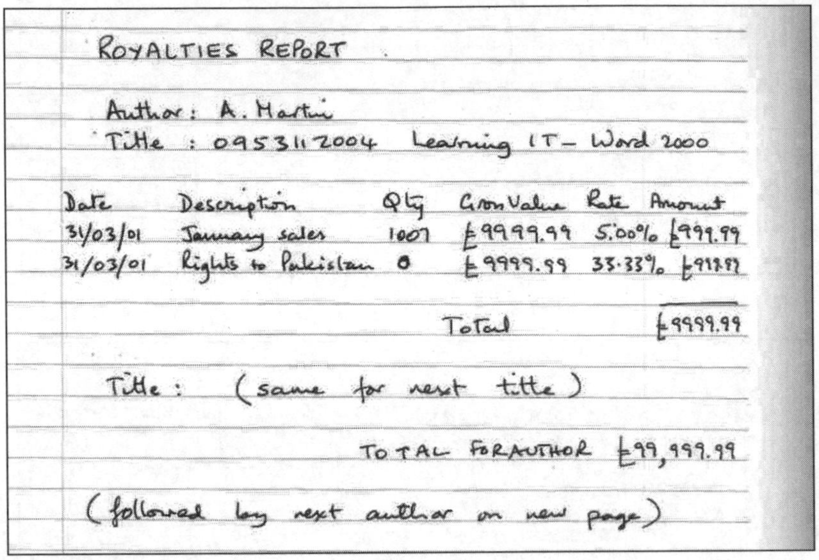

> ROYALTIES REPORT
>
> Author: A. Martin
> Title : 0953112004 Learning IT – Word 2000
>
> | Date | Description | Qty | Gross Value | Rate | Amount |
> |------|-------------|-----|-------------|------|--------|
> | 31/03/01 | January sales | 1007 | £9999.99 | 5.00% | £999.99 |
> | 31/03/01 | Rights to Pakistan | 0 | £9999.99 | 33.33% | £99.99 |
>
> Total £9999.99
>
> Title : (same for next title)
>
> TOTAL FOR AUTHOR £99,999.99
>
> (followed by next author on new page)

Summary report:

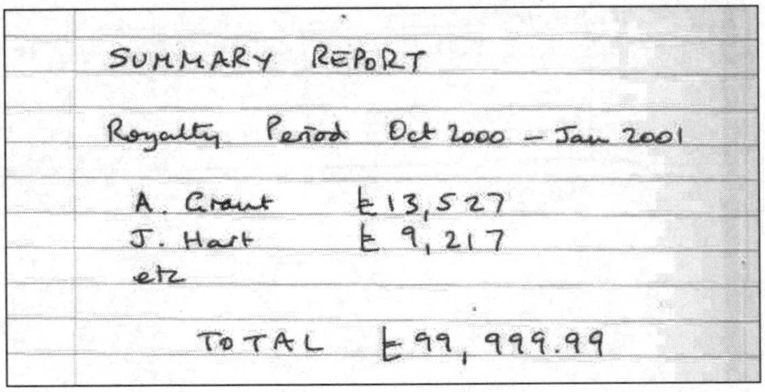

> SUMMARY REPORT
>
> Royalty Period Oct 2000 – Jan 2001
>
> A. Grant £13,527
> J. Hart £9,217
> etc
>
> TOTAL £99,999.99

Book Details:

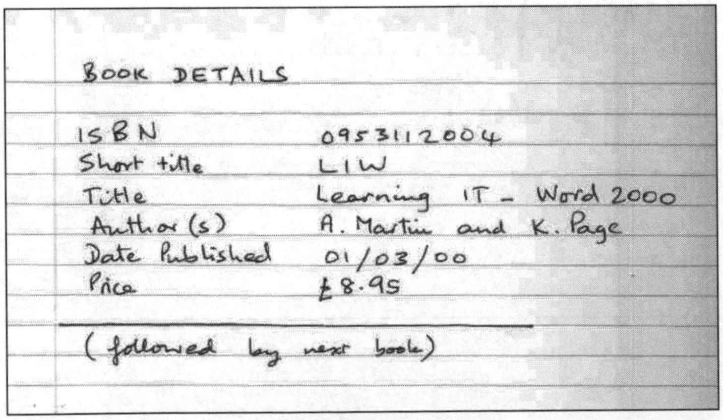

> BOOK DETAILS
>
> ISBN 0953112004
> Short title LIW
> Title Learning IT – Word 2000
> Author(s) A. Martin and K. Page
> Date Published 01/03/00
> Price £8.95
>
> (followed by next book)

Figure 20.7: Report designs

Process specification

Royalty Calculations

To calculate the royalty for a given transaction, a query has to be performed to combine attributes from tblTransaction, tblBook, tblBook/Author and tblAuthor.

The calculation of the Royalty amount is performed as follows:

```
If   TransactionType = 1    (i.e. 'Sales')
then Rate := RoyaltyRate
else Rate := ForeignRoyaltyRate
endif
Amount := Rate * GrossValue
```

These processes will be carried out in qryRoyalty. This query will be the source of both the Royalty report and the Summary report.

Maintenance

Each year, transactions prior to a given date will be copied to an archive file and removed from tblTransaction. This prevents the Transaction file from becoming too large and slowing down the system.

The maintenance will be carried out as follows:

```
Display a dialogue box asking for date prior to which transactions are
to be archived
Accept answer
Run an Append query to append selected records to Archive file
Run a Delete query to delete records from tblTransaction
```

Test plan

Tests will be carried out using valid and invalid data and data at the extremes of acceptable values.

The following test data will be used.

tblAuthor

AuthorID	Surname	FirstName
HARTJ	Hart	Jonathan
MOOREB	Moore	Basil
GRANTP	Grant	Pamela
DESAIM	Desai	Manminder
MARTINA	Martin	Alexander
AYLINGS	Ayling	Stephen
PAGEK	Page	Katherine
PAGEGR	Page	Gilbert

tblBook

ISBN	Short Title	Title	Author(s)	Date Published	Price
0953112004	LIW	Learning IT – Word 2000	A.Martin and K.Page	01/03/2000	£8.95
0953112012	LIE	Learning IT – Excel 2000	A.Grant	01/03/2000	£8.95
0953112020	LIA	Learning IT – Access 2000	J.Hart	01/04/2000	£8.95
0953112039	LIFP	Learning IT – FrontPage 2000	M.Desai	01/05/2000	£8.95
0953112047	LISA	Learning IT – Sage Accounts	K.Page	01/01/2001	£8.95
0953112055	GFE	Going Further – Excel 2000	A.Grant	20/02/2001	£9.95
0953112063	GFW	Going Further – Word 2000	A.Martin	15/03/2001	£9.95
0953112071	GFSA	Going Further – Sage Accounts	K.Page and B.Moore	01/04/2001	£9.95
095311208X	LIAC	Learning IT – AutoCAD 2000	G.R.Page	01/04/2001	£8.95

tblBookAuthor

AuthorID	ISBN	Title	Royalty rate	Foreign Royalty rate
DESAIM	0953112039	Learning IT – FrontPage 2000	10%	66.6667%
GRANTP	0953112012	Learning IT – Excel 2000	10%	66.6667%
GRANTP	0953112055	Going Further – Excel 2000	7%	50%
HARTJ	0953112020	Learning IT – Access 2000	10%	66.6667%
MARTINA	0953112004	Learning IT – Word 2000	5%	33.3333%
MARTINA	0953112063	Going Further – Word 2000	10%	50%
MOOREB	0953112071	Going Further – Sage Accounts	5%	33.3333%
PAGEGR	095311208X	Learning IT – AutoCAD 2000	7%	50%
PAGEK	0953112004	Learning IT – Word 2000	5%	33.3333%
PAGEK	0953112047	Learning IT – Sage Accounts	10%	66.6667%
PAGEK	0953112071	Going Further – Sage Accounts	5%	33.3333%

tblTransaction

Date	ISBN	Transaction Type	Description	Quantity Sold	Gross Value
31/01/2001	0953112039	1	January Sales	580	£5191.00
31/01/2001	0953112012	1	January Sales	423	£3785.85
31/01/2001	0953112055	1	January Sales	1000	£995.00
31/01/2001	0953112020	1	January Sales	1000	£895.00
31/01/2001	0953112004	1	January Sales	234	£2094.30
31/01/2001	0953112063	1	January Sales	532	£5293.40
31/01/2001	0953112071	1	January Sales	100	£995.00
31/01/2001	095311208X	1	January Sales	453	£4054.35
31/01/2001	0953112047	1	January Sales	128	£1145.60
15/01/2001	0953112004	2	Rights sold to Sunrise, Pakistan	0	£400
15/01/2001	0953112012	2	Rights sold to Sunrise, Pakistan	0	£400
15/01/2001	0953112063	2	Rights sold to Sunrise, Pakistan	0	£400
01/02/2001	0953112004	2	Rights sale to LAU, Norway	0	£350
01/02/2001	0953112012	2	Rights sale to LAU, Norway	0	£350
27/02/2001	0953112012	1	February Sales	420	£3759.00
28/02/2001	0953112039	1	February Sales	752	£6730.40

The following tests will be carried out:

Test No.	Test	Purpose	Expected result
1	Select Enter Data from Main menu, then select Books.	To check the menu options work and that the Book form opens at a new record	Book form opens at a new record
2	Enter data from test data set. Try entering an invalid date 31/02/2001	To check that valid data is accepted and invalid date rejected.	All valid data accepted. Invalid date causes error message to be displayed
3	Select Enter Data from Main menu, then select Authors.	To check the menu options work and that the Author form opens at a new record	Author form opens at a new record
4	Enter data from test data set.	To check that valid data is accepted.	All valid data accepted.
5	Try entering an ISBN of 12345 for an author.	Test that no book can be entered unless it exists on Book table	Record rejected
6	Select Enter Data from Main menu, then select Sales.	To check the menu options work and that the Transaction form opens at a new record	Transaction form opens at a new record
7	Attempt to enter a new transaction with date 31/02/2001	To test that the date is validated	Error message will appear on leaving field
8	Attempt to enter a new transaction with ISBN 123456	To test that the transaction is not accepted unless the ISBN is on tblBook	Transaction rejected
9	Select Reports from the Main Menu, then select Book Details	Test the Book reports displays all the books entered	All the books appear on the report
10	Select Reports from the Main Menu, then select Royalties Report	Check that Royalties report is correct	User is asked to enter start and end dates for report. All royalties are calculated correctly
11	Select Reports from the Main Menu, then select Summary Report	Check that Summary report is correct	User is asked to enter start and end dates for report. All totals are calculated correctly
12	Add 2 transactions for dates in 1999. Then select Maintenance from Main menu and specify deletion of records prior to 31/12/1999	Check that Maintenance option deletes records prior to date user enters	The two records are deleted from the table
13	Add a transaction for 31/12/1999. Then select Maintenance from Main menu and specify deletion of records prior to 31/12/1999	Check that Maintenance option deletes records for date user enters	The record is deleted from the table
14	Select Exit from Main Menu	To check that menu option works correctly	Database closes

Development Plan

The planned schedule for development is given below.

Week beginning	Task	Comments
22/01/2001	Detailed design specification	
29/01/2001	Tables created	
05/02/2001	Input forms created	
12/02/2001	Queries and reports created	Reports on books, authors
19/01/2001	Royalties report created	
26/02/2001	Procedures for clearing file developed	clearing records prior to given date
05/03/2001	Testing and modifications	
12/03/2001	Testing and modifications	
19/03/2001	Documentation	
26/03/2001	Installation and entry of master file data	A period of parallel running will follow with reports produced from old and new systems.

Conclusion

The system will be implemented in Access 2000. It will run on any of the existing PCs already installed on the Victory Publishing network.

The database will be accessible from any of the Departments which are responsible for keeping the data up to date, namely the Editorial, Accounts and Foreign Rights Departments.

The system is expected to be tested and installed by the end of March 2001.

Unit 6

Database Design

This unit follows on from the previous unit, although it is possible to do it before covering all the material in Unit 5. However, before starting Unit 6 you need to have covered logical data modelling techniques and normalisation, discussed in Chapter 16. You will also find it useful to look at Chapters 17 and 18 which cover input and output specification.

You will be implementing the MS Access database for which the feasibility study and specification were written in Unit 5, Chapters 19 and 20. You will need to look at these chapters in order to be able to understand what you are trying to achieve!

The unit is assessed through your portfolio work, and you will be required to design and implement a database application and write user and technical documentation.

Chapter 21 – Creating a Database using Access

Objectives

✓ To learn about the different database objects used in Access

✓ To learn the common naming conventions for objects in an Access database

✓ To understand the data types used by MS Access

✓ To design the tables for the Royalties database

✓ To create the tables in Access

✓ To add validation to a field

21.1. Database terminology

You need to know the different terminology used to describe the elements of a database.

❏ A *table* holds information about a single *entity* such as a person, item or sales order, for example. In database terminology a table can also be referred to as a *relation*. (Note that a relation is not the same thing as a relationship.)

❏ A *record* occupies a single *row* of a table. A row is sometimes referred to a *unique entity instance* or, by a few database experts, as a *tuple*.

❏ A column in a database table is sometimes referred to as a *field* or an *entity attribute*.

21.2. The Royalties database

In Unit 5, Chapters 19 and 20 you studied the process of writing a feasibility study and system specification for an application. This unit describes in detail how to create the database and write user and technical documentation. When you have worked through the sample application you will be in a good position to create a database of your own.

In this chapter you will see how to create the tables and relationships specified in the model using MS Access 2000.

21.3. Elements of an Access database

The various elements that you'll be working with in Access are referred to as *objects*. These include:

Tables	for holding information;
Queries	for asking questions about your data or making changes to it;
Forms	for editing and viewing information;
Reports	for summarising and printing information;
Macros	for performing tasks automatically;
Modules	for customising your database using Visual Basic for Applications (VBA).

21.4. Naming conventions

There are various conventions for naming the objects that you use. You don't have to use a naming convention but it will certainly make your database easier to create and maintain, and will probably earn you extra marks in project work. Shown below are the Leszynski/Reddick naming conventions, which will be used in this book.

Level 1

Object	*Tag*	*Example*
Table	tbl	tblCustomer
Query	qry	qryClientName
Form	frm	frmCustomer
Report	rpt	rptSales
Macro	mcr	mcrUpdateList
Module	bas	basIsNotLoaded

Figure 21.1a: Leszynski/Reddick naming conventions

Level 2

Object	*Tag*	*Example*
Table	tbl	tblCustomer
Table (lookup)	tlkp	tlkpRegion
Table (system)	zstbl	zstblUser
Query (select)	qry	qryClientName
Query (append)	qapp	qappNewPhone
Query (crosstab)	qxtb	qxtbYearSales
Query (delete)	qdel	qdelOldCases
Query (form filter)	qflt	qfltAlphaList
Query (lookup)	qlkp	qlkpSalary
Query (make table)	qmak	qmakSaleTo
Query (System)	zsqry	zsqryMacroName
Query (Update)	qupd	qupdDiscount
Form	frm	frmCustomer
Form (dialogue)	fdlg	fdlgInputDate
Form (menu)	fmnu	fmnuMain
Form (message)	fmsg	fmsgCheckDate
Form (subform)	fsub	fsubInvoice
Report	rpt	rptTotals
Report (subreport)	rsub	rsubValues
Report (system)	zsrpt	zsrptMacroName
Macro	mcr	mcrUpdateList
Macro (for form)	m[formname]	m[formname]Customer
Macro (menu)	mmnu	mmnuStartForm

Macro (for report)	m[rptname]	m[rptname]Totals
Macro (system)	zsmcr	zsmcrLoadLookUp
Module	bas	basTimeScreen
Module (system)	zsbas	zsbasAPIcall

Figure 21.1b: Leszynski/Reddick naming conventions

21.5. Data types

In this chapter you will be designing and creating the tables for the Royalties database. Before starting on this you need to understand the different data types that may be used. The table below shows the main data types used in an Access database:

Data Type	Usage	Comments
Text	Alphanumeric data, i.e. any letter, number or other symbol that you can see on the keyboard	A field can be up to 255 characters
Number	Numeric data	Can choose a whole number or a number with a decimal point. Each of these categories has several choices in Access depending on the size of the numbers you want to store – e.g. a whole number can be defined as Byte (0-255), Integer (-32,768 to 32,767) or Long Integer (for larger numbers).
Date/Time	Dates and times	You should always use a Date/Time field for a date, not a text field, because Access can calculate with dates (e.g. find how many days between 03/09/2001 and 25/12/2001) but not with text.
Currency	For all monetary data	
Yes/No	True/False data	Useful when a field can only take one of two possible values such as Yes or No, True or False.
AutoNumber	Often used for a key field – i.e. a field that uniquely identifies a record. No two records ever have the same key field.	This is a unique value generated by Access for each record.
Memo	Used for alphanumeric data	A memo field can be up to 64,000 characters. It is useful for notes that may contain formatting characters such as tabs or line endings (carriage returns).

Figure 21.2: Data Types

21.6. Choosing field names

Access allows plenty of flexibility in the field names you are allowed to use. These can be up to 64 characters long and can include any combination of letters, numbers and special characters except a full stop, exclamation mark, square brackets and a few others. You should avoid using names that are the same as built-in functions, such as **Date**, **Time**, **Now** or **Space**.

You are advised to choose names that do not contain embedded spaces. Some databases such as Oracle do not allow spaces in field names and it is a good idea to make your database as portable as possible.

21.7. Designing the database tables

The next stage is to make a list of exactly what attributes are to go in each table, what data type and length each attribute will be, and any validation checks that can be performed on any attribute to help ensure that only correct data is entered into the database by the user.

The three tables that we need will be named **tblAuthor**, **tblBook**, **tblBook/Author** and **tblTransaction**. The tables will have attributes as shown in Figures 21.3 – 21.6 below.

tblAuthor

Field name	Data Type and length	Comments, Validation
AuthorID	Text (10)	Key field
Surname	Text (20)	
FirstName	Text (15)	

Figure 21.3: Structure of the Author table

tblBook

Field name	Data Type and length	Comments, Validation
ISBN	Text (13)	Key field
ShortTitle	Text (10)	
Title	Text (40)	
Author(s)	Text (40)	
DatePublished	Date/Time	dd/mm/yyyy
Price	Currency	

Figure 21.4: Structure of the Book table

Note that there is a field **Author(s)** in this table, although **Author** is a repeating attribute (i.e. there may be more than one author). It is included here as an attribute because it is convenient to be able to identify a book by both its title and its authors, for example, "Accessible Access 2000" by "Mark Whitehorn and Bill Marklyn". The Author(s) field in this format is no use for the Royalty application but it will be useful for example in creating a price list.

tblBook/Author

Field name	Data Type and length	Comments, Validation
ISBN	Text (13)	Key field
AuthorID	Text (10)	Key field
RoyaltyRate	Number (Single)	Percentage, 2 decimal places, between 0 and 100
ForeignRoyaltyRate	Number (Single)	Percentage, 2 decimal places, between 0 and 100

Figure 21.5: Structure of the Author/Book table

tblTransaction

Field name	Data Type and length	Comments, Validation
TransactionNumber	Autonumber	Key field. Allocated automatically by Access
Date	Date/Time	Date of transaction
ISBN	Text (13)	Foreign key
TransactionType	Byte	1=Sales, 2=Foreign Royalty
Description	Text (50)	Description of Transaction
QuantitySold	Number (Single)	Quantity sold
GrossValue	Currency	Gross Sales value for Transaction type 1, or amount received if type 2 (foreign royalty)

Figure 21.6: Structure of the Transaction table

21.8. Creating a new database

Loading Access

The way that you load Access will depend on which version of Access you are using and whether you are working at home or on a school or college network. There may be an icon in the Main Window or Applications Window that you can click on, or you can click the Access icon in the Office Shortcut Bar at the top of the screen if this is visible. In Windows 95 and later versions you can click on **Start** in the bottom left hand corner and select **Programs, Microsoft Access**.

Opening a new database

When you first start Access, you have the option of either opening an existing database or creating a new one. Access provides many ready-made databases for you to use, and also several wizards to help you to quickly create a database. However in this case, we will create a new database from scratch.

You will see a screen similar to the one shown below.

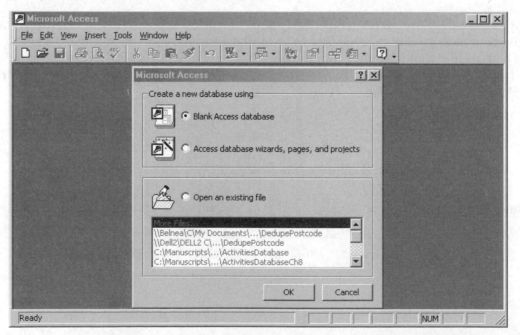

Figure 21.7: Starting MS Access

- Select the **Blank Access Database** option and press **OK**.

A window opens as shown below, asking you to select a folder and a name for your new database. It is a good idea to keep each Access database in its own folder.

- Click the **Create New Folder** button and create a new folder named *VRoyalties*. 
- In the **File Name** box, type the name *Royalties.mdb* and press the **Create** button.

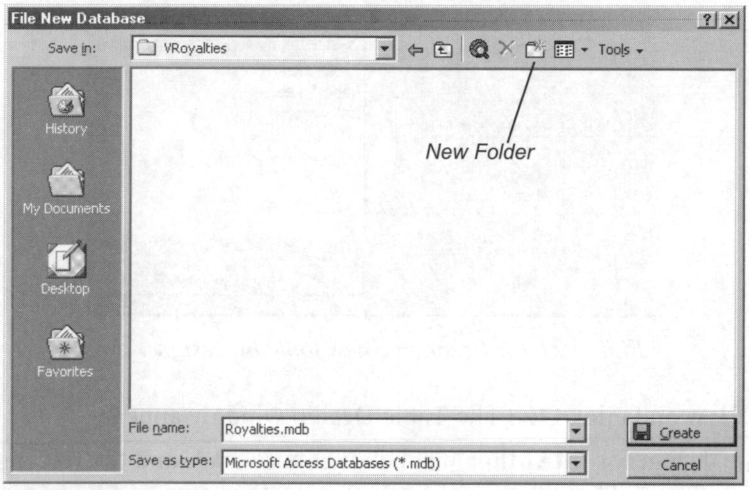

Figure 21.8: Naming a new database

21.9. Defining a new table structure

All data in an Access database is stored in **tables**. A table has a row for each record, and a column for each field. The first thing you have to do is to tell Access exactly what fields you want in each record, and what data type each field is. This is referred to as the database table **structure**. After this has been done and the structure saved, you can start adding data to the database.

The Database window

Every Access database has a database window. The window has buttons (tabs in 7 and 97) for each type of database object: **Tables, Queries, Forms, Reports,** etc. In addition, there are options to open an object, change its design, or create a new object. **Tables** is currently selected and since at the moment there are no existing tables to Open or Design, only the Create options are active.

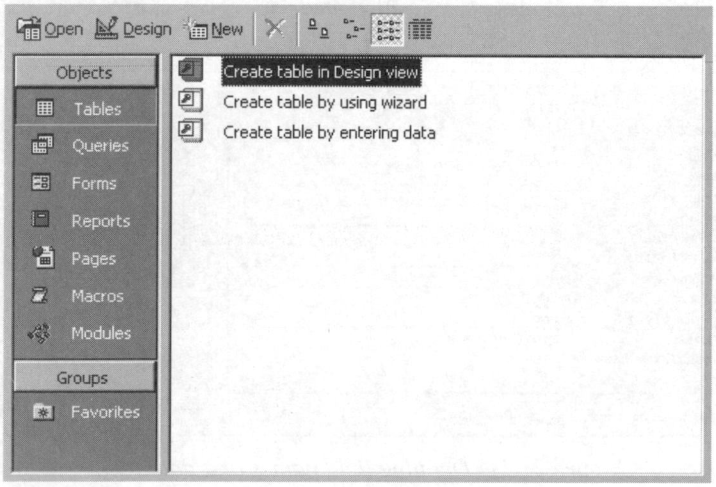

Figure 21.9: The Database window

Creating a new table

In the Database window make sure **Create table in Design View** is selected (in Access 7 or 97, make sure the **Tables** option is selected), and press **New**.

A new window appears as shown below.

Figure 21.10: Creating a new table in Design view

- Select **Design View** and click **OK**. The Table Design window appears.

- Look back at the design for **tblAuthor** just below Figure 20.4, and the relevant entries in the data dictionary (Figure 20.5). These three fields (AuthorID, Surname and Firstname) need to be entered in the new table.

- Enter the first field name, *AuthorID*, and tab to the **Data Type** column.

- Click the Down arrow and select the field type **Text**.

- Tab to the **Description** column and type *This is the Key field*.

- In the bottom half of the screen you can enter Field Properties. Enter *10* for Field Size.

- With the cursor still in the row for the **AuthorID**, press the **Primary Key** button on the toolbar. The key symbol appears in the left hand margin (termed the row selector) next to **AuthorID**.

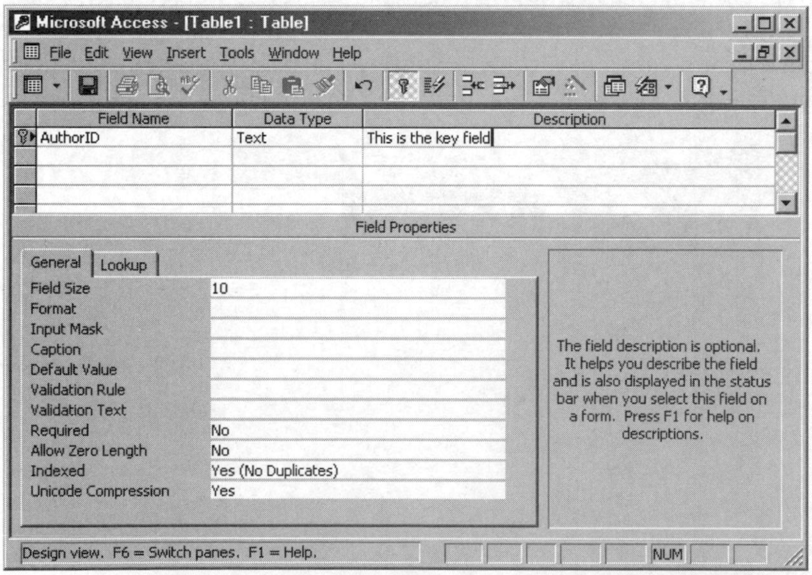

Figure 21.11: Defining field names and data types

Entering other fields

Now you can enter all the other fields. Don't worry if you make a few mistakes – after all the fields are entered, you will learn how to move fields around, delete them or insert new fields. You can correct any mistakes at that point, and it'll be good practice.

- Enter the field name *Surname* in the next row. Tab to the **Data Type** column and the default is **Text**, which is fine. Enter *20* in the Field Size property.

- Enter the field name *FirstName*, data type *Text* and field size *15*.

Your table should look like this:

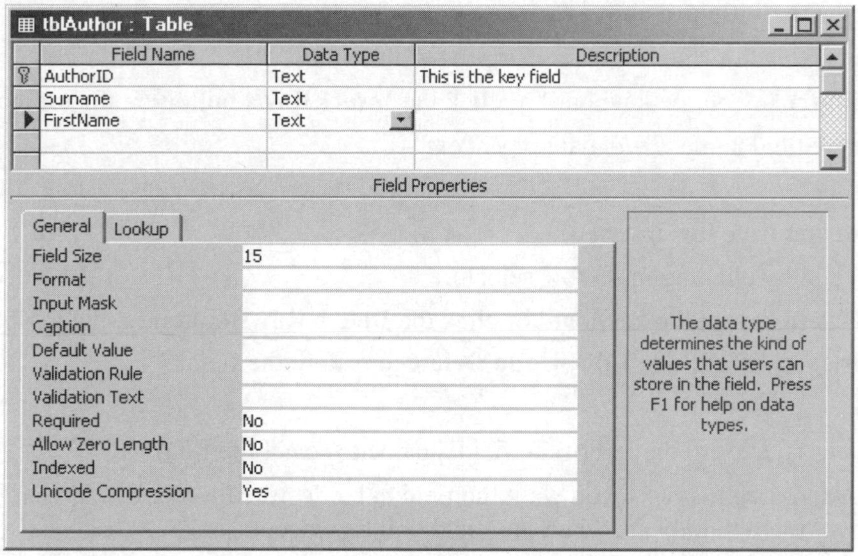

Figure 21.12: tblAuthor

Note that in a real application, you would almost certainly have more information about each author, such as address, e-mail and telephone number. However the three fields above are sufficient to illustrate the principle and use of this table.

Saving the table structure

- Save the table structure by pressing the **Save** button or selecting **File, Save** from the menu bar. Don't worry if you have made some mistakes in the table structure – they can be corrected in a minute.

- You will be asked to type a name for your table. Type the name *tblAuthor* and click **OK**.

Figure 21.13: Saving and naming the table

- Click the **Close** icon (**X**) in the top right hand corner to close the window. You will be returned to the database window.

21.10. Editing a table structure

In the Database window you will see that your new table is now listed.

> **Note:** If you have named the table wrongly, or made a spelling mistake, right-click the name and select **Rename**. Then type in the correct name. You cannot do this later, after you have created forms, queries or reports based on the table, without creating problems!

- Select the table name, click the **Design View** button and you are returned to *Design View*.

Inserting a field

To insert a new row for **Title** just above **Surname**:

- Click the row selector (the left hand margin) for **Surname**.
- Press the **Insert** key on the keyboard or click the **Insert Rows** button on the toolbar.
- Enter the new field name, *Title*, data type **Text**.

Deleting a field

To delete the field you have just inserted:

- Select the field by clicking in its row selector.
- Press the **Delete** key on the keyboard or click the **Delete Rows** button on the toolbar.

If you make a mistake, you can use **Edit, Undo Delete** to restore the field.

Moving a field

- Click the row selector to the left of the field's name to select the field.
- Click again and drag to where you want the field to be. You will see a line appear between fields as you drag over them to indicate where the field will be placed.

Changing or removing a key field

- To change the key field to **Surname**, click the row selector for the **Surname** field and then click the **Primary Key** button on the toolbar.
- To remove the primary key altogether, select the row that is currently the key field and click the **Primary Key** button on the toolbar.
- Sometimes a primary key is made up of more than one field (a *composite* or *compound* key). Select the first field, hold down **Ctrl** and select the second field. Then click the **Primary Key** button.

When you have finished experimenting, restore **AuthorID** as the primary key field of this table. Make any other necessary corrections to leave the fields as specified in Figure 21.3, and save the table structure.

21.11. Creating the other tables

Now create the **tblBook** in the same way.

- Remember to select the correct data type for each field. **DatePublished** has the data type **Date/Time** and **Price** has the data type **Currency**.

Next, create the table **tblBook/Author**.

- You can specify which type of number field you want in the Field Properties at the bottom of the screen. The percentage fields can be formatted as percent.
- To create the composite key field, hold down **Ctrl** while you click the record selector for each of the two fields which make up the key. Then click the **Primary Key** button.

- Make sure the data types and lengths for the foreign keys are defined in exactly the same way as in **tblBook** and **tblAuthor**. You will have trouble setting up the relationships if they are not.

The table structure should look like Figure 21.14.

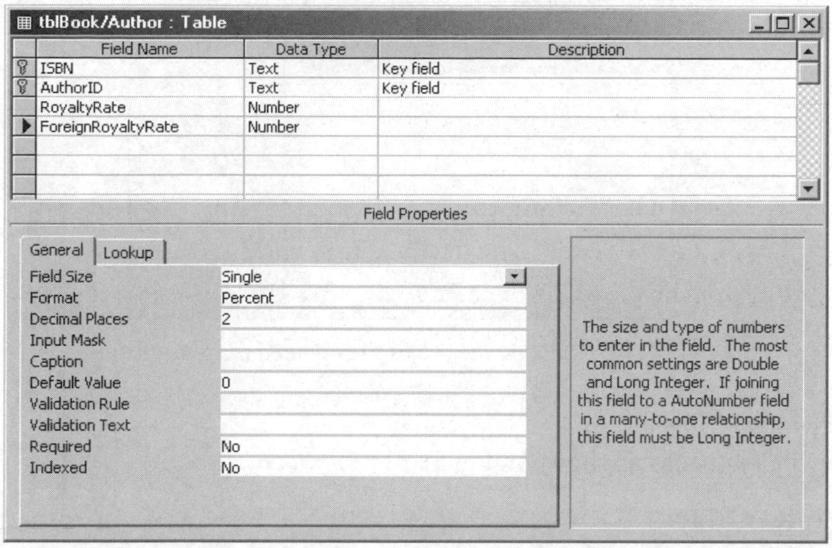

Figure 21.14: The structure of the tblBook/Author table

- Now create **tblTransaction**. Be sure to make **ISBN** Text, 13 characters long and **TransactionType** Number (Byte). (Refer to the data dictionary in the Systems Specification, Chapter 20 Figure 20.5.)

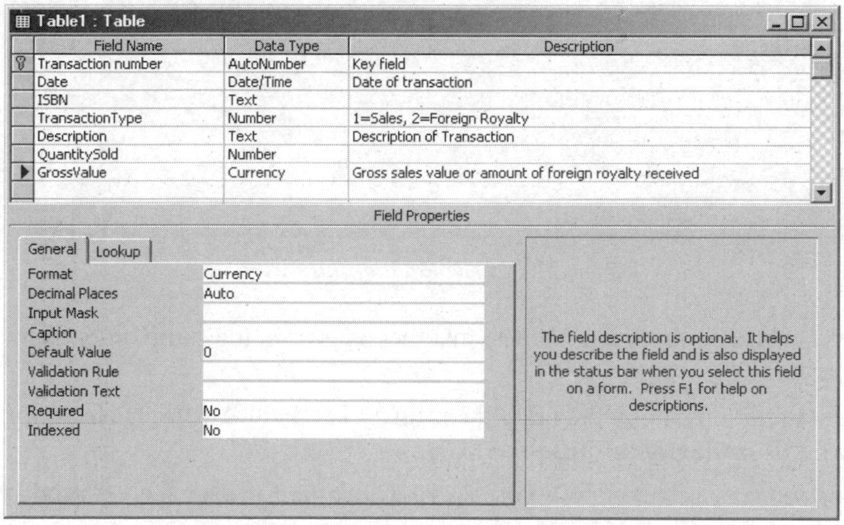

Figure 21.15: The structure of tblTransaction

21.12. Creating relationships

Look back at Figure 20.4. The three one-to-many relationships can be created in Access.

- Close any tables that you have open to return to the database window.
- Click the Relationships button on the toolbar or select **Edit, Relationships** from the menu.

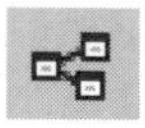

The following window opens. Select all four tables by holding down **Ctrl** while you click each in turn.

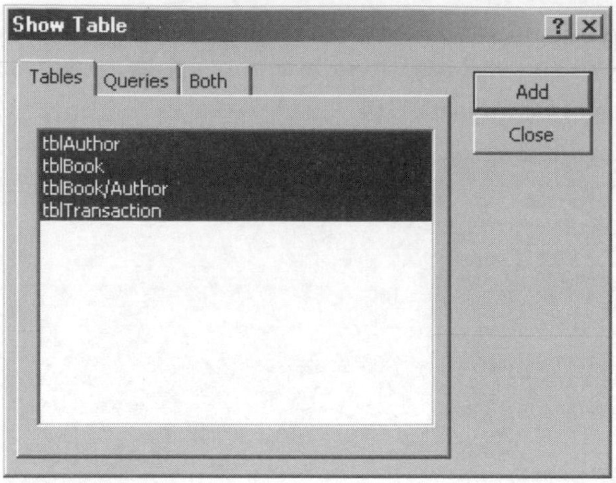

Figure 21.16: Selecting the tables to be joined in relationships

- Click **Add** and then **Close**.

The Relationships window opens as shown in Figure 21.17.

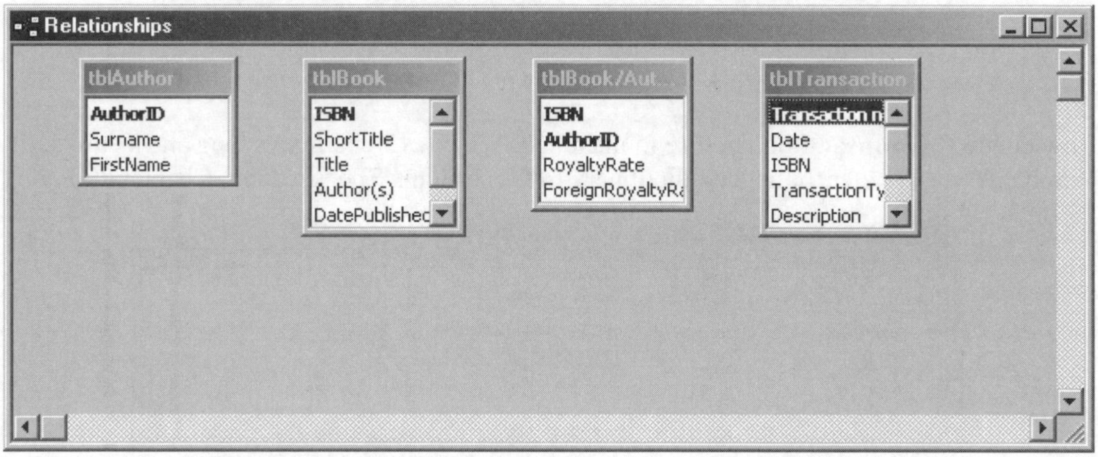

Figure 21.17: The Relationships window

- Rearrange the tables by dragging them so that they appear in the same order as in the ERD (Figure 20.4).
- Create the first relationship by dragging the primary key field **AuthorID** from **tblAuthor** to the foreign key field **AuthorID** in **tblBookAuthor**.
- A new window opens as shown in Figure 21.18. Click the **Enforce Referential Integrity** button.

Enforcing referential integrity means that you will not be able to enter a record for a non-existent author or a non-existent book in **tblBook/Author**. The database will first check that there is a corresponding record in the correct table.

If you choose to tick **Cascade Delete Related Records**, this means that when you delete say, an Author record, any related records in **tblBook/Author** will automatically be deleted. Leave this unchecked, as we are unlikely to need to delete Author records. Leave **Cascade Update Related Records** unchecked too.

Edit Relationships

Table/Query:	Related Table/Query:	
tblAuthor	tblBook/Author	
AuthorID	AuthorID	

☑ Enforce Referential Integrity

☐ Cascade Update Related Fields

☐ Cascade Delete Related Records

Relationship Type: One-To-Many

Create   Cancel   Join Type..   Create New..

*Figure 21.18: Creating a one-to-many relationship between **tblAuthor** and **tblBookAuthor**.*

- Click **Create**.

- Now create a one-to-many relationship between **tblBook** and **tblBook/Author** by dragging **ISBN** from **tblBook** to **tblBook/Author**. (Always drag from the *Many* side to the *One* side of the relationship.)

- Enforce Referential Integrity as before, and click **Create**.

- Similarly, create the relationship between **tblBook** and **tblTransaction**.

The Relationships window will now look like Figure 21.19.

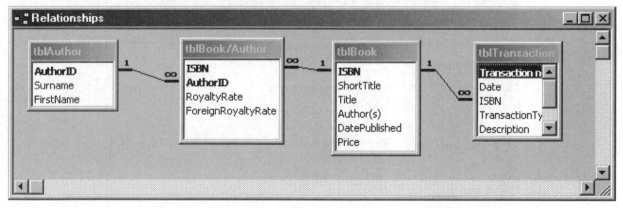

Figure 21.19: The relationships shown

Congratulations! You have laid the foundations of the Royalties database. Save and close the window and the database.

Chapter 22 – Implementing Form Design

Objectives

- ✓ To enter data using Datasheet view
- ✓ To use a wizard to create a screen form for inputting data
- ✓ To use a query to combine fields from two tables into one table
- ✓ To use the query as a source for a data entry form/subform
- ✓ To use the screen form to input data

22.1. Inputting data

In the last chapter you created four tables and relationships joining them.

- Load Access and open the database **Royalties.mdb**.

The database window will open. It should look like the figure below.

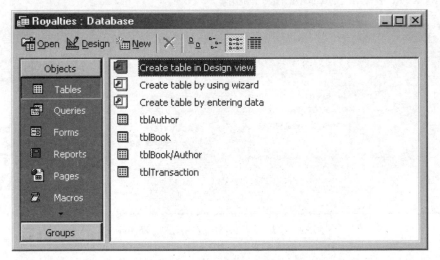

Figure 22.1: The database window

The next stage is to put some data into the tables. There are two different ways in Access of entering data into a table, known as

- ❑ datasheet view
- ❑ form view

Datasheet view

In Datasheet view you can enter data directly into an open table.

- Select **tblAuthor** and click **Open**.

The table will open in Datasheet view and you can enter records directly. Enter records as shown in Figure 22.2, tabbing to move between fields.

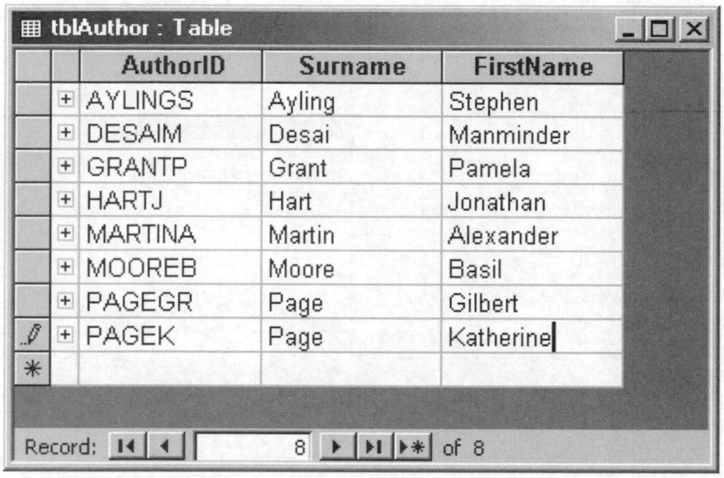

Figure 22.2: Entering records in Datasheet view

- Close the window to return to the Database window. The records will be saved automatically.

Form View

A more finished-looking user interface can be achieved by designing a special screen form for data entry. The user can then use this form to enter records, although they can still enter and edit records in Datasheet view if they prefer. We will create a data entry form to enter and edit book records.

22.2. Creating a simple data entry form

The easiest way to create a data entry form is to use a wizard.

- In the Database window, click the **Forms** tab on the left hand side of the window.
- Select **Create form by using wizard**.

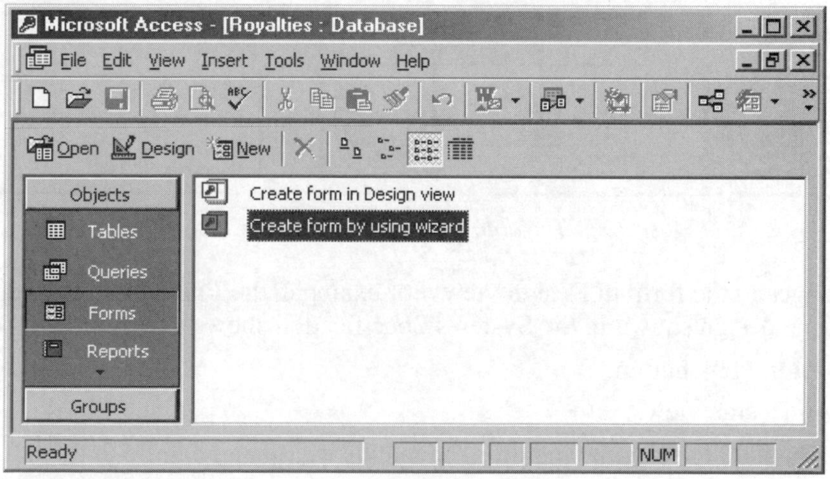

Figure 22.3: Preparing to create a form

- Click **New**.

A window appears as shown in Figure 22.4.

- Select **AutoForm: Columnar**.
- In the list box at the bottom of the screen, select **tblBook**.

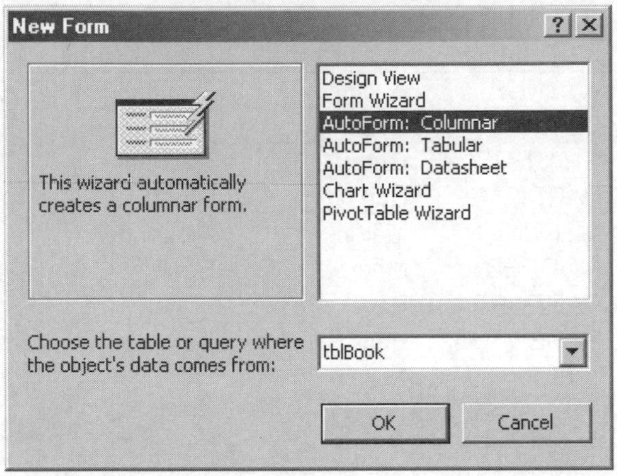

*Figure 22.4: Creating a new form for **tblBook***

- Click **OK**.

A new form is automatically created, which can be used for entering details of books published.

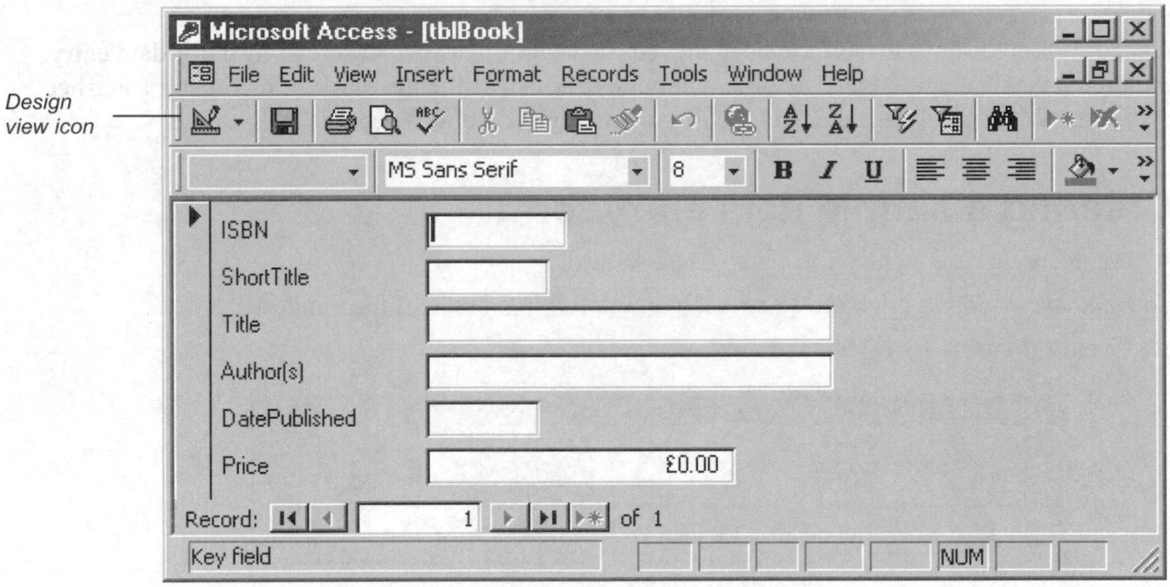

Figure 22.5: The data entry form created by the wizard

You can make changes to the form in Design view. For example, the **Price** field is much wider than it needs to be. Also, the design shown in the Systems Specification shows a form title, BOOKS.

- Click the **Design view** button.

The form appears in Design view.

- Click the **Price** field to select it, and drag the middle right-hand handle to the left to make the field narrower.

Now you can create the heading.

- Drag the bottom edge of the Form Header downwards to make room in the Form Header section.

- Select the **Label** button from the toolbox and drag out a rectangle in the Form Header section.

- Type the heading *BOOKS* and make the text bold, 18point Arial. The form should look like the one in Figure 22.6.

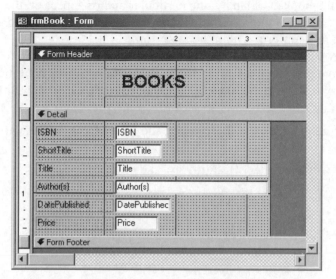

Figure 22.6: The data entry form in Design view

- Click the **Form View** button to see the form in Form view again.
- Enter the following data.

ISBN	Short Title	Title	Author(s)	Date Published	Price
0953112004	LIW	Learning IT – Word 2000	A.Martin and K.Page	01/03/2000	£8.95
0953112012	LIE	Learning IT – Excel 2000	A.Grant	01/03/2000	£8.95
0953112020	LIA	Learning IT – Access 2000	J.Hart	01/04/2000	£8.95
0953112039	LIFP	Learning IT – FrontPage 2000	M.Desai	01/05/2000	£8.95
0953112047	LISA	Learning IT – Sage Accounts	K.Page	01/01/2001	£8.95
0953112055	GFE	Going Further – Excel 2000	A.Grant	20/02/2001	£9.95
0953112063	GFW	Going Further – Word 2000	A.Martin	15/03/2001	£9.95
0953112071	GFSA	Going Further – Sage Accounts	K.Page and B.Moore	01/04/2001	£9.95
095311208X	LIAC	Learning IT – AutoCAD 2000	G.R.Page	01/04/2001	£8.95

Figure 22.7: Book records to be entered

- You can use the record selectors at the bottom of the screen to move between records. Edit any records that contain data entry errors.

- Click the **Save** icon or select **File, Save** from the menu. The Save As window will appear.

- Enter the name *frmBook* instead of the default **tblBook**, and click **OK**.

- Close the form to return to the database window.

The button **Return to Menu** shown in the Systems Specification design (Chapter 20) will be added later, after the menu screen has been created.

22.3. Using a query to combine data from more than one form

To enter the records for **tblBook/Author**, you need to be able to enter several books for one author. It will be convenient if all the books written by one particular author appear on the same screen. This can be done by creating a form with the author's details in the top half of the form, and a list of all the books belonging to that author, in a subform within the main form.

Look back at Figure 20.6 for the hand-drawn form design. The first thing to notice is that the book title appears in the subform, but this is not a field in **tblBook/Author**. Before creating this form, we need to create an extra, temporary table that contains all the fields that appear on the subform.

This is done by means of a Query.

- In the Database window, click the **Queries** tab and select **Create query in Design view**. Click **New**.

- In the New Query window, select **Design view** and click **OK**.

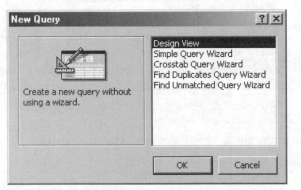

Figure 22.8: New Query window

- Select both **tblBook** and **tblBook/Author** (hold down **Ctrl** while you select the second table) and click **Add**.

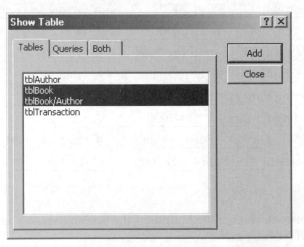

Figure 22.9: Selecting tables for the Query

- Click **Close**, and the Query window opens.
- Drag the fields from the tables in the top half of the screen on to the Query grid as shown in Figure 22.10. Note that **AuthorID**, **ISBN**, **RoyaltyRate** and **ForeignRoyaltyRate** are all from **tblBook/Author**, and **Title** is from **tblBook**. It is important to take the fields from the correct table.

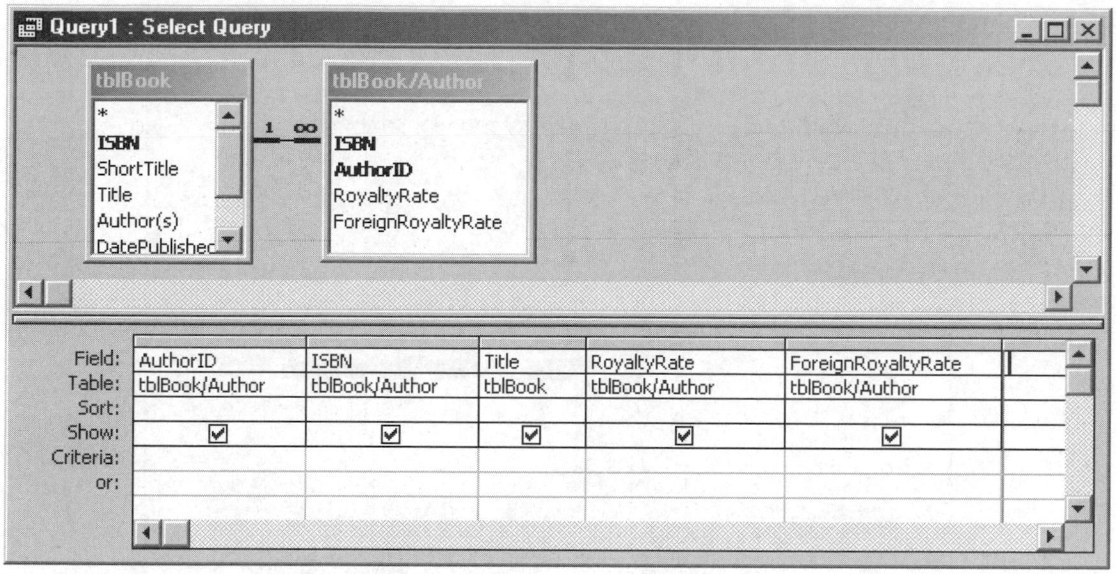

Figure 22.10: Selecting fields for the query

- Now run the query by clicking the **Run** button.

There will be no records in the Results table as we have not yet entered any data for **tblBook/Author**. However, you can see the headings correspond to the selected fields.

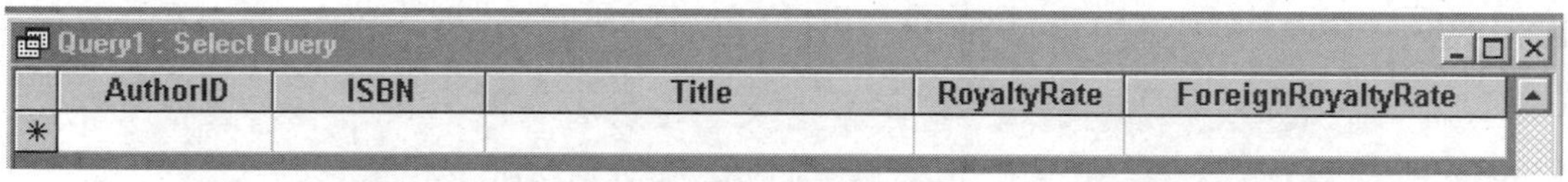

Figure 22.11: The Results table created by the query

This query can be saved and the temporary Results table recreated at any time by running the query. It can then be used as the source of a form or report.

- Click the **Design view** button to return to the Design view of the query.
- Click the **Save** button and save the query as *qryBook/Author*.
- Close the query to return to the Database window

22.4. Creating a form with a subform

- In the Database window, with the **Forms** tab selected, select **Create form by using wizard**. Click **New**.
- In the next window, select **Form wizard** and select **tblAuthor** in the list box at the bottom of the screen. Click **OK**.
- In the next window, you are asked to select which fields you want on the form. Click the double arrow between the two list boxes **Available Fields** and **Selected Fields** to select them all.

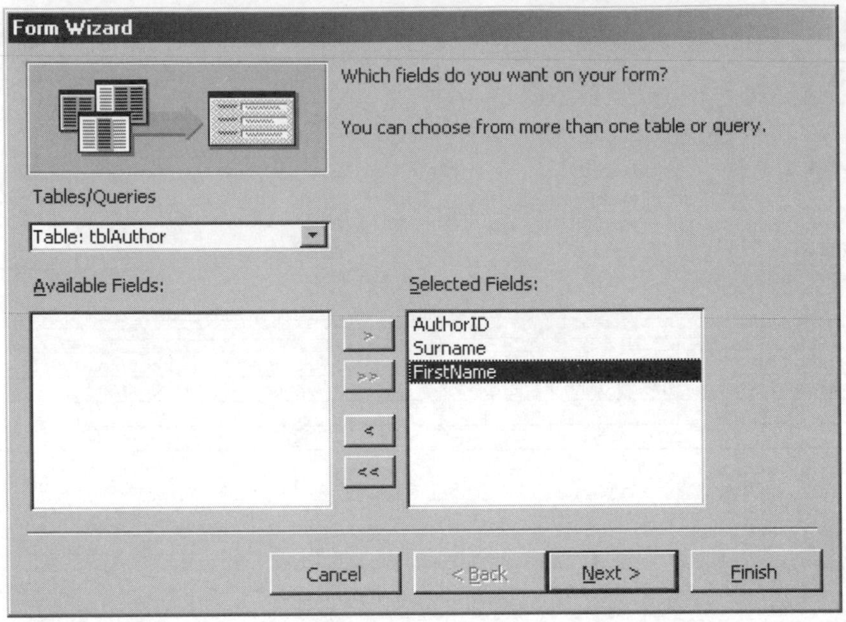

Figure 22.12: Selecting fields for the form

- Now you want to add the fields for the subform. In the list box, select **qryBook/Author**.
- Click the double arrow to move all the fields to the right-hand side. Then click the left arrow to put **qryBook/AuthorID** back in the list of available fields.

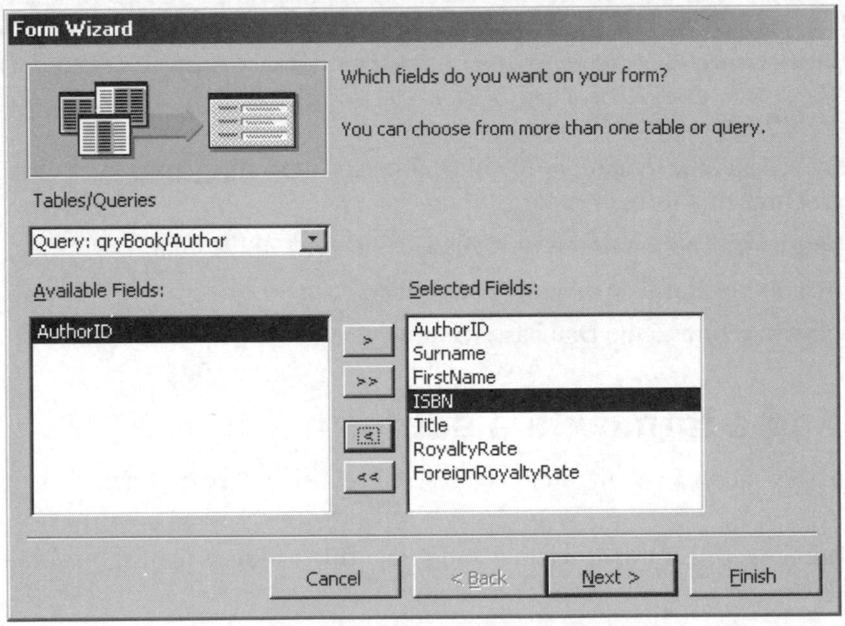

Figure 22.13: Selecting fields for the subform

- In the next window, make sure options are selected as shown in Figure 22.14.

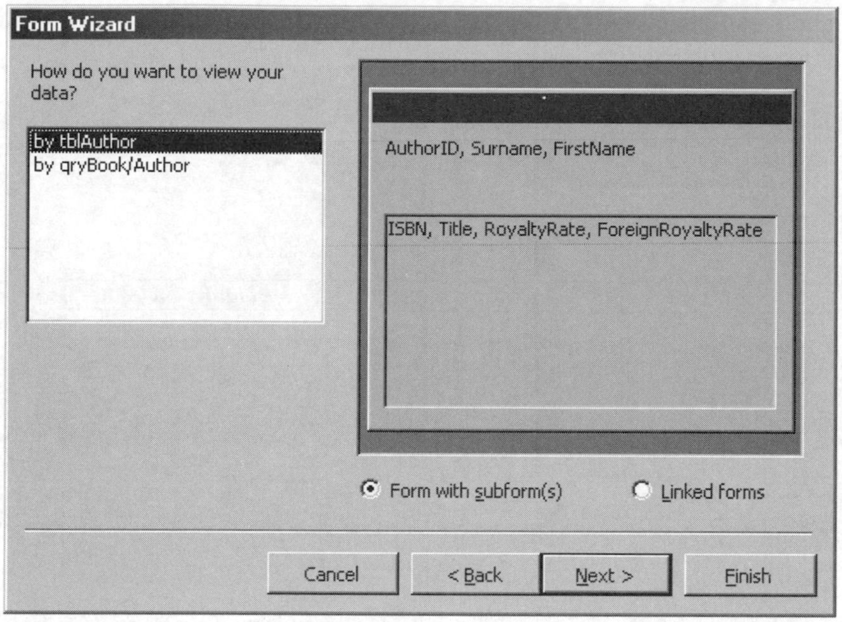

Figure 22.14

- Click **Next**.
- In the next window, select **Datasheet** for the subform layout. Click **Next**.
- In the next window, select **Standard** for the Form style. Click **Next**.
- In the next window, name the form *frmAuthor* and the subform *fsubBook/Author* and make sure the option **Open the form to view or enter information** is selected.

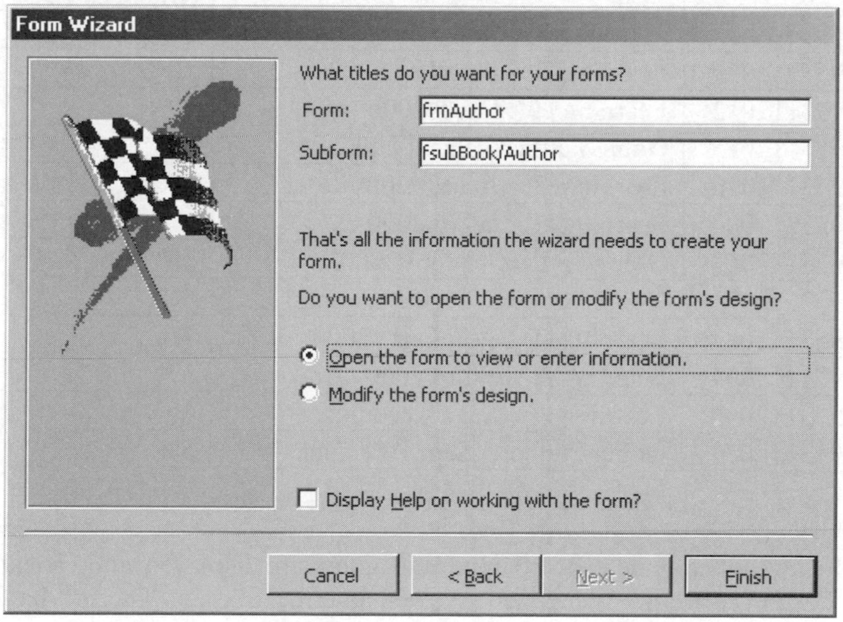

Figure 22.15: the last Form Wixard window

- Click **Finish**.

The form is now created and displayed. Note that you may not be able to see all the fields in the subform – field widths need to be adjusted.

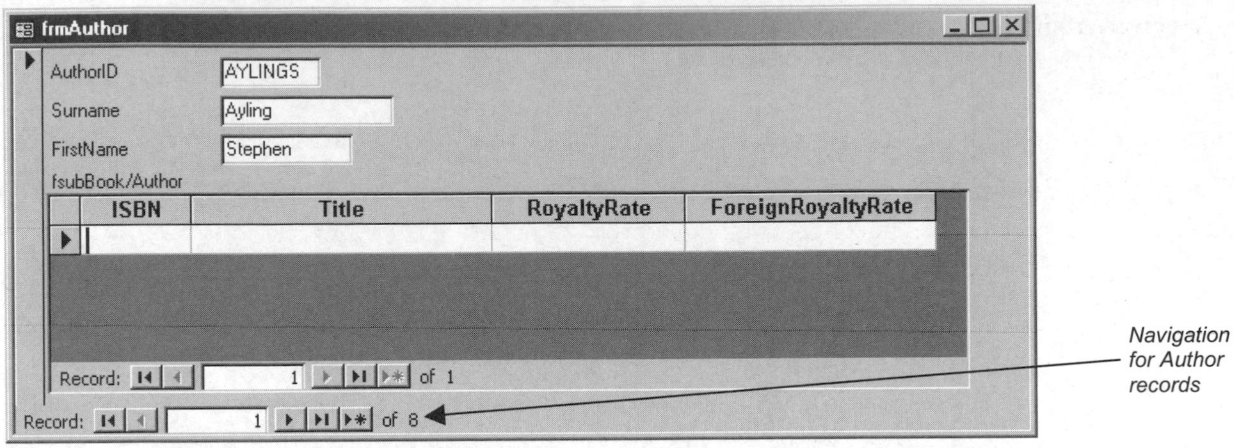

Figure 22.16: The completed form

You can alter the width of the subform by switching to Design view. To change the field widths of the subform you need to edit the subform itself. Field widths of the subform can be adjusted by returning to the Database window and loading the subform in Datasheet view. There is quite a lot that can be done to improve the appearance of this form and you can experiment with different colours and fonts as well as sizing and positioning boxes and setting properties.

- Enter the data from the table below. (Tip: To enter the ISBNs in the second and subsequent records, you can press **Ctrl** and ' to copy the entry in the previous record, then edit the last two digits.)

AuthorID	ISBN	Title	Royalty rate	Foreign Royalty rate
DESAIM	0953112039	Learning IT – FrontPage 2000	10%	66.6667%
GRANTP	0953112012	Learning IT – Excel 2000	10%	66.6667%
GRANTP	0953112055	Going Further – Excel 2000	7%	50%
HARTJ	0953112020	Learning IT – Access 2000	10%	66.6667%
MARTINA	0953112004	Learning IT – Word 2000	5%	33.3333%
MARTINA	0953112063	Going Further – Word 2000	10%	50%
MOOREB	0953112071	Going Further – Sage Accounts	5%	33.3333%
PAGEGR	095311208X	Learning IT – AutoCAD 2000	7%	50%
PAGEK	0953112004	Learning IT – Word 2000	5%	33.3333%
PAGEK	0953112047	Learning IT – Sage Accounts	10%	66.6667%
PAGEK	0953112071	Going Further – Sage Accounts	5%	33.3333%

Figure 22.17: Author records to be entered

Note that once you have entered the ISBN, the title and author are displayed automatically. If you enter an ISBN that is not saved in **tblBook**, Access will give you an error message. This is what is meant by 'data integrity'.

You have to enter the percentages as .1 for 10%, .05 for 5% etc. They are displayed as percentages because of the way the fields were formatted when the table was designed.

- Close the form to return to the database window.

22.5. Creating a form with a list box and option group

The final form that needs to be created is the Transaction form for entering monthly sales and royalties received from foreign publishers. The basic form will be created using a wizard, as for the Books form, using tblTransaction as the source of the form.

- In the Database window select **Create form by using wizard**. Click **New**.
- In the next window select **AutoForm: Columnar**.
- In the list box at the bottom of the screen, select **tblTransaction**. Click **OK**.

The new form will look like the one shown in Figure 22.18.

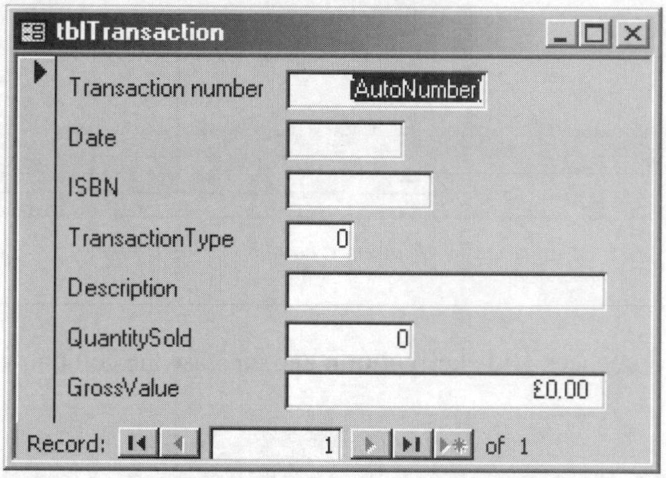

Figure 22.18: The basic transaction form

Looking at the System Specification, Figure 20.6, we need to replace the text box for ISBN with a drop-down list of all the ISBNs stored in the database. We also want to replace the **TransactionType** text box with an option group so that the user can select either Sales or Foreign Royalties. This is one way of validating the user's entries – it will be impossible to put in an invalid ISBN or transaction type. The user will not have to know that TransactionType 1 means Sales and TransactionType 2 means Foreign Royalties, as these values will automatically be stored in the field.

Placing a combo box

- Go to Design view.
- Click in the **ISBN** field and press the **Delete** key to delete it.
- In the Toolbox, check the **Control Wizards** are selected, then select the **Combo box** tool. Drag
  out a rectangle in place of the field you deleted. 
- In the window which appears, select **I want the combo box to look up the values in a table or query**. Click **Next**.
- In the next window, select **tblBook** as the table which will provide values for the combo box. Click **Next**.
- In the next window move **ISBN** and **Title** to the list of selected fields.

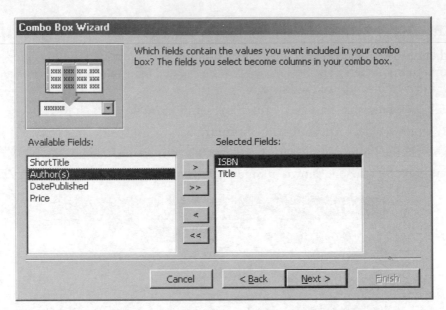

Figure 22.19: Placing a combo box on a form

- Click **Next**.
- In the next window, uncheck **Hide key column** and increase the column width of the **Title** field.

How wide would you like the columns in your combo box?

To adjust the width of a column, drag its right edge to the width you want, or double-click the right edge of the column heading to get the best fit.

☐ Hide key column (recommended)

ISBN	Title
0953112004	Learning IT - Word 2000
0953112012	Learning IT - Excel 2000
0953112020	Learning IT - Access 2000
0953112039	Learning IT - FrontPage 2000
0953112047	Learning IT - Sage Accounts
0953112055	Going Further - Excel 2000
0953112063	Going Further - Word 2000

Figure 22.20

- Click **Next**.
- In the next window, leave **ISBN** selected as the field you want to store. Click **Next**.
- Select **Store that value in this field** and select **ISBN** from the drop-down list. Click **Next**.
- Give the combo box the label *ISBN* and click **Finish**.
- The Combo box will appear on the form. You may need to add a label if you deleted the original one.

At this stage your form should look like the one below.

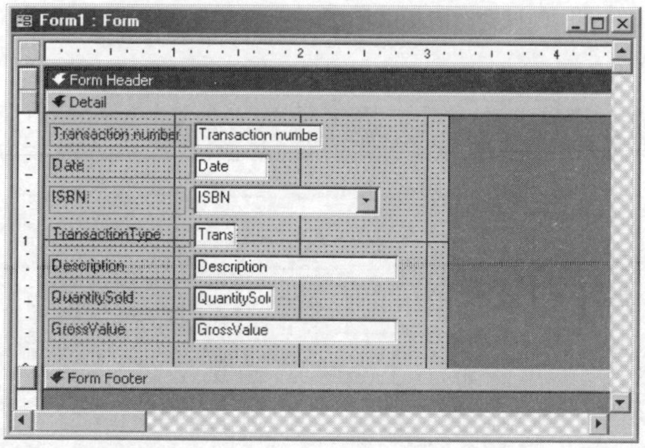

Figure 22.21: ISBN Combo box

Note that if you want the title to be displayed automatically on the form, you could create the form from a query as you did for the subform **fsubBook/Author**. If you then place the field for **Title** on the form the correct title will be displayed automatically when you leave the ISBN field.

Placing an option box

The next stage is to replace the **TransactionType** text box with an option box. First of all you need to create more space on the form.

- Drag the top of the form footer downwards.

- Drag the mouse through all the fields and labels from **TransactionType** through to **GrossValue** to select them, and move them down.

- Delete the field for **TransactionType**.

- Click the **Option Group** button on the Toolbox and drag out a rectangle in place of the deleted **TransactionType**.

- In the window, type the label names as in Figure 22.22. Click **Next**.

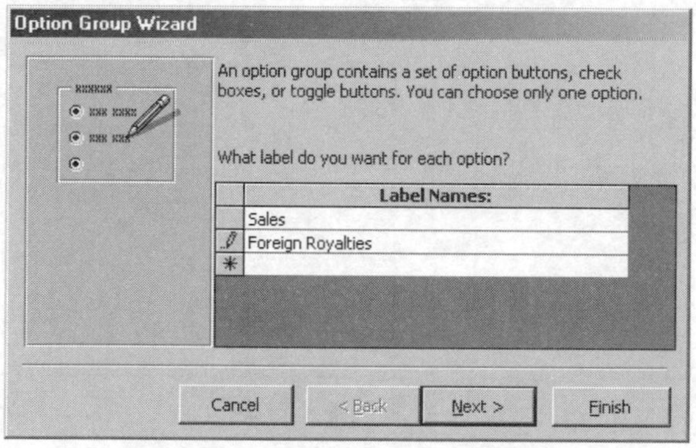

Figure 22.22

- Leave the default choice as **Sales** and click **Next**.

- Leave the values **1** and **2** assigned to the two options and click **Next**.

- Select the option **Store the value in this field** and select **TransactionType** from the drop-down list. Click **Next**.

- Leave the defaults **Option Buttons**, **Etched** in the next window. Click **Next**.

- Specify the caption **Transaction Type** and click **Finish**.

You will need to reposition some of the fields to fit them neatly on the form, which will then look something like the one below:

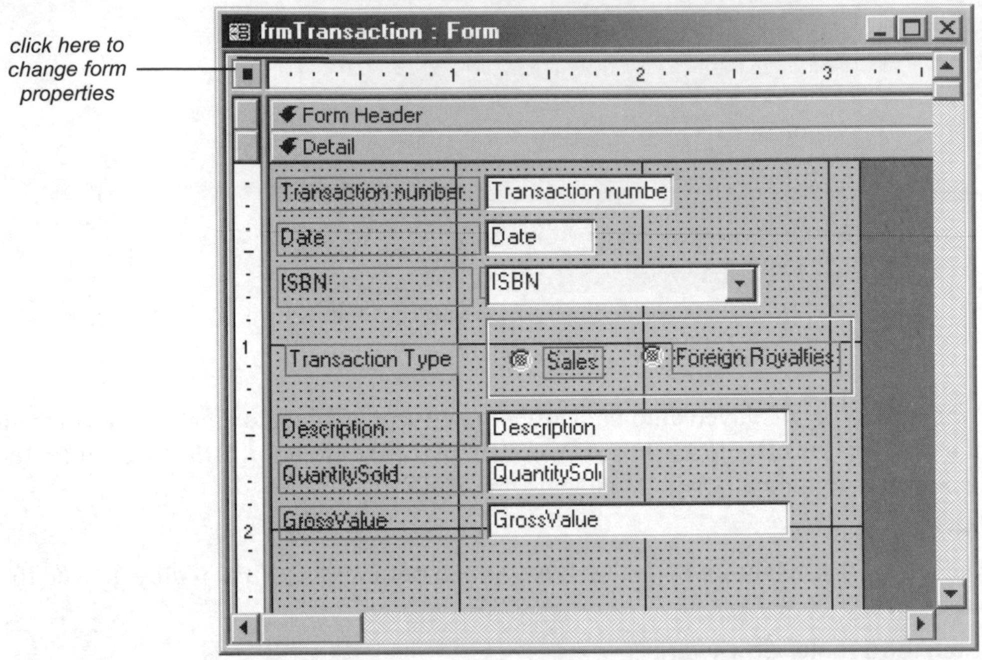

Figure 22.23: Form with combo box and option group

In Form view, the form looks like this:

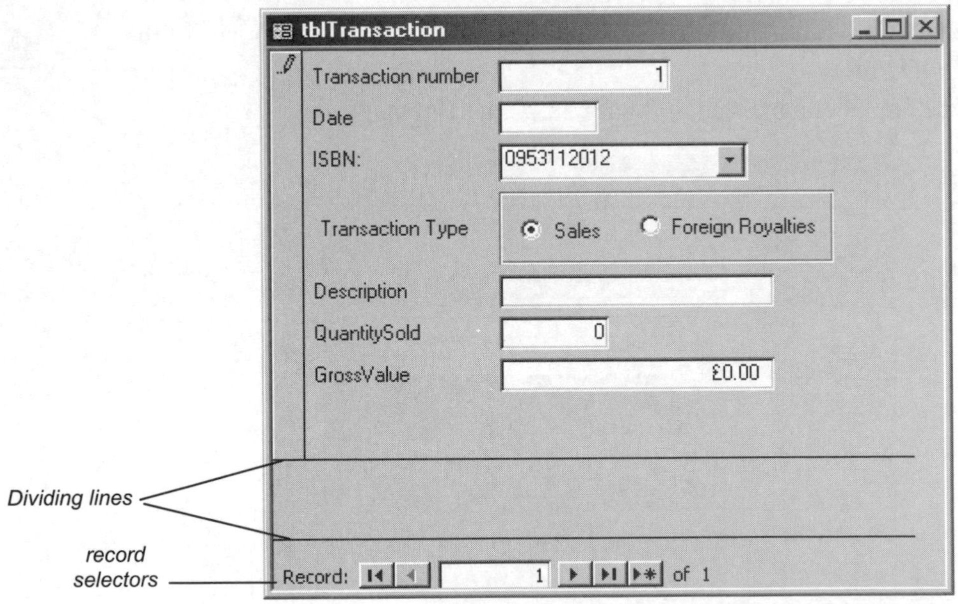

Figure 22.24: Transaction form

To get rid of the record selectors and dividing lines, you need to change some of the form properties.

- In Design view, click the box at the intersection of the ruler lines, as marked in Figure 22.23.
- If the property box is not shown, click the **Properties** button to display it.
- Change the **Record Selectors** and **Dividing Lines** properties to **No**.

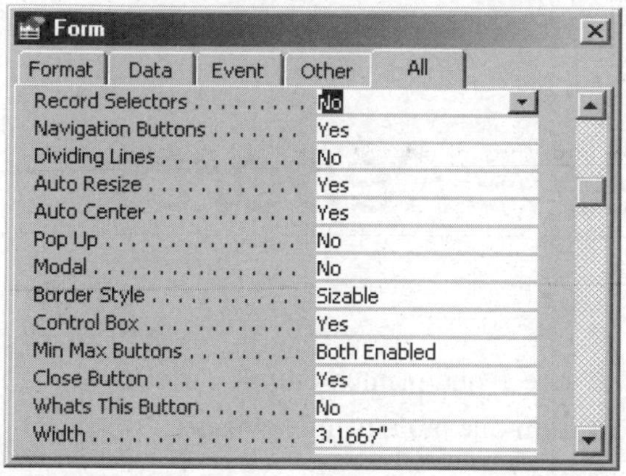

Figure 22.25: Changing form properties

- Save the form as *frmTransaction*.
- Add a heading **Transactions** to the form.

Changing the tab order on a form

Return to Form view and tab through the fields. You will find that the tab order is not right – the fields that we added last are visited last, instead of in their logical order in the form. To correct this you need to change the tab order.

- Return to Design view.
- From the menu select **View, Tab order**.
- In the dialogue box, select **Detail** section and click **Auto Order** as shown below.

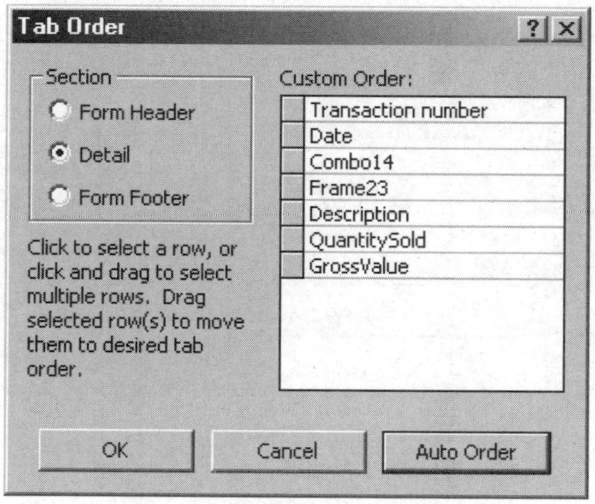

Figure 22.26: Changing tab order

- Click **OK**.
- Save the form again.
- Enter the test data shown in the Test Plan of the Systems Specification (near the end of Chapter 20). Note that to put the same value in a field as in the previous record, you can press **Ctrl-'** (**Ctrl** and ' together).

You will find that Access puts the cursor in the **Transaction number** field, which you cannot alter as it is an AutoNumber field. You can alter the **Tab Stop** property of this field to **No** to prevent this.

You may want to make other minor improvements to your form, or add some colour to it.

Chapter 23 – Reports

Objectives

- ✓ To compare the merits of screen and printed output
- ✓ To create a simple report from one table using a wizard
- ✓ To create a report based on a query
- ✓ To customise the report

23.1. Screen output

Once you have created an input form for inputting your data, this can be used as output as well. If you do not require hard copy, you can search a table using the input form to find a particular record. For example, suppose you wanted to find out which books were written by A. Martin.

- Load Access and open the database **Royalties.mdb**.
- Open the form **frmAuthor**, and click in the **Surname** field.
- Click the **Find** button on the Standard toolbar.
- In the dialogue box, type *martin*.

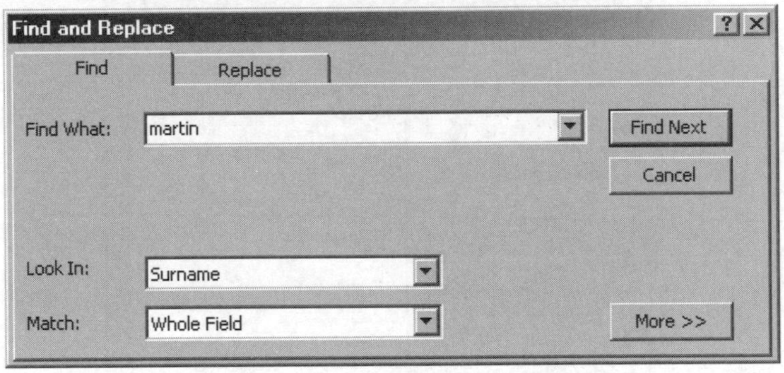

Figure 23.1: Finding a record

- Press **Find Next**. The record for Martin will appear.

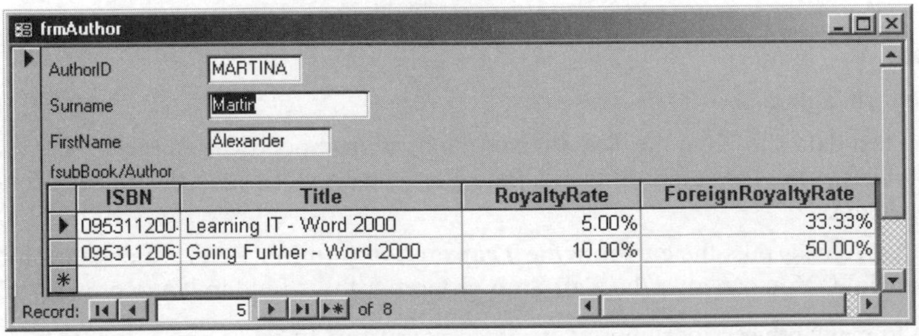

Figure 23.2: Correct record found

23.2. Printed output

Often you will need output in the form of a report which can be viewed on screen and printed if required. Screen forms are not suitable for printing as they are often coloured and usually the wrong shape to fit neatly onto standard A4 paper.

We will create a report of all the books in the database. This report could be useful for sending to a wholesaler to enable them to include the books in their catalogue, for example.

- In the Database window, click the **Reports** tab and select **Create report by using wizard**.
- Click **New**. The New Report window appears. Select **AutoReport: Columnar** and select **tblBook** in the list box near the bottom of the window. Click **OK**.

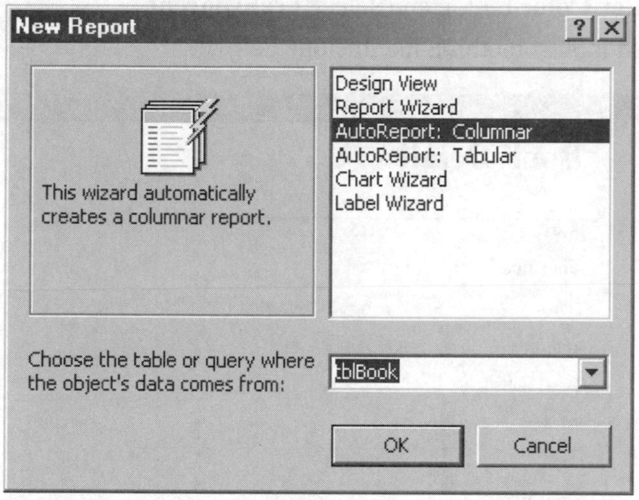

Figure 23.3: The New Report window

A report is automatically generated as shown below.

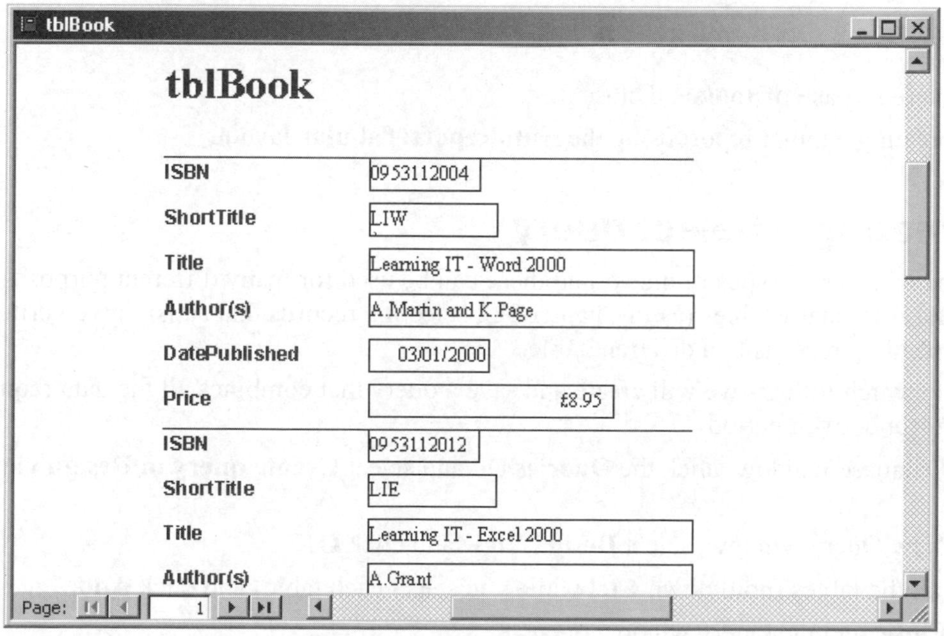

Figure 23.4: A columnar report

23.3. Editing the report

You can click the **Design View** button to edit the format of the report. Referring back to the report design in the Systems specification (Chapter 10), the title should be **Book Details** and there should be spaces in the labels **Short Title** and **Date Published**.

- Change the heading and edit the labels. You can also left-justify the **DatePublished** and **Price** fields to make them look neater.

You can get rid of the borders round each field as follows:

- Drag the cursor around all the fields to select them all. You don't need to completely surround them – it is sufficient to pass through a field to select it.

- Click the **Line/Border Color** button and select **Transparent**.

Your finished report should look something like the one below:

ISBN	0953112004
Short Title	LIW
Title	Learning IT - Word 2000
Author(s)	A.Martin and K.Page
Date Published	03/01/2000
Price	£8.95
ISBN	0953112012
Short Title	LIE
Title	Learning IT - Excel 2000
Author(s)	A.Grant

Figure 23.5: The edited report

- Save the report as **rptBook** and close it.

You can try creating another report using the **AutoReport:Tabular** layout.

23.4. Creating a Select query

Access has many different types of query, and these can be used for many different purposes, including combining data from many tables (as in Chapter 22), selecting records that satisfy given criteria, deleting records or appending records to a different table.

In the example which follows we will create and save a query that combines all the data required for the Royalty report for a given period.

- In the Database window, click the **Queries** tab and select **Create query in Design view**. Click **New**.

- In the New Query window, select **Design View** and click **OK**.

- Select all the tables (hold down **Ctrl** while you select each table) and click **Add**.

- Click **Close**, and the Query window opens.

- Arrange the tables as in Figure 23.6.

- Drag the fields from the tables in the top half of the screen on to the Query grid as shown in Figure 23.6. Note the table that each field is taken from.

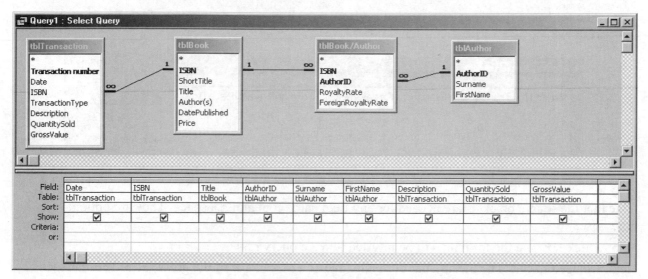

Figure 23.6: Creating the query for the Royalties Report

Now refer back to the Process Specification in the Systems specification given in Chapter 20. The royalty rate used depends on whether the transaction type is 1 (Sales) or 2 (Foreign Royalty). The pseudocode for the calculation is reproduced below:

```
If     TransactionType = 1    (i.e. 'Sales')
then   Rate := RoyaltyRate
else   Rate := ForeignRoyaltyRate
endif
Amount := Rate * GrossValue
```

A calculated field can be inserted into the query grid to perform this calculation.

- Right-click in the top row of the blank column next to **GrossValue** and click on **Build...**
- In the Expression Builder window, type the variable name *Rate:* (the name is followed by a colon) in the top line and press **Enter**.

Figure 23.7: The Expression Builder window

- Select **Functions, Built-in functions** in the left-hand list box, **Program Flow** in the centre box and double-click the **IIf** function in the right-hand list box.

- The format of the expression needed is given at the bottom of the window. Type the formula in as follows:

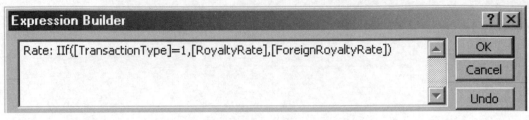

Figure 23.8: The formula for Rate

Note that the square brackets are needed for any field name containing a space. They are optional otherwise.

- Click **OK** and the formula will be inserted into the query grid.

Next, we need to calculate the amount of royalty due as a percentage of the gross sales. This can also be inserted into the query grid as a calculated field.

- In the next column in the query grid, type *Amount: GrossValue*Rate*

- Try running the query. You should see results as follows:

Title	AuthorID	Surname	FirstName	Description	QuantitySo	GrossValue	Rate	Amount
Learning IT - Word 2000	MARTINA	Martin	Alexander	January Sales	234	£2,094.30	0.05000000075	104.715001560
Learning IT - Word 2000	MARTINA	Martin	Alexander	Rights sold to Sunrise, Pak	0	£400.00	0.33333000541	133.332002163
Learning IT - Word 2000	MARTINA	Martin	Alexander	Rights sale to LAU, Norwa	0	£350.00	0.33333000541	116.665501893
Learning IT - Word 2000	PAGEK	Page	Katherine	January Sales	234	£2,094.30	0.05000000075	104.715001560
Learning IT - Word 2000	PAGEK	Page	Katherine	Rights sold to Sunrise, Pak	0	£400.00	0.33333000541	133.332002163
Learning IT - Word 2000	PAGEK	Page	Katherine	Rights sale to LAU, Norwa	0	£350.00	0.33333000541	116.665501893
Learning IT - Excel 2000	GRANTP	Grant	Pamela	January Sales	423	£3,785.85	0.10000000149	378.585005641
Learning IT - Excel 2000	GRANTP	Grant	Pamela	Rights sold to Sunrise, Pak	0	£400.00	0.66670000553	266.680002213
Learning IT - Excel 2000	GRANTP	Grant	Pamela	Rights sale to LAU, Norwa	0	£350.00	0.66670000553	233.345001936
Learning IT - Excel 2000	GRANTP	Grant	Pamela	February Sales	420	£3,759.00	0.10000000149	375.900005601
Learning IT - Access 2000	HARTJ	Hart	Jonathan	January Sales	1000	£895.00	0.10000000149	89.5000013337
Learning IT - FrontPage 200	DESAIM	Desai	Manminder	February Sales	752	£6,730.40	0.10000000149	673.040010029
Learning IT - FrontPage 200	DESAIM	Desai	Manminder	January Sales	580	£5,191.00	0.10000000149	519.100007735
Learning IT - Sage Account:	PAGEK	Page	Katherine	January Sales	128	£1,145.60	0.10000000149	114.560001707
Going Further - Excel 2000	GRANTP	Grant	Pamela	January Sales	1000	£995.00	0.0700000003	69.6500002965
Going Further - Word 2000	MARTINA	Martin	Alexander	January Sales	532	£5,393.40	0.10000000149	539.340008037
Going Further - Word 2000	MARTINA	Martin	Alexander	Rights sold to Sunrise, Pak	0	£400.00	0.5	200
Going Further - Sage Accou	MOOREB	Moore	Basil	January Sales	100	£995.00	0.05000000075	49.7500007413
Going Further - Sage Accou	PAGEK	Page	Katherine	January Sales	100	£995.00	0.05000000075	49.7500007413
Learning IT - AutoCAD 2000	PAGEGR	Page	Gilbert	January Sales	453	£4,054.35	0.0700000003	283.804501208

Record: 1 of 20

Figure 23.9: Query results table

There are some rounding errors but basically the rates should be as they were entered for Sales and Foreign Royalties.

- Save the query as **qryRoyalty** and close it.

23.5. Creating the royalty report

The royalty report can now be created from this query.

- In the Database window click the **Reports** tab.
- Select **Create report by using wizard** and then click **Design**.
- In the Report wizard window select **qryRoyalty** as the source, and click the double arrow to move all the fields to the right-hand list box. Click **Next**.

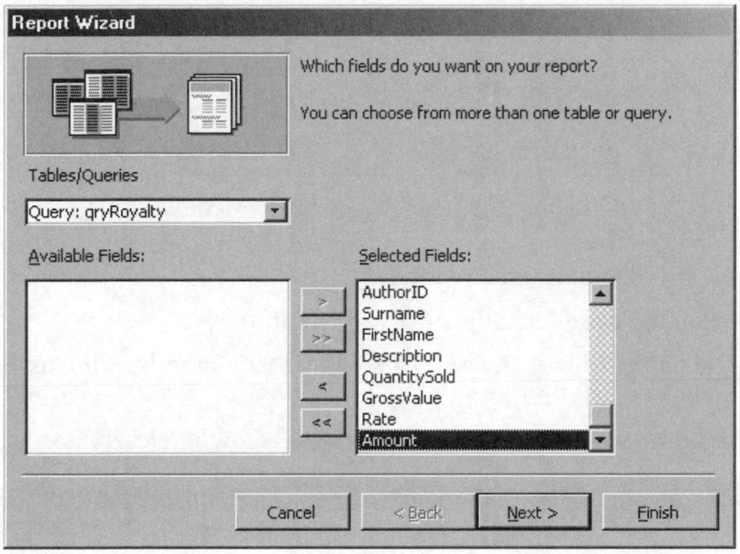

Figure 23.10

- In the next window **ISBN** is already specified as a grouping level. Select **Author** and click the arrow to add a second grouping level. **Author** should come above **ISBN** so click the **Priority** arrow to move it up. Click **Next**.

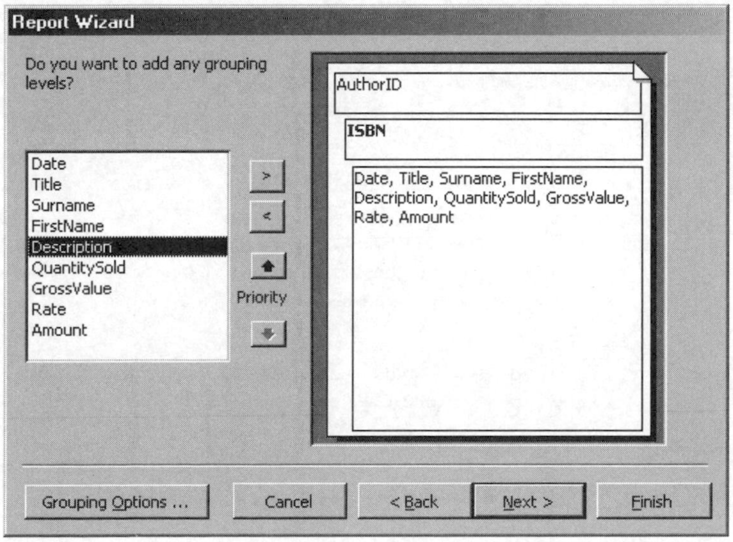

Figure 23.11

- In the next window specify sort fields of **Surname**, **Firstname** and **Date**.
- Click the **Summary** button and specify a **SUM** for **Amount**.

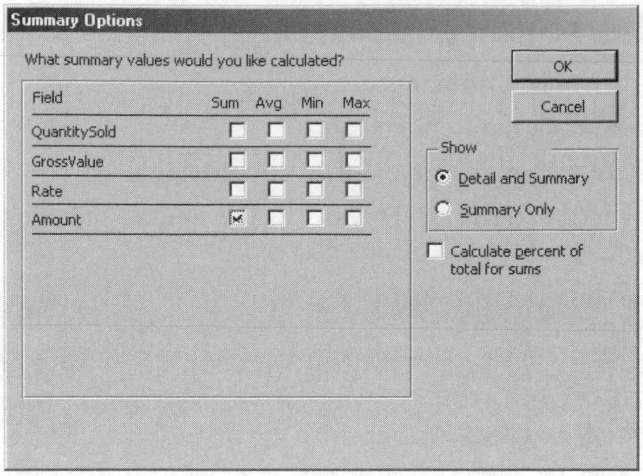

Figure 23.12: Specifying Summary values

- Click **OK**, and **Next** in the Sort Order window.
- Click **Next** to accept the defaults in the next two windows.
- Give the report the name *Royalty Report*. This will be the report heading assigned by the wizard. Click **Finish**.

The report is generated by the wizard and appears as shown below. It clearly needs a lot of work!

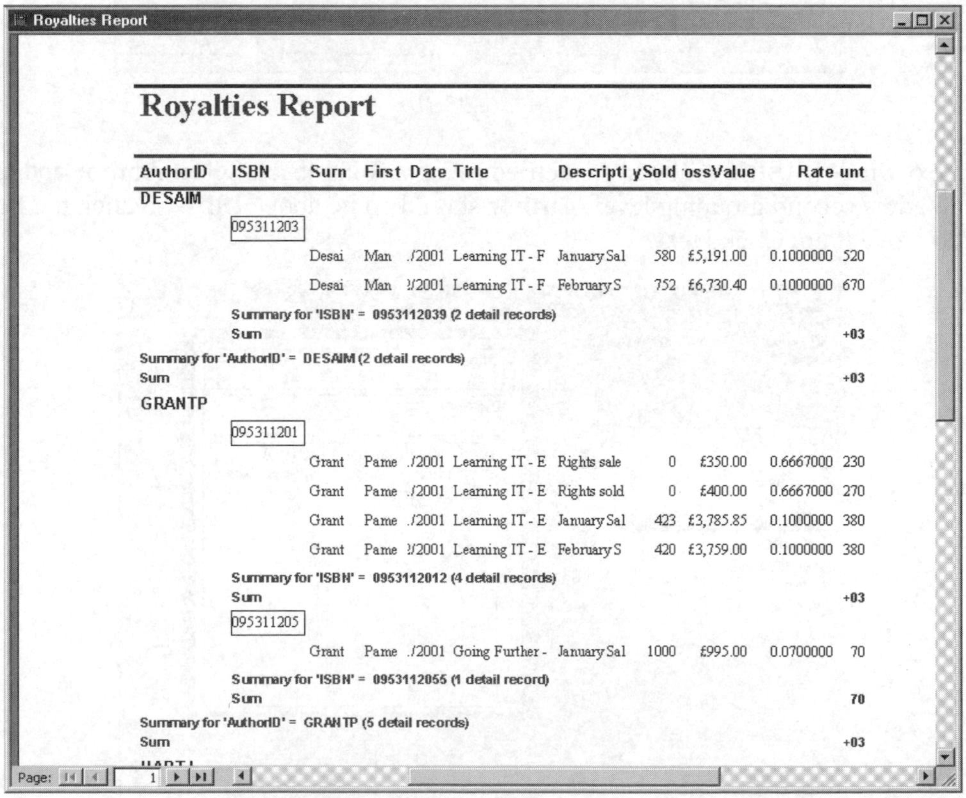

Figure 23.13: Royalties report generated by wizard

- Go to Design view. A multitude of edits are required to get the report looking like Figure 23.14.
- Start by deleting the labels for **AuthorID**, **ISBN**, **Surname**, **Firstname** and **Title**.

- Move labels and fields and adjust widths, checking the report in preview mode to see the effect of your changes.

- Adjust font sizes for Author's name, ISBN and title and make them bold. Make the border round ISBN transparent.

- Edit the summary labels to **Total for title** and **Total for Author**.

- Format all the amounts to **Currency**, **2 decimal places**. (Use the Property box for this.)

- Insert a page break just above the Page Footer section using the **Page Break** tool on the toolbox.

- Enlarge the Page Header section and move the title **Royalties Report** into this section so that it appears on every page. Then move the bottom border of the empty Report Header section up.

Your report should end up looking more like the one below, which shows the second page of the report. It may take trial and error and a lot of patience!

Royalties Report

Date	Description	Qty	Gross Value	Rate	Amount
Grant	**Pamela**				
0953112	**Learning IT - Excel 2000**				
02/01/2001	Rights sale to LAU, Norway	0	£350.00	66.67%	£233.35
15/01/2001	Rights sold to Sunrise, Pakistan	0	£400.00	66.67%	£266.68
30/01/2001	January Sales	423	£3,785.85	10.00%	£378.59
27/02/2001	February Sales	420	£3,759.00	10.00%	£375.90
	Total for title				£1,254.51
0953112	**Going Further - Excel 2000**				
30/01/2001	January Sales	1000	£995.00	7.00%	£69.65
	Total for title				£69.65
	Total for Author				£1,324.16

Figure 23.14: The edited Royalties report

There is one weakness in this report. It does not enable the user to specify the period of the report, or display it. This is not a problem when you only have 2 month's worth of test data, but in a real system you need to be able to specify that only transactions between certain dates are to be included on the report.

This will be looked at in the next chapter.

Chapter 24 – Queries

Objectives

✓ To enable a user to input criteria to a query

✓ To create a summary report

✓ To use a Delete query to delete old records from a table

24.1. Setting criteria in a query

In the last chapter the Royalties report was created from the query **qryRoyalty**. It worked well but there was no means of specifying the period of the report. If **tblTransaction** contained transactions for the last 5 years, all these transactions would be included on the report.

One solution is to allow the user to enter the start date and end date at run time. Only transactions between these two dates will be taken into account.

- Load Access and open the database **Royalties.mdb**.

- Click the **Queries** tab, select **qryRoyalty** and click **Design**. The query opens in Design view.

- We will try a simple query first. In the **Criteria** row in the **AuthorID** column, type *martina*.

- Run the query. Only records with **AuthorID** MARTINA appear.

- Return to Design view.

You can set criteria using the logical operators AND and OR. To use OR, you type the two criteria one underneath the other. To find all records for MARTINA or GRANTP, type *grantp* underneath **martina**.

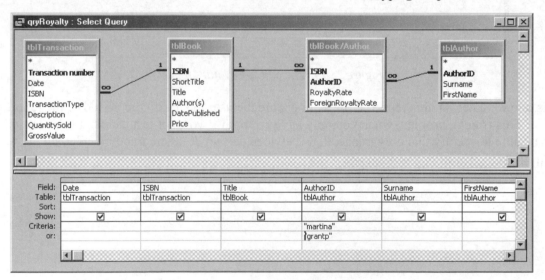

Figure 24.1: Setting criteria in a query

- Run the query. All the records for MARTINA and GRANTP appear.

You can also type the criteria on the same line separated by the word OR.

- In Design view, delete the criteria you entered. We will try entering some different criteria in the **Date** column.
- In the **Criteria** row of the **Date** column, enter the criteria *>15/01/2001 and <= 31/01/2001*
- Run the query. The results should appear as shown below.

qryRoyalty : Select Query

Date	ISBN	Title	AuthorID	Surname	FirstName	Description	Quanti	GrossValue	Rate
30/01/2001	0953112012	Learning IT - Ex	GRANTP	Grant	Pamela	January Sales	423	£3,785.85	0.1000000
30/01/2001	0953112055	Going Further -	GRANTP	Grant	Pamela	January Sales	1000	£995.00	0.0700000
30/01/2001	0953112020	Learning IT - Ac	HARTJ	Hart	Jonathan	January Sales	1000	£895.00	0.1000000
30/01/2001	0953112004	Learning IT - Wo	MARTINA	Martin	Alexander	January Sales	234	£2,094.30	0.0500000
30/01/2001	0953112004	Learning IT - Wo	PAGEK	Page	Katherine	January Sales	234	£2,094.30	0.0500000
30/01/2001	0953112063	Going Further -	MARTINA	Martin	Alexander	January Sales	532	£5,393.40	0.1000000
30/01/2001	0953112071	Going Further -	MOOREB	Moore	Basil	January Sales	100	£995.00	0.0500000
30/01/2001	0953112071	Going Further -	PAGEK	Page	Katherine	January Sales	100	£995.00	0.0500000
30/01/2001	095311208X	Learning IT - Au	PAGEGR	Page	Gilbert	January Sales	453	£4,054.35	0.0700000
30/01/2001	0953112047	Learning IT - Sa	PAGEK	Page	Katherine	January Sales	128	£1,145.60	0.1000000
30/01/2001	0953112039	Learning IT - Fro	DESAIM	Desai	Manminder	January Sales	580	£5,191.00	0.1000000

Record: 1 of 11

Figure 24.2: The Results table

You will notice when you return to Design view that Access puts # characters round the dates in your criteria.

Field:	Date
Table:	tblTransaction
Sort:	
Show:	☑
Criteria:	>#15/01/2001# And <=#31/01/2001#
or:	

Figure 24.3: Date criteria

You can experiment with more complex queries. If for example you type the criterion *martina* under **AuthorID** now, you will get records that apply to **MARTINA** *and* which lie between the specified dates.

24.2. Allowing a user to specify criteria at run time

The next stage is to enable the user to specify criteria when the query (or report based on the query) is run.

- Delete any criteria you have entered.
- In the **Date** column, type *>=[Enter the start date for the report]* (include the square brackets).
- Run the query. A dialogue box appears, into which you can type a date, e.g. 16/01/2001:

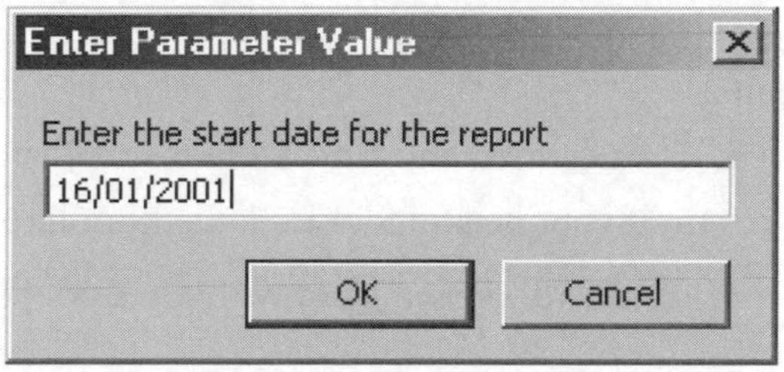

Figure 24.4: Allowing the user to specify criteria

When you press **OK**, the query runs.

- Edit the criteria so that it *says >=[Enter the start date for the report] and <= [Enter the end date for the report]*

Field:	Date
Table:	tblTransaction
Sort:	
Show:	☑
Criteria:	>=[Enter the start date for the report] And <=[Enter the end date for the report]
or:	

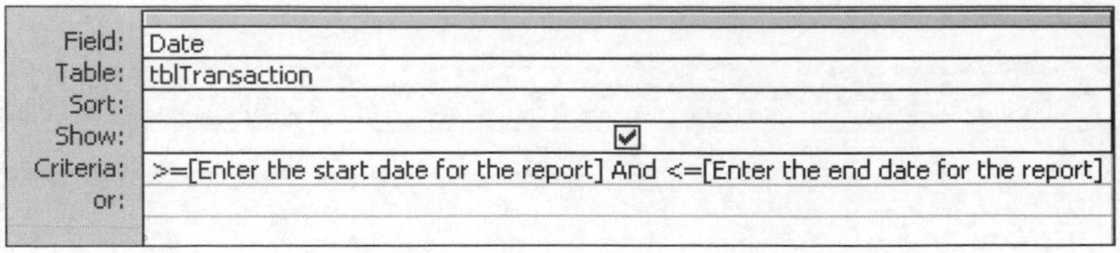

Figure 24.5: Using AND in criteria

- Run the query. Two dialogue boxes appear asking you to enter the start and end dates, and then the query runs as before.

- The entries in the square brackets will be used as field names on the Royalties report, so it would be convenient to shorten them. Edit the criteria to *>=[Start Date] and <= [End Date]*

- Test the query again and then save and close it.

24.3. Entering the criteria on a report

You can make these dates appear on the Royalties report.

- Open **rptRoyalty** in Design view.

- Place two text boxes next to the heading **Royalties Report**. They will each say **Unbound** and have a label associated with them.

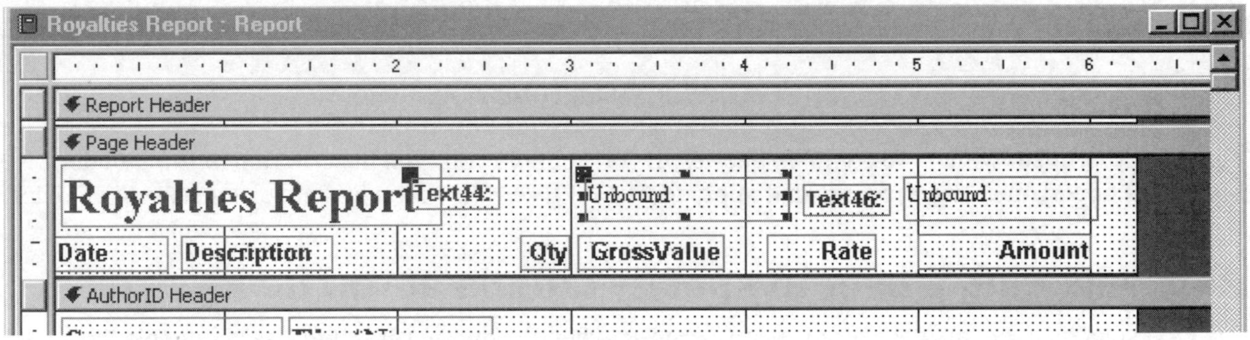

Figure 24.6: Adding text boxes to the report

- Click in the first box that says **Unbound**, and edit it to say *[Start Date]*.

- Click in the second box that says **Unbound**, and edit it to say *[End Date]*.

- Delete the first label (Text 44 in Figure 24.6) and edit the second label to *To*.

- Change fonts and font sizes to match the heading Royalties Report – in Figure 24.7 the font is Times Roman size 20 points.

- **Start Date** is right-justified, **To** is centred and **End Date** is left-justified.

- Reposition and resize boxes until your heading looks something like Figure 24.7.

Tip: Drag the big upper-left corner handle to move a label without its field.

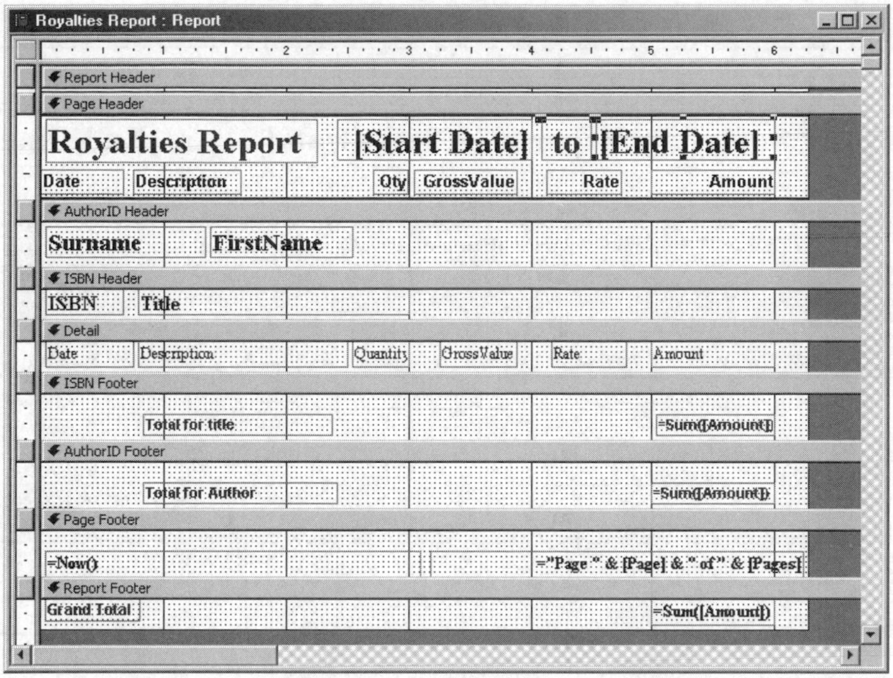

Figure 24.7: The finished Royalties Report in Design view

- Press the **Preview** button to test your report. It should look something like Figure 24.8.

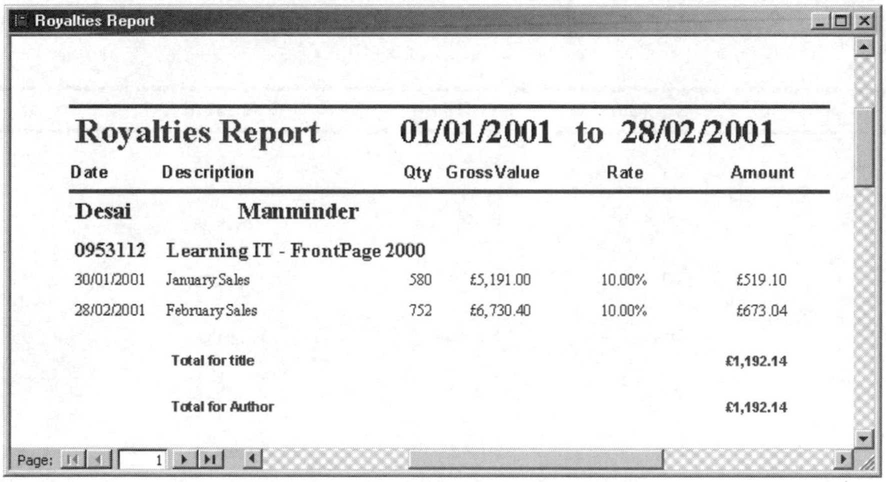

Figure 24.8: The Royalties report in Print Preview

24.4. The Summary report

The Summary report as shown in the Systems Specification (Chapter 20) can be created using a wizard. The source of the report is again **qryRoyalty**, and you need the fields **AuthorID**, **Surname**, **Firstname** and **Amount** for the report. Add a grouping level on AuthorID then select **Summary Only** in the Summary Options and specify that you want the sum of the amounts. You will need to do quite a lot of tweaking to get the report into the desired format: Figure 24.9 shows the report in Design view, and Figure 24.10 shows it in Print Preview.

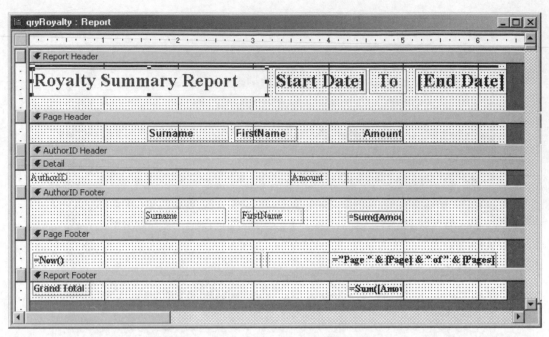

Figure 24.9: Summary report in Design view

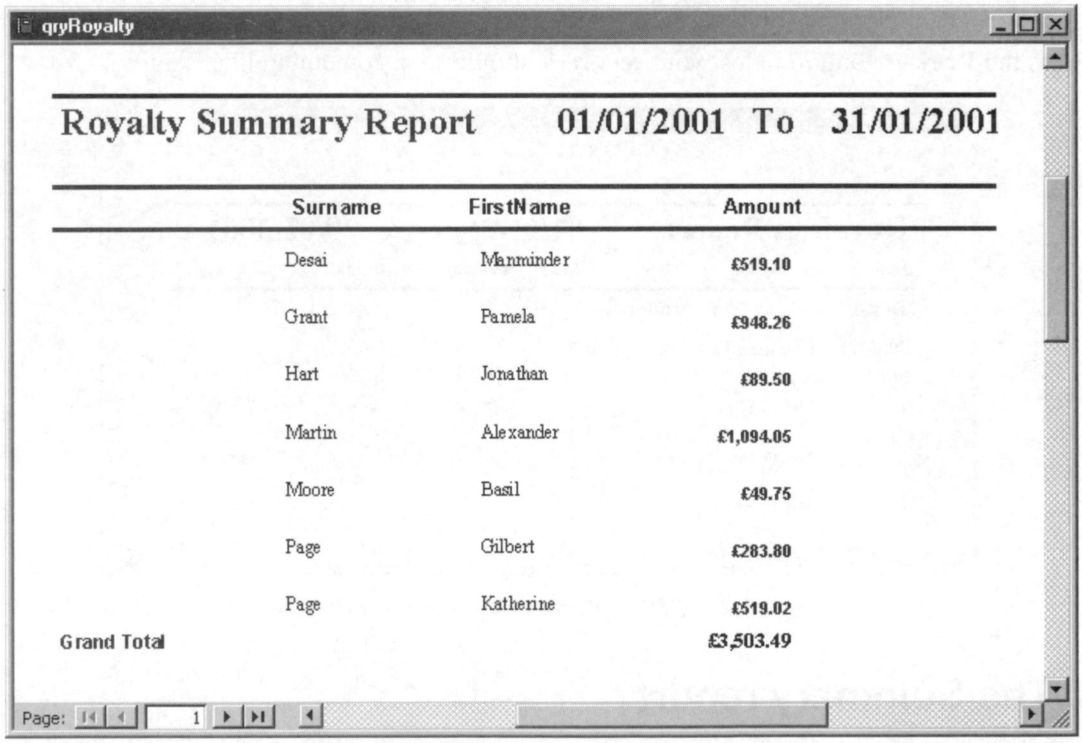

Figure 24.10: Summary report in Print Preview

- Save the report, naming it *rptRoyaltySummary*, and close it. (If it has automatically been saved with a different name, right-click the name and select **Rename** to rename it.)

24.5. Deleting old records from the transaction file

The transaction file cannot be allowed to grow indefinitely. Every so often, perhaps once a year, an archive (backup) copy of the database needs to be made and saved on a tape, floppy disk, CD or zip disk, carefully labelled and stored in a safe place. Of course, this is in addition to the daily, weekly or monthly backups that will be routinely made.

Once the backup has been made, transactions that are over, say, one year old may be deleted. We will allow the user to specify the date prior to which transactions are to be deleted. Access has many different types of query in addition to the Select Query type which you have already seen, and one of these is a Delete query, which instead of displaying the selected records in a Results table, deletes them from the original table.

- Start by adding some more transactions to the file, dated 1999. These will be deleted when the maintenance routine is tested. Add about 3 transactions – it does not matter what they are so long as they have dates in 1999. Use the Transaction form and remember to go to a new blank form at the end of the records to add a new transaction. Close the Transaction form.

- In the Database window create a new query in Design view as before, and add the Transaction table to the Query window.

- Double-click each field in turn to place each field on the query grid.

- From the menu select **Query**, **Delete Query**. (You will have to click the double-arrow to display this option.)

- Enter a criterion in the **Date** column:

    <=[Delete transactions prior to which date?]

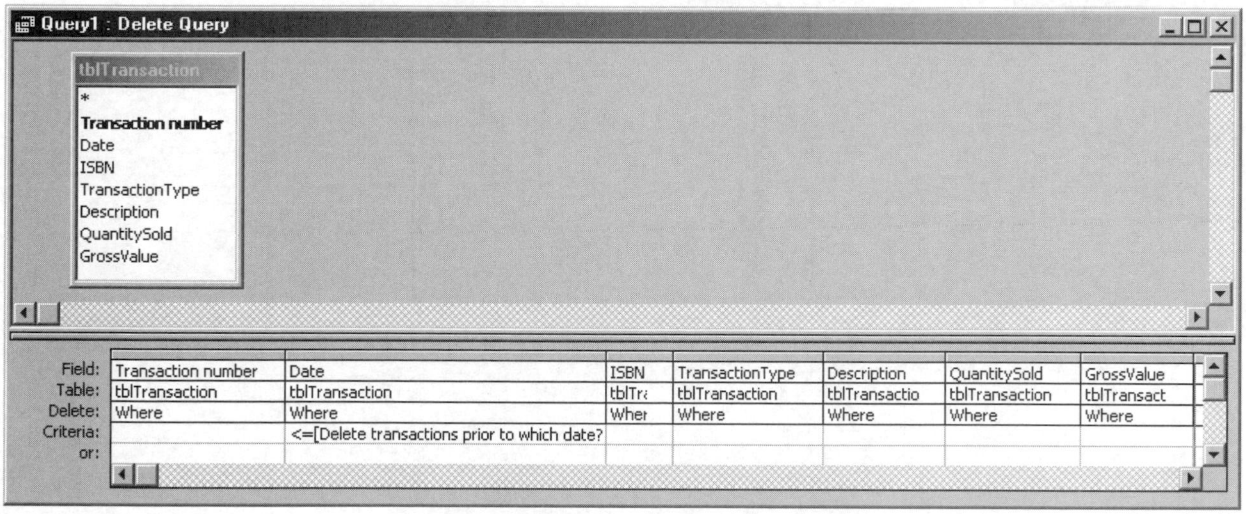

Figure 24.11: Creating a Delete query

- Run the query. You will see a dialogue box, into which you can type a date:

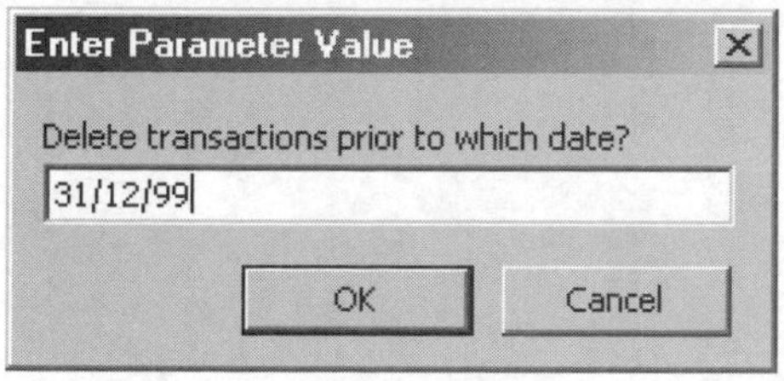

Figure 24.12

Another dialogue box now appears, telling you that you are about to delete three records, or however many satisfy the criteria.

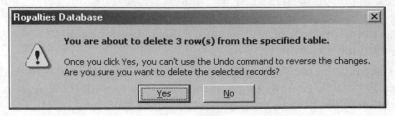

Figure 24.13

When you click **Yes**, nothing appears to happen but if you open **tblTransaction**, you will find that all records prior to the specified date have disappeared.

- Save the query as *qdelTransactions* and close it.

You have now completed all the forms, reports and processes required for this application. All that remains is to construct the menu which gives the user an easy and obvious way to perform all the functions in the database.

Chapter 25 – Macros, Menus and Command Buttons

Objectives

- ✓ To create a simple macro
- ✓ To create the menu structure
- ✓ To add a button to an input form
- ✓ To display the main menu on starting the application

25.1. Creating a macro

A macro is a small program that tells Access to perform one or more actions such as running a query, opening a form or printing a report. Once you have written the macro you can save it and run it from the Database window, or you can attach it to the event property of a form or command button.

The macro that we are going to create will run the Delete query **qdelTransactions** to delete transactions over a given age.

- Load Access and open the database **Royalties.mdb**.
- In the Database window select the **Macros** tab and click **New**.
- You will see the Macros window. To add an action, you click the drop-down arrow on the first line under **Action** and select an action.
- Scroll down the list of actions and select **OpenQuery**.
- In the **Action Arguments** list, select **qdelTransactions** as the query name. Leave the other two arguments with their default values.
- Add a comment to say what the macro does. This does not affect the running of the macro but provides useful documentation.

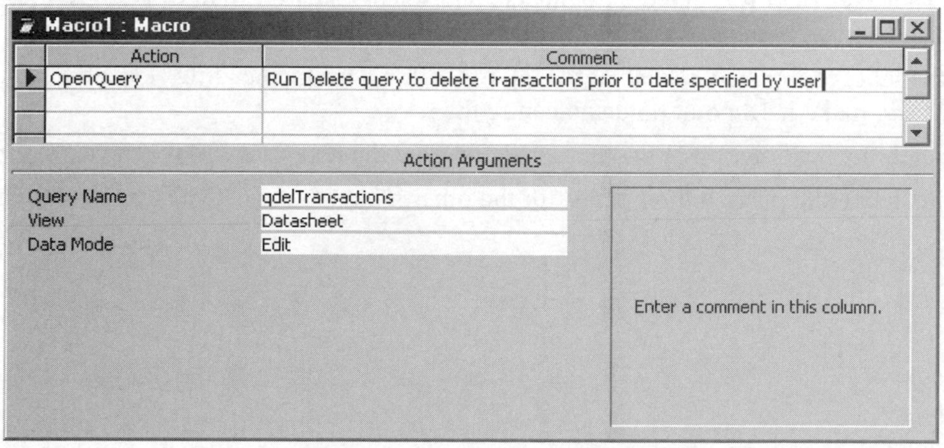

Figure 25.1:Creating a macro

- Save the macro, naming it **mcrMaintenance**. Close it to return to the Database window.

- Before you can test the macro, you will have to add one or more transactions with dates prior to, say, 31 December 1999 which you can then delete. Do this now.

- Test the macro by running it. Be careful not to delete test records that you wish to keep!

25.2. Attaching a macro to an event property

We will create one more macro which will be attached to the Open Event Property of **frmBook**, **frmAuthor** and **frmTransaction**. The macro will cause a new record to be displayed when the form is opened.

- In the Database window select the **Macros** tab and click **New**.

- Scroll down the list of actions and select **GoToRecord**.

- In the Action Arguments list, select **New** as the **Record** argument.

- Save the macro as *mcrNewRecord* and close it.

- Open **frmBook** in Design view.

- Right-click the square at the intersection of the ruler lines and select **Properties**.

- On the **Event** tab in the Properties Box, click the **On Open** event. Select **mcrNewRecord** as the event procedure to run when the form opens.

- Save and close the form.

- Open the form again to test it. It should display a new blank record.

- Follow the same steps to attach the macro to the forms **frmAuthor** and **frmTransaction**.

25.3. Creating a menu

Access has a special Add-In called the Switchboard Manager which allows you to quickly create a series of 'switchboards' or menus. This is accessed from the menu by selecting **Tools, Database Utilities, Switchboard Manager** or in earlier Access versions, **Tools, Add-Ins, Switchboard Manager**. However, as this is not always installed, we will use an alternative method of creating menus, which is to place command buttons on blank forms to perform tasks such as opening or closing forms, previewing reports, or running queries.

Refer back to Figure 20.3 in the System Specification. We will start by creating the Data Entry menu.

- In the Database window, click the **Forms** tab and select **Create Form in Design View**. Click **Design** and a new, blank form appears in Design view.

- Using the label tool, create a label at the top of the form for the heading. Type the heading *Data Entry Menu*, make it 18 point bold and centre the text.

- Underneath the heading, place another label and type the text *Sales*. Make the text 12 point.

- Copy this label and paste it three times for the other menu options. Type text as shown in Figure 25.2.

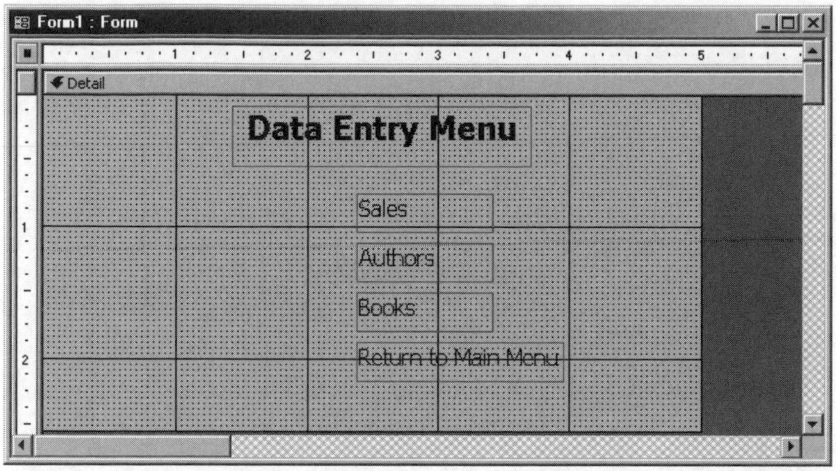

Figure 25.2: The beginnings of the Data Entry submenu

- Have a look at the form in Form view. It has scroll bars, record selectors, dividing lines, navigation buttons, Max Min buttons and is sizeable. All these properties need to be changed using the form's property box.

- Return to Design view. Click at the intersection of the ruler lines and set the form's Format properties as follows:

Property	Setting
Caption	Data Entry Menu
Default View	Single Form
Views Allowed	Form
Scroll Bars	Neither
Record Selectors	No
Navigation Buttons	No
Dividing Lines	No
Border Style	Dialog
Max Min buttons	None

The next step is to place command buttons to open the relevant form. The last option will simply close this submenu.

- Place a command button to the left of the first menu option, **Sales**. A dialogue box will open.

- Select **Form Operations** in the left-hand list and **Open Form** in the right-hand list. Click **Next**.

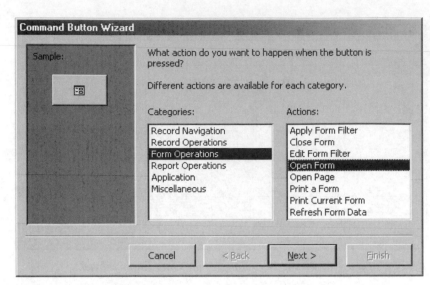

Figure 25.3: The Command button wizard

- In the next window, select **frmTransaction** and click **Next**.
- Select **Open the form and show all the records** and click **Next**.
- Click the **Text** option but delete the text as shown below. Click **Next**.

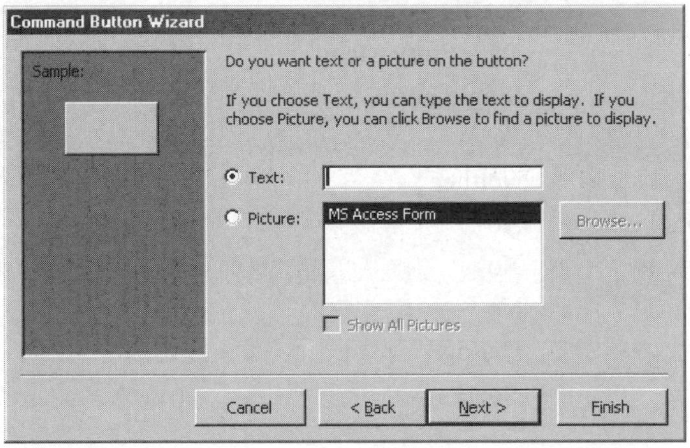

Figure 25.4

- Give the button the name **Sales** and click **Finish**.
- Go to Form view and try out the command button. The Transaction form should open.
- Close the transaction form and return to Design view.
- Add 2 more command buttons and go through the steps to open the Author form and the Book form.
- Add the final command button. The action associated with this button is simply to close the form. The main menu will be visible when it has been created.
- Select all the buttons and from the menu select **Format**, **Align**, **Left** to get them neatly lined up.

The menu should look like Figure 25.5. You can add colour or borders, etc.

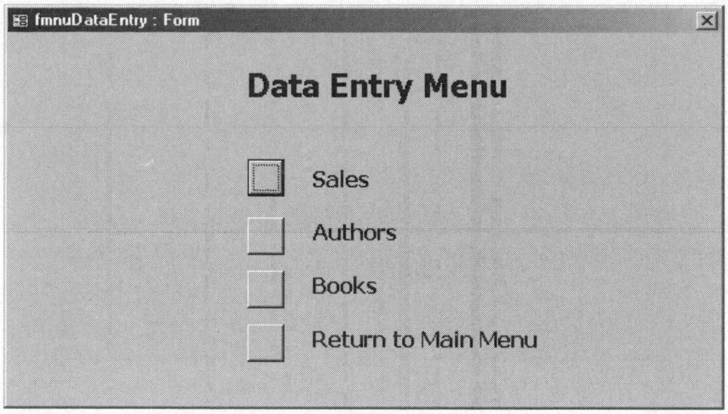

Figure 25.5: The Data Entry menu

- Save the form as *fmnuDataEntry*.
- Test each of the options before closing it.
- Create the **Reports** submenu in the same way, opening each report in preview mode.

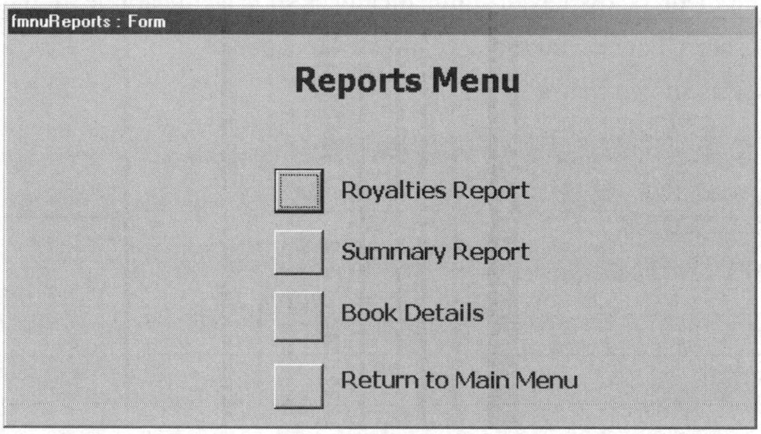

Figure 25.6: The Reports menu

Now the main menu can be created. The **Enter Data** option opens the Data Entry submenu and the **Reports** option opens the Reports submenu. The **Maintenance** option runs the query **qdelTransactions**. The **Exit** option will quit the database.

- Open a new form in Design view and set all the properties as for the other menus.
- Place the heading and labels on the Main Menu form.
- Place the first command button, and specify **fmnuDataEntry** as the form to open.
- Place the second command button, specifying **fmnuReports** as the form to open.
- Place the third command button. In the first window select **Miscellaneous**, **Run Macro** and click **Next**.
- Select **qdelTransactions** and click **Next**.
- Proceed as before, giving the button a suitable name.
- Place the fourth command button and select **Application**, **Quit Application** in the first window.
- Save the menu and test it.

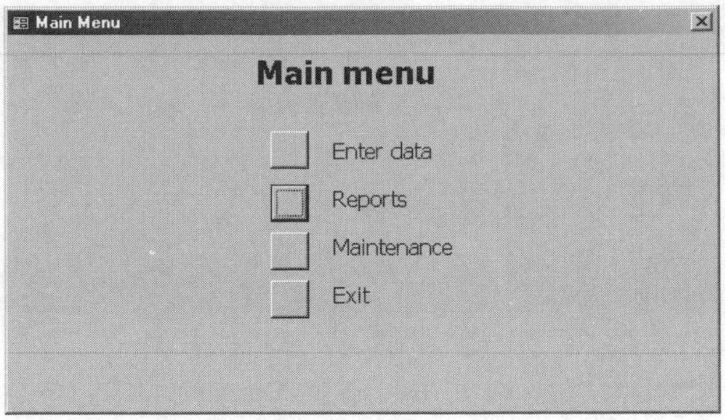

Figure 25.7: The Main Menu

You can add command buttons to each form if you wish, to return to the main menu. The action required is simply to close the current form, as the menu will be open underneath it.

25.4. Setting Startup options

You can make the main menu be displayed automatically as soon as the application is loaded.

- From the menu select **Tools**, **Startup**. A dialogue box appears.
- Fill in the entries as shown below.

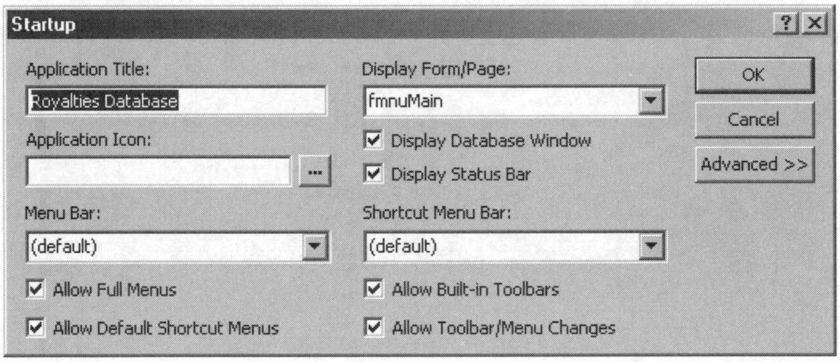

Figure 25.8: Setting Startup options

- Click **OK**.
- You will have to close the database and reopen it to see the effect. The main menu should appear automatically.

Well, that's the main essence of the database. It's a little rough around the edges but you should have the general idea. The next thing is to test it thoroughly, using your test plan.

Chapter 26 – The Technical Report

Objectives

✓ To define the contents of technical documentation

✓ To implement and write a report on the test plan in the technical documentation

26.1. The contents of the technical documentation

The technical documentation records the design and development of the database. It is intended for specialists who may need to refer to it when any changes or enhancements are to be made to the database. It may include the following:

❑ a copy of the specification agreed with the user

❑ details of the hardware, software and other resources required

❑ a detailed entity-relationship diagram

❑ a detailed data dictionary

❑ details of any program code

❑ details of validation and verification procedures

❑ details of all input and output screens and printed reports

❑ copies of the test specification.

The technical documentation has much of the same contents as the system specification. However, the system specification is a design document, produced before you even start to implement the database. The technical documentation records how you actually implemented the database as opposed to how you originally planned to do so. Inevitably, as you develop the database, you will hit snags and have to do things in a different way from how you planned them.

You may not have a lot of actual program code in your application. However, you can show screenshots of your queries and macros, and explain how and why they are used. One of the aims of this document is to prove to the moderator that you have used the advanced features of the package and that you can 'use technical language fluently, make good use of graphic images and use annotated screen prints to create effective (user instructions and) technical documentation'.

While evidence of thorough testing does not necessarily form part of the technical documentation, your teacher may advise you to include screenshots of test output as evidence that the database works as it is supposed to.

On the following pages extracts from sample technical documentation are given. For obvious reasons the systems specification is not included, as this can be found in Unit 5, but you should include either a systems specification or analysis and design sections.

26.2. Sample technical documentation

Systems Specification

(Description of the proposed system, DFDs, data model, data dictionary are all given in the System Specification in Unit 5. These should be included here as part of the analysis. Likewise, include the Input, Process and Output specification. The test plan and test data as given in the System Specification should be included in a Design section.)

Details of Processing

The following objects are used in the application.

Queries

qryBook/Author

The purpose of this query is to combine the fields from **tblBook** and **tblBook/Author** that are required for the subform **fsubBook/Author**. This subform appears on the data entry form **frmAuthor** used for entering details of authors and the books they have written.

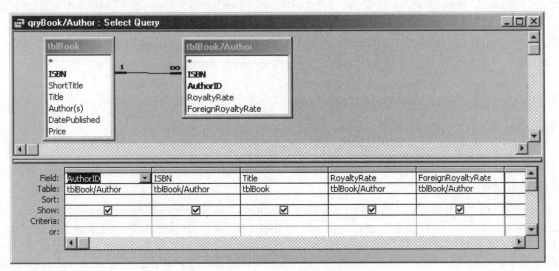

*Figure 26.1:The query **qryBook/Author***

qryRoyalty

The purpose of this query is to:

- ❑ combine the fields from various tables required for the royalties report
- ❑ determine on the basis of whether this is transaction type 1 or 2, which royalty rate to use
- ❑ calculate the royalty amount
- ❑ allow the user to enter the start and end dates to determine which transactions are to be included on the report.

The statement which determines which royalty rate to use is

Rate: IIf([TransactionType]=1,[RoyaltyRate],[ForeignRoyaltyRate])

The calculation of the royalty is carried out using the following statement:

Amount: [GrossValue]*[Rate]

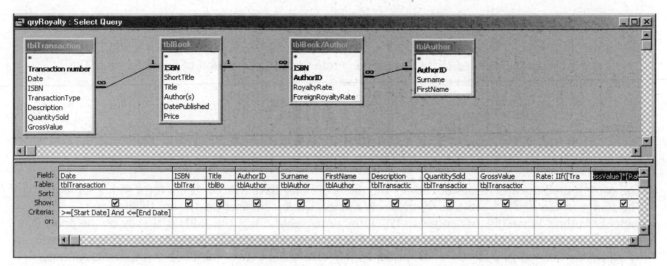

*Figure 26.2: The query **qryRoyalty***

qdelTransactions

The purpose of this Delete query is to delete all transactions prior to the date specified by the user. This prevents the file becoming too large over a period of several years.

The Date criteria is specified as follows:

<=[Delete transactions prior to which date?]

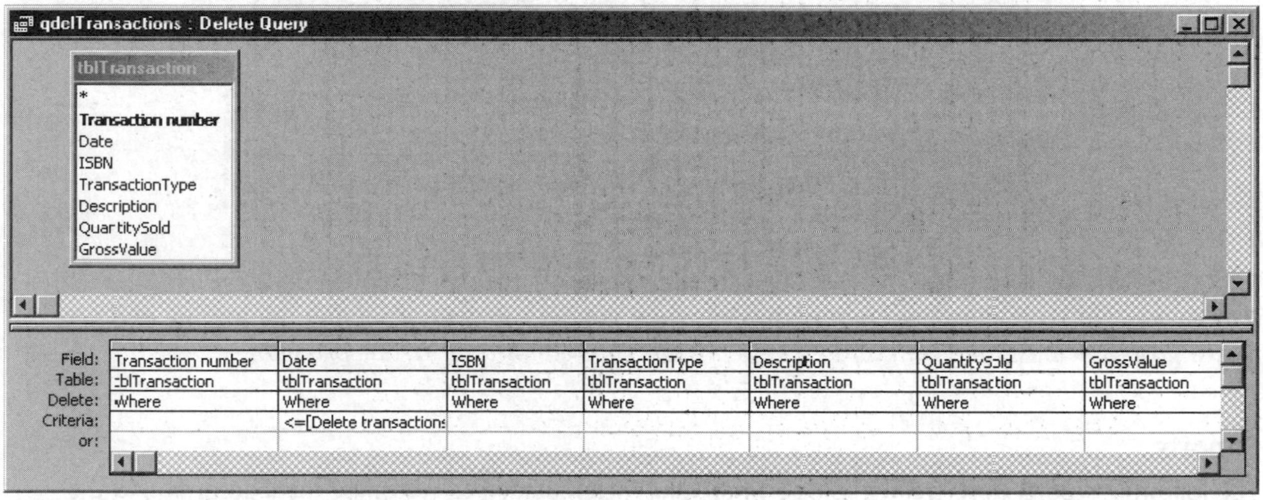

*Figure 26.3: The Delete query **qdelTransactions***

Macros

The following macros are used:

mcrNewRecord

This macro causes a blank form to be displayed when a form is opened, ready for the user to enter a new record. The macro is attached to the On Open Event property of the data entry forms **frmBook, frmAuthor** and **frmTransaction**.

mcrMaintenance

This macro runs the delete query **qdelTransactions**. It was necessary to write a macro to do this because a Delete query cannot be specified in the Command Button wizard as the action to be performed. The Maintenance option on the main menu calls this macro.

Forms

The following forms were created for data entry:

frmAuthor

This form is used to enter details of authors and the books they have written. It is a form with a subform. The source of the subform is the query **qryBook/Author**, which combines fields from **tblBook** and **tblBook/Author**. When the user enters an ISBN, the system checks that this ISBN is already on the Book table. If it is, the title is displayed automatically. If it is not, an error message is displayed. (This is achieved by specifying Referential Integrity when setting up the relationship between **tblBook** and **tblBook/Author**).

The Design view of the form is shown below:

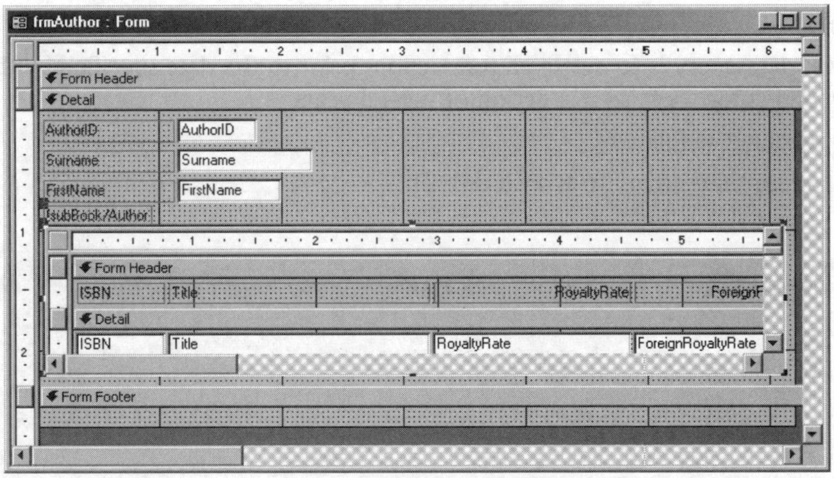

Figure 26.4: **frmAuthor** *with subform in Design view*

(Go through each of your forms in turn. Emphasise where you have used counter fields, date and time fields, drop-down list, and validation. These are all required for an A Grade project.)

Reports

The following reports were created using a wizard and then modified to customise them according to the system specification.

rptRoyalty

This report has as its source **qryRoyalty**. Customisation was carried out as follows:

❑ Some fields were moved from the detail section into header sections, and other fields spaced out.

❑ Extra fields **Start Date, End Date** were added as part of the report title.

❑ All currency amounts were formatted as Currency, two decimal places by altering field properties in the Properties box.

❑ Each author's report is started on a new page. This is done by inserting a page break (this is a tool on the Toolbox) just above the page footer – it shows as a short dotted line at the left margin.

❑ Subtotals for each title and grand totals for each author are printed on the report. Labels were adjusted to meet the specification.

The Design view of this report is shown below.

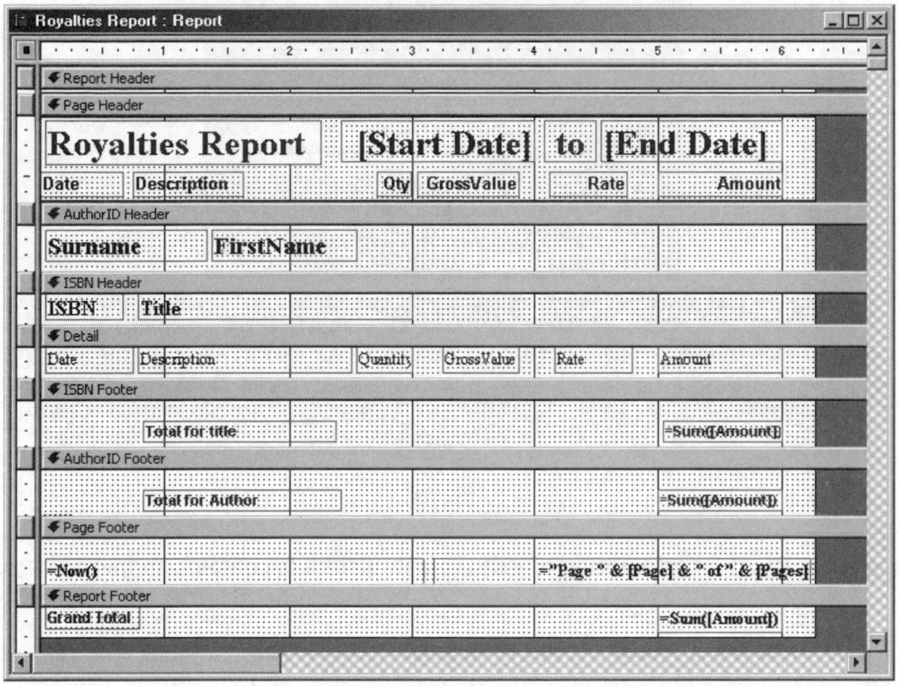

*Figure 26.5: **rptRoyalty** in Design view*

(Document each of the reports in your system, describing the customisation that you carried out.)

Testing

(You will find that a screen capture utility is very useful for both the technical manual and the user manual. The utility program Screen Print Gold from Software labs (www.softwarelabs.com) is downloadable free from the Internet. Alternatively, press Print Screen on the keyboard to send a screenshot to the printer.)

The test plan and test data as detailed in the Systems Specification was used. Results of testing are shown below.

Test 1: Select Enter Data from the main menu

The Data entry menu opens and the Book form opens at a new record.

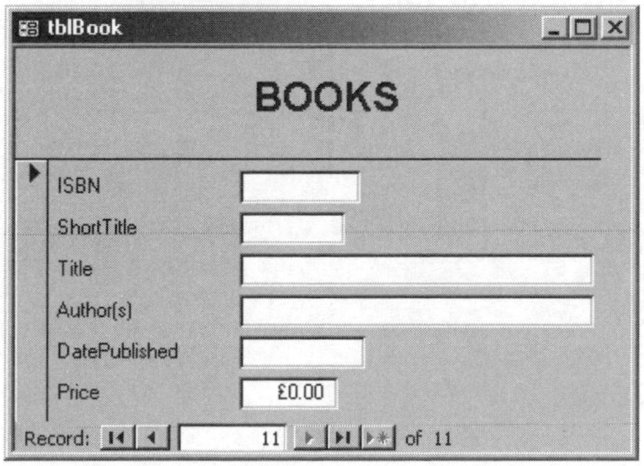

Test 1

Test 2: Enter a record with an invalid date

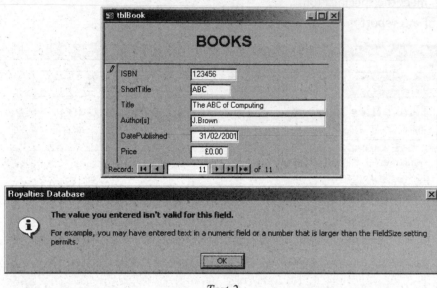

Test 2

An error message is displayed on attempting to exit the date field if it contains an invalid date.

Test 3: Select Enter data from Main Menu, then select Authors.

(You should go through each test in the test plan and show a screenshot of the result. Comment on anything that needs mentioning. For reasons of space no more test output is shown here.)

Conclusion

The system works well and achieves the objectives described in the Systems Specification. It would be possible at a later date to expand the application to include details of foreign publishers and foreign rights.

(You can discuss here any modifications, weaknesses or enhancements that could be made to the database.)

Chapter 27 – The User Manual

Objectives

✓ To understand the purpose and contents of user documentation
✓ To write a user manual for an application

27.1. The user manual

The user manual is aimed at the end user of your database, who may be a manager or one of the clerical staff. You cannot assume they know anything about Access and, if your application is well-written, it should not be necessary for them to do so. Your user manual should explain clearly and simply what your application does and how to use it.

It could include:

❑ an introduction giving an overview of the application
❑ instructions on how to start the database
❑ a screenshot of what appears when the database is started up
❑ for each menu option, a screenshot showing what the user will see and instructions on how to perform the selected task, e.g. inputting a new record or printing a report
❑ samples of data-entry screens and reports
❑ advice on how to respond to error messages
❑ advice on backing up
❑ advice on who to contact if technical problems arise.
❑ a title page and Table of Contents.

27.2. Word processing your user manual

In Unit 1 you will have learned how to set up styles so that you can generate an automatic Table of Contents. You will also need to use headers and footers to specify what the document is, the page number, your name etc. Make sure you know how to do these things before you begin!

27.3. Sample user manual

Sample extracts from a user manual for the Royalties database are given on the next few pages. The title page and table of contents are omitted but you should include them in your documentation.

Royalties Database – User Manual

Introduction

The Royalties Database is designed to provide a record of all titles published by Victory Publishers, and details of all authors. One of the main functions of the system is to calculate the royalties due to each author for each 6-month period. There are two sources of data for calculating royalties:

❑ Monthly sales figures of each title, keyed in by the Sales Department

❑ Foreign Royalties received, keyed in by the Foreign Rights Department. The royalty rates received by an author for each of these different types of royalties is recorded on the database and used in calculating the royalties payable.

Starting the application

To start the application, load MS Access.

- Click on **Open an existing file** and select **Royalties**.

The opening menu will be displayed as shown in the figure below.

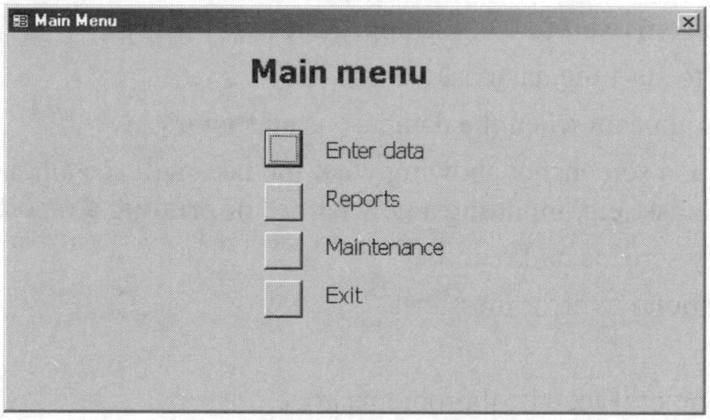

Figure 27.1: The opening menu

The Enter Data submenu

To enter data about books, authors or transactions relating to royalties, click the **Enter Data** button. This will cause a further menu to be displayed.

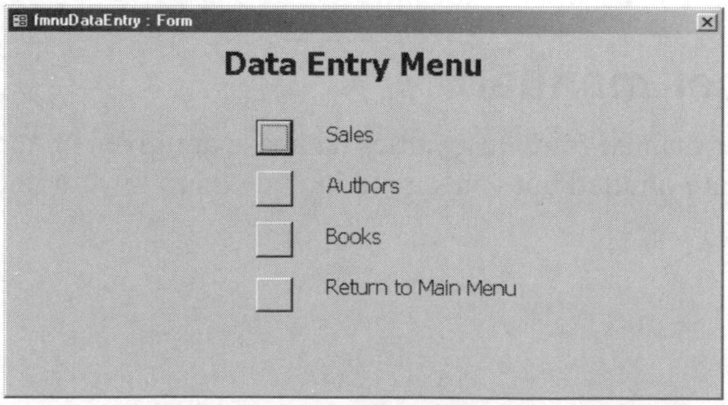

Figure 27.2: The Data Entry menu

Entering sales

Select the **Sales** option to enter details of monthly sales or receipts from foreign publishers relating to the sale of publishing rights to titles.

You will see the data entry screen open ready to enter a new record as shown below:

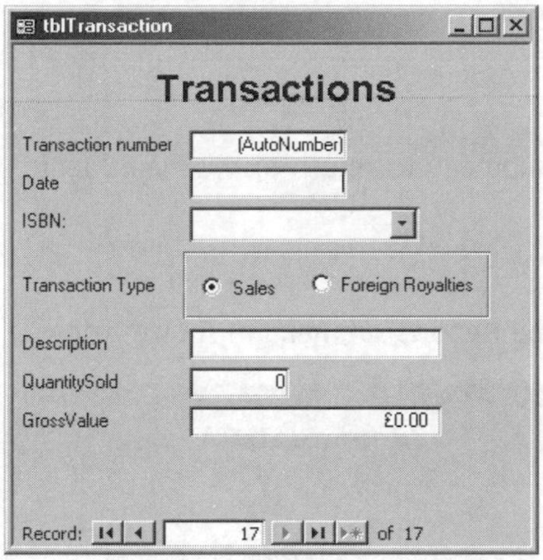

Figure 27.3: Data entry screen for Sales transactions

- The description field is used to enter a description of the transaction, e.g. 'February Sales' or 'Royalties received from LAU (Norway)'.
- When you tab out of the last field you will be taken to a new record. When you have entered all the records, close the form to return to the menu. The new records will be saved automatically.

Entering authors

Select the **Authors** option to enter details of new authors or edit details of existing authors. Note that you cannot enter a royalty rate for a title until that title has been entered using the **Books** option.

You will see the following data entry screen.

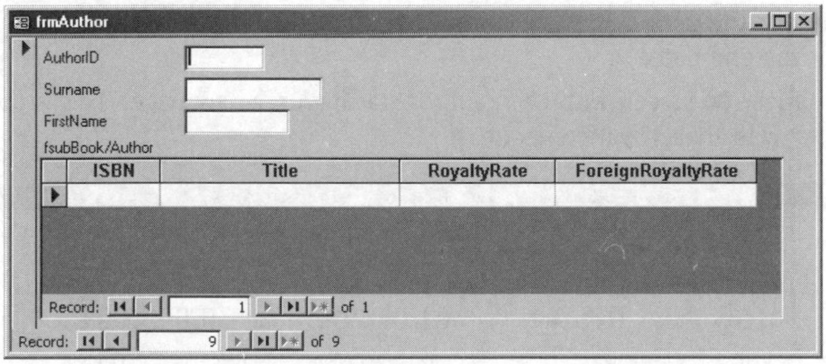

Figure 27.4: Data entry screen for new author

Notes:

- **AuthorID** is a unique ID of up to 10 characters. You can use, for example, the author's surname (or first 9 characters) plus first initial – e.g. MOOREB for Basil Moore.
- You can enter as many ISBNs as needed for one author. When you tab out of the ISBN field, the book title will be automatically displayed.
- You will not be able to enter an ISBN which has not already been entered using the data entry screen for **Books** – an error message will be displayed when you attempt to save the record or tab to the

next line. Either correct the ISBN or press Esc to abandon the record if you have not yet entered the book details.

Entering books

Select the **Books** option to enter details of new books or edit details of existing books.

(Describe this option in a similar manner.)

Return to main menu

Selecting this option will close the submenu to return to the Main Menu.

The Enter Reports submenu

Selecting this option will bring up the Reports submenu as shown below.

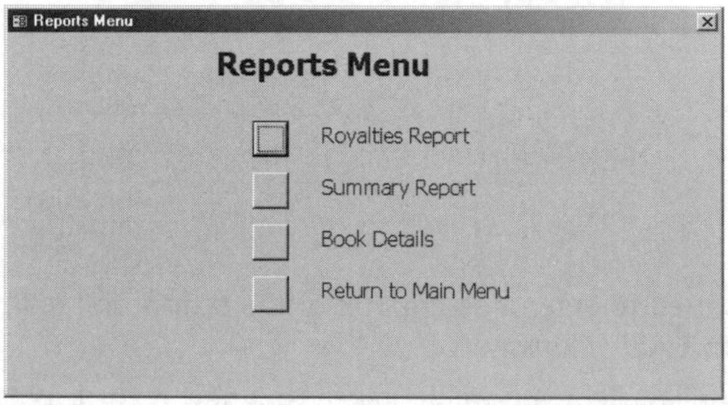

Figure 27.5: The Reports submenu

Royalties report

This option will normally be run every 6 months, although it can be run at any time. When you select this option, you will be asked to enter a start date and an end date for the report. For example if this report relates to royalties due for the period January-June 2001, you should enter 01/01/2001 as the Start Date, and 30/06/2001 for the end date.

The report will then appear on screen with each author starting on a new page. This is the report that will be sent out to each author with their royalty cheque.

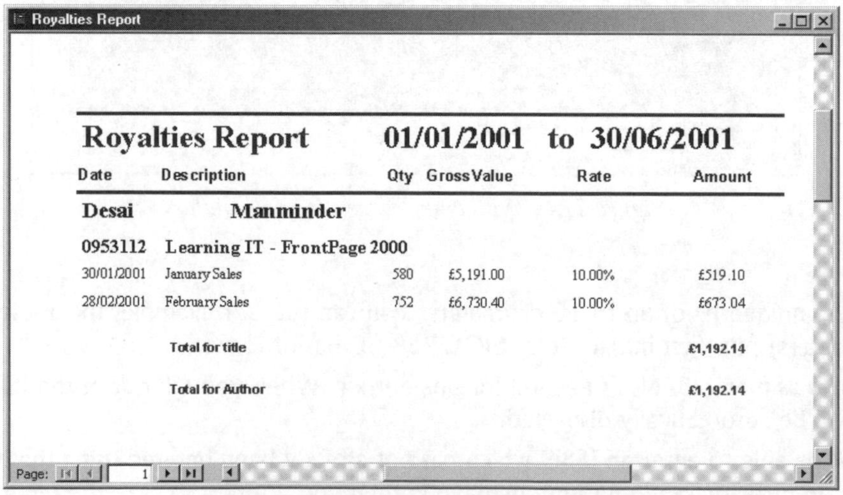

Figure 27.6: The Royalties report

Notes:

❑ Press the **Print** button on the Standard toolbar to print the report.

Summary report

(Go through the rest of the reports in a similar manner.)

The Maintenance option

*(Go through the **Maintenance** function, explaining how and why it is used.)*

The Exit button

*(Explain what happens when you press **Exit**..)*

Backup

It is important to back up the database at the end of every day if you have made any changes or added new data. This should be done from Windows Explorer with the database closed. You should back up the database file **Royalties.mdb** onto a floppy disk or zip disk and store it in a secure location away from the computer.

User Support

If you have any problems using the database, please contact User Support on **01234 123456**.

Appendix A – Standard Ways of Working

Introduction

Every organisation has rules about the way it operates. These may not be formal rules and regulations that are written down – they may just be conventions and ways of working that all members of staff adhere to. Standard ways of working are important when working with ICT systems because they can help to protect three of the organisation's most important assets: information, equipment and employees.

Managing your work

Planning

Often, whether you are at School/College or in the workplace, you will be faced with a number of tasks that need to be completed. If you can plan your work effectively you will be more likely to complete those tasks successfully. Spending some time drawing up a plan to organise your work will pay off in the long run and is something you should become used to doing as a matter of course. The plan will depend on you clearly identifying the task to be completed and discussing the details with whoever has set it. You need to establish the priority of the task, how long it is likely to take you and what deadline has been imposed. If you feel that the deadline is unrealistic it is always worth trying to renegotiate it, but you will have to be able to put up a good case! It is often useful to identify 'milestones' leading up to a deadline so that you can check your progress and that you are on target for completing in time.

Working with files

Almost all of the work that is created using a computer is stored in a file. These files are stored in folders on a storage device – often the hard drive on your computer. Every file is given a name and it is important that you use sensible filenames that remind you of the contents. Once you are in the workplace the files that are created and stored belong to the organisation. This means that they need to be accessible to other people within the organisation so a well-organised file structure is vital.

My Documents is a desktop folder that provides you with a convenient place to store documents, graphics, or other files you want to access quickly. On your desktop it is represented by a folder with a sheet of paper in it. Often users will create their own subfolders within My Documents creating a simple path to where their files are stored.

Fault Logging

Many problems can arise when working with ICT systems. Often many of the 'faults' are not problems with the system but arise because users do not fully understand how to operate them or what messages mean. This is why initial user training and good user documentation are vital to the success of a new ICT system.

However the resolution of many true faults can be speeded up if clear and precise information is passed on to the technical people supporting the system. When reporting a fault the following information should be provided:

- ❑ The way the fault manifests itself. If there is an error message, it should be relayed exactly as it appears on the screen.
- ❑ The exact sequence of events that gave rise to the fault.
- ❑ Details of the equipment and its precise location.

A fault log should always be kept near to a PC and all details of the problem entered neatly. These records can help to identify equipment that has a recurring fault and provide information on how the fault has been fixed in the past.

Keeping information secure

Computer systems must have adequate controls to ensure that only authorised personnel have access to data. There are a number of ways in which this can be achieved:

Passwords

Most networks require a user to log on with their password before they can gain access to the computer system. Additional passwords may be required to gain access to certain programs and data. For example, in an organisation everyone may be able to access word processing programs and files, but only people working in the Finance department may be able to access the accounting system. It is clearly important that these passwords are not divulged to other people and it is recommended that passwords are frequently changed. In fact many systems are set up to automatically prompt you after a set number of days to change your password.

Communications controls

These controls ensure that only authorised people can connect to a computer from an external link. Some organisations have dial-back systems: when someone attempts to log on to the remote computer, they are positively identified and the computer disconnects them and immediately dials them back to ensure they are an authorised user.

Virus checks

Viruses are generally developed with a definite intention to cause damage to computer files or, at the very least, cause inconvenience and annoyance to computer users. The first virus appeared at the University of Delaware in 1987, and since then the number of viruses has escalated to over 9000 different variations in 1997. The virus usually occupies the first few instructions of a particular program on an 'infected' disk and relies on a user choosing to execute that program. When an infected program is executed, the virus is the first series of instructions to be performed. In most cases the virus's first action is to copy itself from the diskette onto the PC and 'hide' within obscure files, the operating system code or within unused disk blocks which are then marked as being 'bad' and unavailable for reuse. The virus can then proceed to perform any of a number tasks ranging from the irritating to the catastrophic such as reformatting the hard disk.

Some viruses lie dormant, waiting to be triggered by a particular event or date – the 'Friday 13th' virus being a well-known one. The virus then infects other diskettes, perhaps by modifying operating system programs responsible for copying programs. From there, the next PC to use the diskette will be infected.

Virus checkers need to be installed on all computer systems so that they automatically check for any infected data when the computer is started up. Manual checkers can also be used to check for viruses on floppy disks.

Backup systems

Routine back-ups of the computer system should be made so that in the case of serious emergency, the system can be recreated to the last full back-up. Back-ups can be made to a variety of media – magnetic tape, CD-ROM, Zip drive etc. They are made on a daily, weekly or monthly basis depending on the importance of the data to be backed up. The back-up media must be clearly labelled and should be stored in a fire-proof safe, or better still on a different site, so that should a disaster or emergency occur, the backup media will be safe.

Copyright

Computer software is copyright material – that means it is protected in the UK by the Copyright, Designs and Patents Act 1988. It is owned by the software producer and it is illegal to make unauthorised copies.

When you buy software it is often supplied in a sealed package (e.g. CD ROM case) on which the terms and conditions of sale are printed. This is called the software licence and when the user opens the package they are agreeing to abide by the licence terms.

Software licences usually permit the user to use one copy on any single computer. It is considered to be in use if it is loaded into either the computer's temporary memory (RAM) or onto the hard disk drive. With network licences the software is often loaded onto the file server and the licence specifies how many users on the network can access it at any one time.

It is illegal to make copies of the software except for backup purposes, so you are breaking the law if you copy some software from a friend to use on your own computer.

Data that is held on computer is often subject to copyright. For example not everyone has the ability or opportunity to draw or to take photographs and you often want to include copies of someone else's work in your documents. These images may well be copyright and belong to the original artist or photographer. If this is the case it may be possible to contact the publisher for permission to use the material, but this can be a lengthy process. To be outside the copyright law, the artist/photographer/writer has to have been dead for 70 years. If this is the case and you would like to use, for example, some old photographs, you may do so freely, but it is often best to acknowledge the source somewhere in your document.

Computer Misuse Act 1990

In the early 1980s in the UK, hacking was not illegal. Some universities stipulated that hacking, especially where damage was done to data files, was a disciplinary offence but there was no legislative framework within which a criminal prosecution could be brought. This situation was rectified by the Computer Misuse Act of 1990 which defined three specific criminal offences to deal with the problems of hacking, viruses and other nuisances. The offences are:

- ❑ Unauthorised access to computer programs or data.
- ❑ Unauthorised access with a further criminal intent.
- ❑ Unauthorised modification of computer material (i.e. programs or data).

To date there have been relatively few prosecutions under this law – probably because most organisations are reluctant to admit that their system security procedures have been breached, which might lead to a loss of confidence on the part of their clients.

Principles of Data Protection

The Data Protection Act 1998 came into force on 1 March 2000. It sets rules for processing personal information and applies to paper records as well as those held on computers. It strengthens and extends the rules about data protection laid down in the Data Protection Act 1984, which it now replaces.

The rules

Anyone processing personal data must comply with the eight enforceable principles of good practice. They say that data must be:

- ❑ Fairly and lawfully processed.
- ❑ Processed for limited purposes.
- ❑ Adequate, relevant and not excessive.
- ❑ Accurate.
- ❑ Not kept longer than necessary.
- ❑ Processed in accordance with the data subject's rights.
- ❑ Secure.
- ❑ Not transferred to countries without adequate protection.

Personal data covers both facts and opinions about a living person. It also includes information regarding the intentions of the data controller towards the individual, although in some limited circumstances exemptions will apply. For more information on Data Protection visit the following web site: www.dataprotection.gov.uk

Working safely

Computers and health

Computers can be held responsible for a whole raft of health problems, from eyestrain to wrist injuries, back problems to foetal abnormalities, stomach ulcers to mental collapse. Articles appear regularly in the newspapers relating stories of employees who are suing their employers for computer-related illnesses.

Not so long ago it was thought that the widespread use of these fantastic machines, that could perform calculations and process data with lightning speed and complete accuracy, would free up humans to work maybe only two or three hours a day, while the computer did the lion's share. In fact, people seem to be working harder than ever, trying to keep up with the output of their computers. Human beings are the weak link in the chain, needing food, rest, a social life; prone to headaches, stress, tired limbs and mistakes.

Figure 1: Stress at work

Stress

Stress is often a major factor in work-related illness. Simply thinking about computers is enough to cause stress in some people. It is stressful to be asked to perform tasks which are new to you and which you are not sure you can cope with. It is stressful to know that you have more work to do than you can finish in the time available. It is stressful, even, to have too little to do and to be bored all day.

The introduction of computers into the workplace can have detrimental effects on the well-being of information workers at many different levels in an organisation. For example:

- Some companies may use computers to monitor their workers' productivity, which often increases their stress levels. Symptoms include headaches, stomach ulcers and sleeplessness.

- Many people are afraid of computers and fear that they will not be able to learn the new skills required, or that their position of seniority will be undermined by younger 'whizz kids' with a high level of competence in ICT.

- It can be almost impossible for some people to get away from work. Pagers, mobile phones, laptop computers and modems mean that even after leaving the office, there is no need to stop work – indeed, should you even *think* of stopping work? As a busy executive, can you afford to waste 45 minutes on the train to Ipswich reading the newspaper or just gazing out of the window, when you could be tap-tap-tapping on your laptop, or infuriating your fellow passengers by holding long and boring conversations on your mobile phone?

- 'Information overload' means that managers are often bombarded with far more information than they can assimilate, producing 'information anxiety'. Try typing the words 'Information Overload' into one of the World Wide Web's search engines and within seconds, it will have searched millions of information sources all over the world and come up with thousands of references all presorted so that those most likely to be of interest are at the top.

- A survey of 500 heads of ICT departments revealed that over three quarters of respondents had suffered from failing personal relationships, loss of appetite, addiction to work and potential alcohol abuse. The continuing developments within ICT ensure that it is always in the minds of business executives and also that it is blamed for most corporate problems. The very speed of development, for which ICT is now famous, and the need to keep pace with this is also a major contributing factor to ICT stress-related illness.

Repetitive Strain Injury (RSI)

RSI is the collective name for a variety of disorders affecting the neck, shoulders and upper limbs. It can result in numbness or tingling in the arms and hands, aching and stiffness in the arms, neck and shoulders, and an inability to lift or grip objects. Some sufferers cannot pour a cup of tea or type a single sentence without excruciating pain.

The Health and Safety Executive say that more than 100,000 workers suffer from RSI.

Eyestrain

Computer users are prone to eyestrain from spending long hours in front of a screen. Many computer users prefer a dim light to achieve better screen contrast, but this makes it difficult to read documents on the desk. A small spotlight focussed on the desktop can be helpful. There is no evidence that computer use causes permanent damage to the eyes, but glare, improper lighting, improperly corrected vision (through not wearing the correct prescription glasses), poor work practices and poorly-designed workstations all contribute to temporary eyestrain.

Extremely low frequency (ELF) radiation

In normal daily life we are constantly exposed to ELF radiation not only from electricity mains and computer monitors but also naturally occurring sources such as sunshine, fire and the earth's own magnetic field. Research into the effects of ELF radiation is increasing and seems to indicate that it may be connected to some health problems. Several studies have tried to establish whether there is a link between monitor use and problems in pregnancy such as early miscarriages. The results are not clear-cut, because although some studies seem to show a correlation between an increased rate of miscarriages and long hours spent at a VDU in the first trimester of pregnancy, other factors such as stress and poor ergonomic conditions could have played a part.

Computers, health and the law

Occupational health and safety legislation in Britain is researched, guided and structured by the Health and Safety Executive (HSE), a government body. An EEC Directive on work with display screen equipment was completed in the early 1990s, with member states required to adapt it to become part of their own legislation. As a consequence, the Health and Safety at Work Act of 1974 incorporated legislation pertaining to the use of VDUs, and the relevant section is now referred to as The Health and Safety (Display Screen Equipment) Regulations 1992.

This legislation is intended to protect the health of employees within the working environment, and employers, employees and manufacturers all have some responsibility in conforming to the law.

Employers are required to

- Perform an analysis of workstations in order to evaluate the safety and health conditions to which they give rise.

- Provide training to employees in the use of workstation components.

- Ensure employees take regular breaks or changes in activity.

❑ Provide regular eye tests for workstation users and pay for glasses.

Employees have a responsibility to

❑ Use workstations and equipment correctly, in accordance with training provided by employers.

❑ Bring problems to the attention of their employer immediately and co-operate in the correction of these problems.

Manufacturers are required to ensure that their products comply with the Directive. For example, screens must tilt and swivel, keyboards must be separate and moveable. Notebook PCs are not suitable for entering large amounts of data.

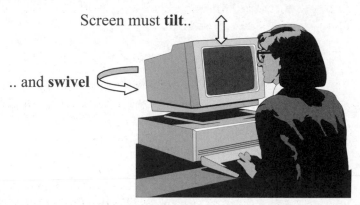

Screen must **tilt**..

.. and **swivel**

Figure 2: Workstations must be ergonomically designed

The ergonomic environment

Ergonomics refers to the design and functionality of the environment, and encompasses the entire range of environmental factors. Employers must give consideration to

❑ **Lighting**. The office should be well lit. Computers should neither face windows nor back onto a window so that the users have to sit with the sun in their eyes. Adjustable blinds should be provided.

❑ **Furniture**. Chairs should be of adjustable height, with a backrest which tilts to support the user at work and at rest, and should swivel on a five-point base. It should be at the correct height relative to a keyboard on the desk.

❑ **Work space**. The combination of chair, desk, computer, accessories (such as document holders, mouse and mouse mats, paper trays and so on), lighting, heating and ventilation all contribute to the worker's overall well-being.

❑ **Noise**. Noisy printers, for example, should be given covers to reduce the noise or positioned in a different room.

❑ **Hardware**. The screen must tilt and swivel and be flicker-free, the keyboard must be separately attached.

❑ **Software**. Software is often overlooked in the quest for ergonomic perfection. The EEC Directive made a clear statement about the characteristics of acceptable software, requiring employers to analyse the tasks which their employers performed and to provide software which makes the tasks easier. It is also expected to be easy to use and adaptable to the user's experience.

Appendix B – Assessment Evidence for Units 4-6

Unit 4: System Installation and Configuration

ASSESSMENT EVIDENCE

You need to produce:

- a specification for a complete ICT system to meet user requirements, together with an operational system

- a specification for an upgrade to an ICT system that requires the installation of at least two items in the processing unit and configuration of software, together with an operational system. You must also show you can remove the installed items and use uninstall procedures to restore the system to its original state

- records of set-up, installation, configuration and test activities.

Your configuration of software must include setting up a toolbar layout, a menu, a template and a macro. (Hardware installation tasks may be undertaken with a small group of colleagues.)

To achieve a grade E your work must show:	*To achieve a grade C your work must show:*	*To achieve a grade A your work must show:*
E1 definitions of user requirements and clear specifications for the ICT system and the upgrade, including for each full details of hardware, OS, applications software and configuration E2 selection of suitable hardware and software and correct: - connection of hardware - installation of items in the processing unit - installation of software - setting of ROM-BIOS parameters - configuration of OS and software E3 design and implementation of a suitable toolbar layout, menu, template and macro to meet user requirements E4 the upgraded ICT system correctly restored to its original state E5 clear records of work done that include suitably annotated printed copy or screen prints of your toolbar, menu, template and macro, together with details of a suitable system configuration check, test procedures, problems experienced and solutions implemented.	C1 through your records of practical work a systematic approach to specifying and constructing an operational ICT system C2 clear definition and implementation of test procedures to check each task undertaken and how you overcame problems or limitations found as a result of using the test procedures C3 that you can work independently to produce your work to agreed deadlines.	A1 good understanding and imaginative use of options for customising applications software, such as keyboard configuration, toolbar layout and menu design, by providing users with facilities that improve efficiency A2 an imaginative use of design and attention to detail in the creation of a template and macro that clearly enable users to improve their efficiency and effectiveness A3 effective use of system diagnostics, system monitoring procedures and uninstall routines, implementing adjustments as necessary to ensure correct system operation A4 records kept in an organised way and indexed to enable easy reference to the problems experienced and the solutions implemented.

Note: The Edexcel Board does not number the grade criteria. This has been done to make it easier to refer to a particular criterion.

Unit 5: Systems Analysis

ASSESSMENT EVIDENCE

You need to produce:

- a feasibility report
- a system specification to meet the requirements.

(You must also show evidence of data modelling with an entity-relationship diagram that has at least three related entities.)

To achieve a grade E your work must show:	To achieve a grade C your work must show:	To achieve a grade A your work must show:
E1 a clear statement of purpose and user requirement for the system, including a definition of scope and a high-level (contextual view) dfd	C1 good understanding and effective use of structured analysis tools in the development of your dfds, the identification of events and the production of process specifications	A1 a systematic approach to your analysis of the existing system, investigation of potential improvements and selection of priorities for development
E2 appropriate low-level dfds to describe the main system events		A2 a clear definition in your input specification of appropriate sources of data, methods of data capture, layout of screen data-input forms and validation and verification techniques
E3 an erd and a data dictionary that clearly lists and describes the entities, their attributes and the relationships	C2 good understanding and method in the development of your erd and data dictionary to resolve problems and ensure first normal form	
E4 accurate input and output specifications and details of resource implications	C3 that you can work independently to produce your work to agreed deadlines.	A3 a clear definition in your output specification of the information to be output in screen or printed reports and appropriate ways of organising and presenting it
E5 suitable process specifications using an appropriate method		A4 clear specification in your conclusion of the possible alternatives, constraints, risks and potential benefits, and a cost-benefit analysis to support your recommendations.
E6 a conclusion that makes recommendations for development.		

Unit 6: Database Design

ASSESSMENT EVIDENCE

You need to produce:

- a relational database to a given specification requiring at least three related tables
- design and analysis notes for the database
- annotated printed copy and test results for the database
- a user guide and technical documentation.

To achieve a grade E your work must show:	To achieve a grade C your work must show:	To achieve a grade A your work must show:
E1 the initial draft design and final data model correctly normalised to at least first normal form E2 clearly the entities, attributes, keys, relationships, and internally generated or processed data in your design notes E3 a working relational database that allows users to append, delete and edit data, initiate queries and print reports E4 suitable and correct data-input forms E5 a user guide that enables novice users to make efficient use of the database E6 clear and accurate definition, in the technical documentation, of: - the database structure and data relationships - a data dictionary - the range of acceptable data - example output from queries and reports - test procedures E7 printed reports and screen prints that clearly demonstrate the operation of the database, annotated to explain their purpose.	C1 reports that make correct and effective use of queries, grouping, mathematical formulae and related tables C2 fluent use of technical language, good use of graphic images and use of annotated screen prints to create effective user instructions and technical documentation C3 that you can work independently and meet agreed deadlines by carrying out your work plans effectively.	A1 detailed design and analysis notes that include graphic images to define the data model clearly and demonstrate that it is correctly normalised to third normal form A2 effective use of validation and of automatic counter, date or time fields in data-input forms A3 test procedures, designed and implemented, that check reliable operation, including rejection of data outside the acceptable range A4 user-friendly, well-laid out screen data-input forms with title labels, field names, set widths, pull-down lists and instructions as appropriate to enable data entry into multiple tables.

Index